A Dangerous Liaison

Baroness Sheri de Borchgrave

A Dangerous Liaison

One Woman's Journey into
a World of Aristocracy,
Depravity, and
Obsessive Love

A DUTTON BOOK

DUTTON

Published by the Penguin Group
Penguin Books USA Inc., 375 Hudson Street, New York, New York 10014, U.S.A.
Penguin Books Ltd, 27 Wrights Lane, London W8 5TZ, England
Penguin Books Australia Ltd, Ringwood, Victoria, Australia
Penguin Books Canada Ltd, 10 Alcorn Avenue, Toronto, Ontario, Canada M4V 3B2
Penguin Books (N.Z.) Ltd, 182-190 Wairau Road, Auckland 10, New Zealand

Penguin Books Ltd, Registered Offices:
Harmondsworth, Middlesex, England

First published by Dutton, an imprint of New American Library,
a division of Penguin Books USA Inc.
Distributed in Canada by McClelland & Stewart Inc.

First Printing, September, 1993
1 3 5 7 9 10 8 6 4 2

 REGISTERED TRADEMARK—MARCA REGISTRADA

LIBRARY OF CONGRESS CATALOGING-IN-PUBLICATION DATA:
Borchgrave, Sheri de, Baroness.
A dangerous liaison : one woman's journey into a world of aristocracy, depravity,
and obsessive love / Baroness Sheri de Borchgrave.
p.   cm.
ISBN 0-525-93637-8
1. Borchgrave, Sheri de, Baroness—Marriage.   2. Borchgrave,
Jacques de, Baron.   3. Journalists—United States—Biography.
4. Abused wives—United States—Biography.   5. Suicide victims
—United States—Biography.   6. Nobility—Belgium—Biography.
I. Title.
CT275.B584518A3   1993
973.92'092'2—dc20   93-6725
                                                                  CIP

Printed in the United States of America
Set in New Baskerville and Snell Roundhand

Designed by Steven N. Stathakis

*To my mother,
my Auntie Elly,
and
my Uncle Oscar,
and to my Club Med family,
who gave me a chance to recover
in their faraway villages.*

Acknowledgments

Many thanks to the three most important women in my life: Ruth Pomerance of Lee Rich Productions who first showed enthusiasm for the book and then directed me to Suzanne Gluck of ICM, the most terrific literary agent; and my editor at Dutton Jennifer Enderlin, whose great insight and talent brought my manuscript to a new level.

With special thanks: to my close friends Annijge Luns Hebben in Amsterdam, Alix Lemarchand in Paris, and Sallie Motsch in New York, and to my adopted sister and brother, Wha Youn Kim Boulton and Benjamin Ashton, whose great spirit and encouragement has sustained me; and to some ardent supporters along the way, Allan Barnard, Albert Goldstein, and Rick Hunter Garcia.

In the course of writing this book, I decided to change the names of certain people in the story. I also changed the names of all the family castles, residences, and the areas around Brussels where events took place. I wrote the first draft and the final draft of the book on Fire Island, where the island residents and the beautiful beach provided a lot of inspiration.

$\mathcal{P}$rologue

1989

"Sheri, are you sitting down?" The overseas call from my Belgian lawyer came at 3:00 A.M.

"The Baron de Borchgrave has committed suicide. This past summer. You are a widow, Sheri, and ironically you are the baroness of the family for life."

I was stunned, but managed to ask him how and when it happened.

"At the beginning of August. He did it with a hunting rifle, a shot right through the temple. A neighbor found him in his bedroom. A gruesome sight, I'm afraid. He was lying in a pool of his blood, gun still in hand. Definitely a suicide. The family tried to hide it. Of course, they kept it out of the newspapers. The family is saying that it was a heart attack, I've heard, but their attorney couldn't lie to me about the real cause of death."

"How could they hide it?" I asked. "Jacques was not exactly an unknown figure."

"Probably because it happened on August sixth, Sheri, when everyone, literally everyone, in the noble circle was away at their summer haunts and even the hottest gossip wouldn't find its way to their lands of Sybaris."

The baron's sister Isabelle later told me, "I'm proud of my brother. He died like a nobleman. A perfect shot through his temple. Clean. He could even have an open-coffin wake."

Jacques had been a perfect shot and had loved going to the famous hunting events in France. Proficiency in the hunt was a talent that Belgian nobles valued above most other sports. And he had been the best.

Baron de Borchgrave had been only in his mid-forties and had seemed to have everything in the world. He was handsome—six foot six with a slim, muscular build—and wealthy. His family, considered one of Belgium's top members of noble society, owned four castles. (When his father died at a young age in a military accident, the King of Belgium honored him. The country observed a silence; even the public transportation system stopped for a minute of respect.) The baron had an international business in yachts and cranes, was the father of two teenage sons, and had a beautiful mansion as well as his own family castle. He was a connoisseur of pleasures: food, wine, women, sex, and rock and roll; a collector of seventeenth-century Flemish paintings.

And he had lived happily on the edge, though a different edge than is generally thought. The edge of the cushioned, untouchable world of the noble circle, so removed from what reality is to most people. Life was to be used primarily in the pursuit of pleasure, and to attain that ultimate pleasurable existence he had lived with noble license to do exactly as he pleased, even if it meant some rather dangerous games. He had still lived as if there were "the common people" and "the king and his nobles" in a world of dangerous liaisons. Sometimes he had gone over the edge. He had been an irresistible man and I had been seduced.

But why did he commit suicide? I know. I was married to him. And he destroyed my life just as surely as he put a bullet through his head. For two years, I couldn't face anyone. I, his baroness.

When I met Baron de Borchgrave I was a recent Barnard College graduate working at a contemporary art gallery in New York City's SoHo. This was the late seventies. An exciting time in the art scene and in New York City. Life was fast; "live for today" was what everyone practiced. Relationships with men were also live-for-today. The men I met through college and just after never thought of the future. No one felt the need to commit. Then I met Baron de Borchgrave, who immediately wanted a future with me. I think it would have been hard for most women of my age to resist him. He completely mesmerized and enraptured me, and once he had me under his seductive spell, he took me with him to the dark side. And this is my story. I'm not a heroine, but a woman who was swept away into a dangerous adventure.

Chapter 1

1977

$\mathcal{T}$ransylvania felt like a film noir, I thought as I sat in the ·Romanian airline jet on my way back to New York. I was too deep in reviewing my impressions of my trip to have noticed anyone sitting down next to me in the airline's unique all-one-class seating, and I was startled when I felt a large presence to my left.

As the Tarom Airlines plane abruptly pulled back from the gate, I was aware of the tall, handsome man in the seat next to me watching me intently. I smiled, then turned to gaze out of the window, but when I glanced up a while later, my eyes once again met his. He looked to be in his mid-thirties, with classic good looks, intense green eyes, thick, straight light-brown hair, a straight chiseled nose, and an angular structure to his cheeks, chin, and jaw. He was dressed in an elegantly tailored three-piece cashmere suit.

He nodded, then introduced himself, his deep, rich voice telling me that he was Jacques de Borchgrave. In return, I introduced myself in French as Sheri Heller. "Ah, you are American," he said with a smile, determined to engage me in conversation. "What is your final destination?"

"New York."

"We were lucky to get on this flight. We might have been stuck here for days. They predict an airplane strike. I cut my business short, and I'll probably have to return before summer," he continued, his expression pained at the prospect.

This was the spring of 1977, and an earthquake had hit Bucharest several months earlier. He told me his business was selling cranes to the Romanian Government to rebuild high-rise buildings that had been destroyed.

I, in turn, told him that I had been on tour through Romania, Transylvania, and the Black Sea Coast with my mother and that she had continued the tour to Istanbul, but I had to return to my job at a contemporary art gallery.

Our nonstop conversation, in a halting mixture of French and English, was open and sharing, the easy chat that transpires between strangers who think they will never meet again. He confessed that he had been traveling constantly, not only to expand his business's international operations, but to recover from the breakup of his marriage. I could sympathize with him. My mother and I had also been traveling often, to help us both recover from the sudden death of my beloved father, a prominent Massachusetts attorney, who had died of a stroke right in his law office less than a year earlier.

We came down in Brussels to an especially rocky landing, and my new acquaintance insisted on escorting me to my gate for the flight back to the United States; we exchanged business cards. I didn't look at his card until I was on the plane to New York, and I was startled to see that it read "Baron de Borchgrave, Brussels, Belgium." What an irony, meeting a European of the noble class on a flight from a Communist country. Now I realized why he'd seemed somehow different. He was an aristocrat. A European noble. I couldn't wait until Mother arrived home to tell her and to tell my friends. It was a fascinating interlude on a long flight.

Back in New York City, I was caught up once again in my fast-track life in SoHo, the center of the contemporary art world. My career, working for the prestigious Sonnabend Gallery, was interesting. Robert Rauschenberg, Jasper Johns, Roy Lichtenstein, and Andy Warhol walked in and out of the gallery daily; there were endless rounds of exciting opening-night parties; performances given by artists like Gilbert and George; dinners at artists' lofts with a sprinkling of critics, film stars, and musicians as guests; spectacular evenings at newly opened discos. My circle of friends was growing daily, and I was finally settling into my beautiful high-rise apartment in a doorman building in the fashionable East Fifties. The only thing missing, I thought late one night as I returned from a dinner party, was a man willing to make a commitment for longer than an evening, for longer than his immediate quest for pleasure lasted.

My conversation with the baron had become a brief memory when he telephoned one evening a month later. He spoke slowly in English, repeating parts of certain sentences in French, to be certain I understood him.

"I have not been able to stop thinking of you, Sheri. I am completely fascinated by you. It has never been so easy for me to converse with anyone as I openly spoke with you. I would like to see you again. I'll arrange a business trip to America and stop in New York. Very soon! I promise. I'll write you a letter with all the details."

The stunningly handsome baron had reentered my life, and now he was always on my mind. His express letter soon arrived from Belgium, inviting me to come to St. Tropez in late July to spend two or three weeks with him. His invitation took me by surprise. I had thought he might come to New York and visit for a few days, but I had never expected to be invited to summer in the South of France! Unable to resist such an adventure, and curious to learn more about the baron, I cabled my acceptance.

He was pleased that I would be joining him in St. Tropez, he wrote in his next letter, and, almost intuiting my thoughts, assured me that he'd arranged for separate rooms, and was mailing me my plane ticket.

I felt more comfortable reading his letter, and reasoned that if any relationship developed between us later, I'd have had the opportunity to get to know him first.

In July, Jacques met me at Charles de Gaulle Airport in Paris. Wearing tight jeans and an open shirt, he looked younger and sexier than when I'd met him on the plane, and when he kissed me on both cheeks, then lightly on the lips, I felt an immediate, powerful "click."

We left Paris, already in its summer slumber, and headed towards the Autoroute du Sud, destination the Côte d'Azur, in Jacques's speedy white BMW 520.

I noticed the car's speedometer often registering 180 kilometers, or about 110 miles an hour, and I don't know whether it was the speed or the sheer daring of being on such an adventure that got me so excited. I often glanced at Jacques while he was driving, and I couldn't quite believe that I was in a car heading to the South of France with this strikingly handsome man.

As we conversed easily, using both French and English words and phrases in the oddest combinations of the two languages, discussing our route and forthcoming vacation, his eyes often flashed at me with a sensuous warmth, and I almost had to pinch myself to believe that this was actually happening.

As Jacques enthusiastically described the wonders of St. Tropez and repeated how anxious he was to show them to me, I just knew that this would be the best time in my life. I felt an overwhelming attraction between us.

The force of this magnetism made me shy at first, and I found myself covering my nervousness with much laughter and giggling. But after a couple of hours of driving our high-pitched excitement calmed a bit.

Toward the middle of France, near Lyon, we dined at Les Frères Troisgros, one of the eight best restaurants in the world—three stars from the experts Gault and Millau. A divine experience, and I could see that Jacques had taken great pains to plan a trip that would be an extraordinary discovery for me—and for us.

We arrived at sunset at a charming small hotel set in the hills above St. Tropez, where our rooms had private gardens and patios overlooking the village. This first night we went down and walked around the harbor, stopping in at various spots to greet Jacques's acquaintances. Then, after a light dinner at a brasserie in the Place d'Elysées—fresh oysters, steak *au poivre*, a bottle of wine, and the traditional *tarte au pomme*, St. Tropez's hot apple tart with Calvados poured over it—we browsed the trendy boutiques, where Jacques bought me an exquisite dress in transparent layers of white organza. "In St. Tropez, Sheri, the chic women wear a different-style dress every night of the week," he said, "showcasing fashion trends for all of Europe. I want to buy you everything so that you'll have the latest St. Tropez look for our vacation."

I told him I couldn't accept, but he just smiled and said, "You can accept. It would make me very happy to buy you beautiful clothes."

The next morning we awoke in our charming rooms, furnished in white rattan with a full wall of sliding glass doors leading out onto the flower-filled patio. Jacques joined me for croissants and coffee in the garden, in full bloom in red, orange, and yellow flowers, as were the gardens that dotted the surrounding hills; the air was fragrant with their scent, which mingled with the many herbs and spices that this southern region was famous for. The warm Mediterranean atmosphere seduced us with its cloudless azure sky, its twisted-branched Provençal olive trees, and the white stucco houses with their red-tiled roofs that spread before us in the village below. The setting was right out of a Cézanne painting.

The beach club at which Jacques had decided we would spend our days was Voile Rouge, the Red Sail, where the umbrellas and beach mats were red and placed in orderly rows along the beach. In the past years he had gone with his wife to Club Cinquante-Cinq (55), with its white umbrellas, but chose for us this equally chic club, where he was not known.

The club had an open-air restaurant with only a thatched roof as a cover against the hot sun, and a panoramic view of the beach and ocean, the beautiful white yachts at anchor offshore.

The first morning, Jacques took me to a thatched hut on our beach where the famous St. Tropez bathing suits were sold, and picked out two minuscule string bikinis, which the girls custom-fitted to me. When I insisted on buying the tiny top, he laughed. "In St. Tropez the bottom alone is quite sufficient. I will transform you into the Sheri of St. Tropez," he teased. "And in a week, you'll only cover your front with a little V."

From that very first day at the beach club we established

a daily itinerary which we repeated throughout the three-week stay. We arrived around eleven o'clock at Voile Rouge and were taken by the attendant to a front-row spot, where our mats were arranged and our red umbrella opened. After basking in the drenching Mediterranean sun and taking a swim in the warm, almost lake-calm clear blue water, we lunched at the beach club. It was always an elaborate full-course lunch of southern French cuisine with young chilled rosé wine from the local region, Provence. Most women dined topless in their string bikinis. Even the owner and the waiters wore the barest strings, covering only their genitals. They were all paragons of masculine bodies. Yet, amusingly, the service was formal; they brought the wines and champagne with a white napkin draped on one arm and presented the food in French style with a flourish from their serving trays.

While dining, we watched the serene beach scene and admired the landscape of perfect bodies. Voile Rouge, among the most exclusive of St. Tropez beach clubs, attracted high society as well as European celebrities, all spectacularly attractive, with perfectly formed, slim, suntanned physiques.

During lunch, balladeers went from table to table softly serenading the diners with Provençal folk songs or classical Spanish guitar tunes. After lunch, we often took a nap in the sun, had another long swim in the ocean, and stayed to sunbathe until the late afternoon.

From the beach club it was a ten-minute drive to the village where the harbor was. Outdoor cafés and restaurants lined the street that ran the periphery of the semicircular harbor, which was ringed with yachts. Hundreds of people strolled, seeing and being seen: truly a perfected art of the French. The late-afternoon dress for this ritual was the "just from the beach" look, with people throwing all types of innovative racy covers over their bathing suits. Jacques took me to his favorite café bar, Gorille, where we had our aperitifs and watched the parade of the chic and not-so-chic, that is, the day-tripper or camping contingent. The walking streets and cafés emptied out within two hours, except for day tourists, and people dispersed to their homes and hotels to ready themselves for the late-night scene. The harbor section came alive again after ten o'clock at night.

The evening itinerary featured a ten o'clock dinner at one of the fabulous restaurants, followed by several hours of dancing at one of the discos or nightclubs and an early-morning drink at the then quiet harbor.

Returning from the first day at the beach to our hideaway hilltop hotel, I sensed that the moment was nearing when we would make love for the first time. The sun was low in the sky, bathing the surrounding hills in a soft golden light, as Jacques brought our drinks out into the garden. The air was balmy, holding the intoxicating perfume of spices and flowers. He took my hand and we walked quietly around the hilltop garden; then we sat down and he studied me for a moment, his warm eyes searching mine. "Sheri, I wanted to bring you here to my favorite place . . ." He paused. "Ever since that day on the plane together, I couldn't get you out of my mind." He gazed at me again with such an intensity that I felt naked. "Your sparkling eyes, so alive, so exotic with their slight upward slant. That cute little upturned nose. Your soft, perfectly heart-shaped face and beautiful, sensuous, smiling lips. Your sweet smile lighting up those brown eyes, looking up at me, listening to me with such intensity, exuding such energy. I'd never seen a face like that. You don't look like the European women I know."

"Jacques," I gasped. I could only look at him, transfixed. Never had an American man spoken to me like this.

"And now that I've seen your body on the beach, your soft curves, your perfect hips and legs, I want to caress those curves. And your long silky hair sweeping your shoulders and back. Sheri, I desire you furiously," he whispered. In English, this may sound melodramatic, but in French, the language of love, it was perfect.

He drew me up and took me into his arms, kissing me all over my face and my eyelids. His body was still warm from the day in the sun and smelled of the wonderful summer scent of salt, tanning lotion, sun, and sweat. He pulled the strings of my tiny bikini, and the top and bottom dropped off in unison; then he guided me with his hand to help him off with his suit. We kissed for a long time in our private garden, feeling the warm outdoor breezes against our naked skin. He led me inside and we went into the shower, where we soaped each other's bodies, exploring each other for the first time. Jacques was incredibly handsome, Indian brown, with tight muscles all over his lean six-foot-six body. His legs were so long that they ended near my waist.

Then he lifted me onto the bed and slowly kissed my body, wrapping his legs around me with a delicate touch. He kissed my upper thighs and then, gently separating my lips with his fingers, he kissed me between my legs.

He sat up.

"I want to savor this first time together," he said tenderly. "Let me look at you." And he traced my body with his hands.

"Jacques, I . . . I am feeling the same . . ." He kissed my mouth, as if to tell me I need say no more.

I kissed his taut stomach and legs, his chest, his lips.

After a few moments he lifted me on top of him and very slowly eased into me, holding his breath as if to feel the sensation completely. We moved in a slow and cautious rhythm as he prolonged our pleasure, stopping and changing or slowing the tempo. After he brought me to an explosive climax, he followed with a powerful surging motion and held me in a tight embrace.

Then came a sweet, humorous moment—one of a sort that often happens to people who don't speak the same language.

"*Fais le bouchon*," he whispered into my ear.

"What? . . . In English, please?"

"I'll try to translate: Put the cork into the bottle. Do you understand?" he whispered, a little embarrassed.

"No . . . I'm sorry," I said, also embarrassed.

"I must be technical now. I am trying to say, create a stopper—you know, put your hand down there when I pull out of you, to catch the liquid," he said, forcing out the explanation in both English and French.

"Oh, I see." I giggled and obliged him.

We lay still for the longest time. And then he sweetly kissed me on the cheeks and eyes and with his hand gently brushed away the moisture on my face.

When he did this I suddenly became aware of how right this felt. Funny that I hadn't had a moment of hesitation over whether or not to make love with him. Always in the past I had gone through a whole dialogue in my head, a nagging debate with myself; usually it was resolved with a restraining order. Though my sexual experience was limited to a few boyfriends in college, I had never had a love affair, or what I consider a genuine, passionate, all-encompassing experience. Already I sensed I could fall in love with Jacques.

Never had sex felt like a passionate emotional moment; it had always felt rather like a pleasurable sport that ended in mutual satisfaction. The whole scenario of meeting Jacques on a plane and now being with him in the South of France, in one of the world's most romantic enclaves, made me wish that this had been my very first time with a man. But then again, I reasoned, it actually was—my college-age sex partners were just boys at play; Jacques was my first real lover.

As he left my room to dress for the evening, he asked, "May I now tell the hotel owner we'll be needing just one room? The one with the private pool?"

"Yes, great!" I smiled, envisioning making love with him in the pool in the middle of the night.

While dressing for the evening in the new white dress Jacques had bought me, I was deeply enveloped in a dreamy romantic state. We drove back to the village, leaving the car on the outskirts, since cars cannot enter the narrow alleyways that wind through the village. As we walked the narrow cobblestone streets, I started to feel like a St. Tropez woman, a *Tropézienne*. Not exactly like Brigitte Bardot, but getting close.

Dinner was followed by a midnight walk around the harbor section, and by this hour the festivities aboard the yachts were in full swing. On the back decks mammoth floral arrangements indicated that parties were in progress, and planks were lowered onto the walking street to admit guests.

Then from the harbor it was off to the nightclubs. Cave du Roi at Hotel Byblos was still the hot spot this year, as it had been for many years. It was the gathering place of the so-called Rich and Powerful, the International Set, the Jet Set, or whatever the current term, and the nightclub was charged with glamour and sparkle. Although it was not a private club, only certain people were admitted by the door attendant.

On the nights when we didn't go to a nightclub or disco, we had a late drink at the harbor or in the village square. All types of brass bands and entertainers moved from café to café entertaining the patrons. There were fire-eaters, acrobats, Spanish guitar players, and Senegalese dancers.

It was not difficult to become infatuated with the man who initiated me into this marvelous existence. This schedule was repeated, with slight variations, every day and night for our entire three-week stay in St. Tropez. Variations were tennis or windsurfing on the breezy Mediterranean and playing the French lawn-bowling game *pétanque*, an equivalent of the Italian boccie, in the village square during the cocktail hour.

I was fascinated by the baron's desire to make me into his ideal image. He admitted he treasured women, their glorious femininity. With each new dress he bought me, his interest in the way I carried it off grew stronger. He advised me on different hairstyles to suit the various dresses. Often he preferred my hair to fall freely in a mass of untamed curls. He even loved handling my hair, seeing how it looked back, up, or to one side. I laughed to myself as I tried to imagine how unthinkable it would have been for any of my past boyfriends to do this. God, I mused, European men are certainly different! Or was it European noblemen?

More intimate, even touching, was hearing Jacques try to describe in English the hairstyles he had in mind. The word for hair is plural in French (*les cheveux*), and he always spoke about my hair in the plural and without pronouncing the "h," to my amusement and despite my occasional corrections. "Your hairs, take them to one side and now do a crisscrossing several times like your American Indians and clip them up and around. Oh! Your hairs are so sparkling, my *chérie*."

In addition to this attention, Jacques was also mesmerizing me sexually. It was almost frightening to feel my body so drawn to another, to the point where his mere touch on my knee or shoulder at a restaurant might set off in me a sexual craving.

It fascinated me how he noticed smells and savored sensory stimulation. "The smell of the skin after spending weeks in the sea and sun and dining on Provençal rose garlic and spiced foods gets into the pores and scents the whole body," he told me in the final week during our late-afternoon love-making session. "And there is nothing more arousing for a man than smelling the natural body perfumes of a Mediterranean girl—sea smells, sweat flavored with garlic, herb scents and salty air. The most natural aphrodisiac. Nothing is as sensual. There are times I could climax just by lying near you and smelling you."

By the second week of our vacation, Jacques, feeling more and more comfortable with me, began to tell me more about himself. "We are very private people . . . in my circle, that is. We never talk openly about our lives. Not even with a lover. It's part of the code, you might say. It's baffling to me that I really want to tell you so much."

He revealed that he was the first person in his family who actually worked for the purpose of making money. All of the other Borchgraves had had diplomatic posts or positions in the military, but not in business. Most nobles collected income on their lands and sustained their financial position and maintained their castles. Now, in inflationary modern times, it became necessary to earn more money to support the castles and lifestyles.

Jacques admitted he resented the changed times. His company, started by an older cousin, imported construction equipment from the United States and sold it in various parts of the world, and also had a division that built yachts in the Philippines, which they sold in the South of France. Jacques called this activity "his little stab at business."

One night at dinner he finally spoke about his marriage. "We were married too young. Then Claudine immediately got pregnant. Two children, far too soon. As the years went on our relationship grew more and more distant. I had to end an intolerable situation. All the men were after her perfect body, I'm sad to say."

It surprised me that he was so open with me, but I

assumed that there was much more involved in this situation. He seemed to be a very principled man with a strong code of honor, and unfaithfulness had to be a cardinal sin to him.

Later, he explained to me that it was expected of him to behave in an exemplary fashion because he had to carry on his family's name and line; he had been trained for this role all his life. "Our titles in Belgium are the most pure of all those in Europe. They can only be granted by the King. And they are very important to us. I take my title and my role in the family very seriously."

He then confided in me something he claimed was his deepest guilt, speaking in a tone that he might use in the confessional.

"A fifteen-year-old girl committed suicide in my home and I was indirectly responsible. She had worked for me as a maid's assistant. Because I found her so competent with my two young sons, I paid attention to her and included her in family activities. Apparently she fell in love with me. When I discovered this I gave her notice to leave. Despondent that she would be discharged from service, she spread rumors that I had had an affair with her. It was ghastly! Soon after, we found her dead in her quarters in our home; she had committed suicide." He turned his face away momentarily, as if to hide his emotion. "The girl's parents accused me of forcibly violating their daughter, and it took a little money to quiet them. Their charges were utterly ridiculous. The whole affair was hushed up by my family, but naturally the word did seep out. I had a couple of very uneasy years over this, and to this day I feel a gnawing guilt that I might have treated her wrong."

I asked him whether he had thought the girl a disturbed person before the incident.

"No," he said quickly.

"Was she very lonely?"

"Well, no; she had the boys with her all the time," he said. His eyes focused inward, his expression tightening. I decided it was not my business to interrogate him. Suicide was such a frightening concept. Only once had it touched my life, when my fifth-grade teacher killed himself. His death affected me for years. I knew Jacques must be riddled with guilt.

His confession seemed to bring us even closer, adding a new depth to our relationship. And his masculine attentiveness and overwhelming tenderness—he kissed me at every opportunity very publicly throughout the day and night, and embraced me even while we were in the sea—grew to a fiery intensity by the last week. I had not a doubt that this was more than simply a summer fling for him; we both yielded equally to falling in love.

As the last day approached, we were in a turmoil, knowing that our idyll had come to an end. He assured me that we would see each other often, and he began speaking about the future, whispering over late-night drinks at the harbor that he would like to spend the rest of his life with me. Before he put me on my plane in Paris he again assured me that our romantic adventure was only the beginning of a long life together. Our parting was an emotional scene with all the drama of embraces, tears, and final kisses. I knew this would be one of many tearful airport farewells.

After my St. Tropez romance it was difficult for me to come back to earth. I threw myself into work at the gallery, but Jacques was constantly on my mind. Although there was a steady flow of mail between us, the distance made our relationship seem unreal. I was to join him in Paris for a week after New Year's.

Jacques chose a charming hotel in St. Germain des Prés, on the Left Bank of Paris. It was an incredibly romantic week as well as another sublime adventure, and Jacques showed me the nightlife as I had never seen it before—days full of top restaurants, nightspots, private discothèques, and even a high-class sex cabaret; another nonstop gourmet feast at lunch and dinner, another continuous high on the finest champagnes and wines.

It seemed as if our relationship had entered a second phase, the phase when a couple feel natural with each other and when the pressure of having to be "on" at every moment disappears. Language was also easier; we had come close to perfecting a bilingual method of speaking. We had widened our knowledge and could talk in complete sentences.

As the week progressed, Jacques's questions about my life became more searching, as did mine about his. I asked him why he had requested that I not call him on weekends, and he answered that he couldn't take any calls because his wife and sons visited every weekend at his home.

"Sheri, Sheri," he smiled, sensing my mood. "I stay on good terms with her so that she'll be more agreeable to a divorce by mutual consent and will appear at the hearings. Once a couple agrees to divorce, they live separately for at least a year. Then within the following year they must meet three times before a magistrate to announce that they have not changed their minds about divorcing. If one party decides not to appear for the final hearing at the end of the year, the whole process repeats itself all over again. Three times in front of a judge to say you still want a divorce. Unless one party finds grounds to divorce the other, then it is a different process, much more complicated than a divorce by mutual consent."

The week passed quickly. We spent the days going to art galleries in St. Germain des Prés and museums including the Louvre, the Rodin museum, and the Petit Palais French Impressionist collection. On our shopping tours Jacques bought me luxurious gifts: perfume, designer scarves at Hermès, the famous sexy Parisian lingerie, a Gucci pocketbook. And his generosity was exhibited even further at restaurants, where he ordered the finest champagnes and the oldest cognacs.

One night as our week together was nearing an end, Jacques poured us a cognac and became very sentimental.

"It will be difficult without you for the next five months, *ma chérie*. I wish I could ask you to come to Belgium and live with me now but my divorce procedure prevents that." Tears welled up in his eyes. "I have never been so happy—not for years. No one brings me such joy as you. You're so exciting to be with, always enthusiastic and happy. You are giving me new life, a new start. When you live with me in Belgium, I will make it a paradise for you. We'll travel constantly. I'll take you to Cannes and St. Tropez every summer, to hunting weekends in France in the fall. Perhaps we'll buy a home in St. Tropez."

"Oh, Jacques, it sounds like a dream life," I said.

"I know you are not the type to spend your time idly, so I'll arrange a position for you in my company. Yes, you'll handle something like, let's say . . . the business dealings with America and England. Would you like that?"

"Oh, yes, definitely. I could help you! I'd love that!" I was happy that he realized I needed a professional role, even if not in my chosen career. I knew that most women he spoke about in his circle didn't work.

"We'll make a life together that will make up for all the years I've lost. Life with you will be a dream, my Sheri. I love you."

Jacques drew me close to him in our large four-poster bed and threw back the quilt. "Lie back and let me give you pleasure; let me make love to you. Just take from me. A man sometimes wants to take joy in just your pleasure.

"Now just relax and enjoy me," he whispered.

He turned on the radio to slow, melodic French ballad music. I lay still, as he had asked, while he started massaging my feet and then putting my toes into his mouth and swirling his tongue between them with a suction that grew more and more enveloping, creating the most pleasurable feeling from this unusual erogenous zone. He moved slowly up first one leg, then the other, kissing and massaging each inch with varied stimulating touches: first with hard pressure from both his tongue and fingers, then with only his fingertips, barely touching my skin and bringing me to extreme excitement.

"Jacques, please, please let me kiss and touch you."

"Sh . . . Sh. I'll tell you when. Just think of your pleasure. Don't be afraid to let me show you how. Close your eyes." He took my ostrich-feather boa from the closet. "Close your eyes," he repeated in a hushed tone. He slowly moved the boa around my body, turned me over onto my stomach, and gently moved it along my back. Again trying to give me a sensation I had never felt before, he moved his tongue around the full curves of my buttocks and along the crevice. His tongue explored those sensitive areas and he pressed my buttocks firmly against the side of his face. He moved his head and tongue around and down with increasing suction and rhythm until I was shaking with pleasure. Suddenly he whispered something in my ear that, oddly enough, sounded like "Are you Jewish?" but at that moment I wasn't ready to ask him what he had really said. Then he entered me and climaxed while I was still shivering with the aftermath of my own orgasm.

Never had I had a lover like this. It almost frightened me that bodies could be brought to such pleasure.

"When you live with me in Belgium I'll teach you about sex, real lovemaking, and different pleasures that I'm sure you've never even fantasized about. There's a whole range, my girl. We've just started."

We spent our last day in Paris planning a year of meetings. He said he might pass through New York in the spring on the way to the Midwest on business. Then in July he planned to take me again to St. Tropez. He said perhaps he could arrange for me to arrive in Belgium and stay at his home overnight before leaving by car for the South of France.

When it came time to say goodbye at the airport, we were both desolate at the thought of having to leave each other.

"These partings are impossible," Jacques said. "I hope soon we will never have to face these long separations. I am deeply in love with you."

Early in March, the owners of the gallery asked me to deliver a small but valuable painting to a gallery in Paris. I flew there the next day and called Jacques. He was ecstatic about this unplanned visit and asked me to take a train to Belgium to visit him on the coming weekend.

I took the TransEurope Express to Brussels, and Jacques picked me up at the station. He brought me to the Hotel Amigo in the center of the Old City of Brussels, right on the Grand Place, explaining to me it would be dangerous for us to be seen together in his home.

He was glowing with happiness and took my coming as a sign that I couldn't wait to see him again. He had already planned to take me to his uncle's castle, which he had considered home since his father died. His uncle was like a father, and was also his confidant and knew all about me. And to my great surprise he had also arranged a lunch at his mother's home. She too knew about our love affair and wanted to meet me, but the thought of being presented to these two important people in his life made me more than slightly nervous.

In the early evening, as we left for our dinner at the castle, Jacques sensed my nervousness, and he advised me to act naturally, saying that his relatives were very unassuming and relaxed.

We drove about a mile into the property and crossed a drawbridge over a moat to arrive at the castle. It was a mammoth, ancient, gray structure with four corner towers. Because I could not be fully accepted and received in the proper style while Jacques was still married, we were not greeted at the door; instead we walked through the first atrium into a big reception hall filled with sculptures and tapestries, and then into a side tower. There, in a circular study, sat his uncle and aunt in front of a fireplace. It was an intimate room where aperitifs were served before dinner.

They greeted me warmly. Jacques's Uncle Gérard spoke fluent English, while his aunt could not speak a word of it. We all drank kir before dinner. I had a rare attack of shyness, but as the evening went on I started to converse easily with the uncle, a man about seventy years old, slightly built, balding and fine-looking, with clear blue eyes. He was friendly and charming and, at the same time, highly formal and reserved. He explained that he spoke English so well because he had lived in Washington, D.C., where his father had been a diplomat. The aunt was a small woman with an angelic face and manner. She was in her late fifties or early sixties. She spoke very softly and had a warm, receptive manner. Neither one had any of the haughtiness I had expected. Jacques had explained to me that she was of the highest nobility, with one of the loftiest titles in Belgium: marquise. Her family had always been close to the King and Queen.

The butler came into the tower and announced that dinner was ready. We passed through what seemed an endless succession of reception halls and ballrooms filled with treasures, and finally entered a large dining room which had a very high ceiling with ornate designs. We were served by a couple. The dinner was the traditional French: a multi-course meal, each course accompanied by a different old fine wine. Jacques's uncle and aunt told us of their plan to sell the castle, not for financial reasons but because it was too cold and damp for an older couple during the long, rainy Belgian winters. They were in the process of converting a three-hundred-year-old farmhouse into a much more livable home than the castle.

From the comfortable, easy way they treated me that evening I felt I was being accepted as Jacques's fiancée, and his uncle indicated that he expected I would be present at many family events. After dinner Jacques and his uncle took me on a tour of the castle. The furniture, artworks, carpets, and tapestries were of museum quality. There were five salons of different degrees of formality, each with an ornate fireplace and precious antique clocks on every mantel. These clocks were the most extraordinary works of art—some were in pure gold with a series of mythological figures around the face; others were of porcelain, again with delicately sculpted figures in a landscape, and still others had figures that moved each time the clock chimed. Many of the halls, salons, and ballrooms were not in use during the winter and were barely heated; in some, the furniture was draped with protective coverings. There were marble floors of intricate design and coloration throughout the first floor. One grand staircase led to the main bedrooms and living quarters; along the steps stood marble and bronze sculptures and large Flemish Master paintings. There were also French School Orientalist paintings and Italian Renaissance paintings, all in gilded, ornate frames.

In the second-floor sitting rooms, studies, and bedrooms, huge tapestries of court, hunting, and pastoral scenes covered entire walls. The bedrooms were furnished in fine French period furniture; some beds were of unique baroque and rococo design. Every window looked out onto meadows and forests.

I was overwhelmed at the opulence. The experience of spending an evening at a castle where people actually lived made me more completely aware that I was truly in a world very different from mine.

The next day was the scheduled luncheon with Jacques's mother, and, needless to say, I was very nervous. We drove into the best section of Brussels, comparable to Fifth Avenue on the park in New York City, where Jacques's mother owned an apartment which took up a whole floor of the building.

His mother wanted to speak to me alone first, and Jacques dropped me off, saying he'd join us within the hour. A maid opened the door and led me into the salon, where the baroness was waiting for me.

Jacques's mother was stately, very pretty, with soft features and light hair. She was about sixty years old and around five feet, seven inches in height, dressed in impeccable taste, wearing elegant jewelry. Her most noticeable feature was her penetrating blue eyes, which seemed to assess me in one moment. If not for those eyes, her face would have been gentle. In contrast to the sweet and noble aunt, she looked and acted just as one would expect an aristocrat in Europe's highest circles to do. She moved and gestured with authority and assurance.

The opulent salon was fitted with family heirlooms and sixteenth- and seventeenth-century Flemish paintings of pastoral and interior scenes done in vivid reds and earth colors, giving the apartment real warmth.

I had the distinct sense that this meeting would determine my future with Jacques, that the baroness's approval or disapproval could affect a decision in any matter of importance. She spoke slowly and clearly, and soon covered my family background, education, and even my attitude about children. I answered all her questions directly and openly, without hesitation, and began to sense that she liked me, possibly because I was not intimidated by her.

She seemed to approve of my appearance and diplomatically expressed her relief that I was not "the brash American," rather that I had a European manner about me. By the time Jacques arrived we were feeling somewhat relaxed with each other.

Soon after we finished our aperitifs we sat down to a fine formal lunch, served by the maid, who was also the cook. Throughout the meal Jacques's mother watched me closely as if to observe my table manners. Because my mother grew up in Europe and taught me to handle utensils in both the European and American styles, I chose the European.

Our luncheon conversation was very cautious; subjects were American politics, which always seemed to fascinate Europeans, New York lifestyles, and food. She seemed interested to know whether American couples lived together without marriage. She said it was the new trend in Belgium. She also wanted to know the prices of luxury apartments in New York, as she was aware of the investment potential. She asked me questions about stocks, bonds, and other money instruments, as if to test my familiarity with finance.

Jacques had rarely brought up the subject of money and investments, and never the subject of cohabitation. I was relieved when the lunch was over and couldn't wait to return to the hotel to spend some relaxing time alone with him.

That evening Jacques and I savored each other's company with a deepened feeling. After the meetings with his relatives, our relationship seemed to have entered a new phase.

There were a few phone calls from the family, who obviously knew where we were staying, and Jacques beamed after each call. After one from his mother he said simply, "She liked you very much." I was dying to hear more and questioned him, but he only added, "My mother was surprised at how well you spoke French and she thinks you are very pretty and intelligent." He seemed relieved and happy that his mother had given me the stamp of approval. He said that his uncle and aunt were enchanted with me.

The night was another exercise in abandon and sexual rapture, and I felt as if we were falling deeper and deeper in love. After a light supper in a restaurant hidden away in the Old City, we made good use of the huge penthouse terrace off our presidental suite at the Amigo. I knew from the first moment when Jacques spotted the terrace that he would be inspired to sexual creativity.

"I never want you to forget your first times making love with me in Belgium," he said, leading me onto the terrace to face a sweeping view of turrets, towers, red-tile roofs, and narrow winding streets. "Don't look around," he said as he kissed me on the back of the neck and then held me from behind in a tight embrace. "Do you promise?"

I giggled as I felt him lift up my dress, unfasten my back garters, and slip down my panties. "I promise."

"Now I just want you to concentrate on feeling me inside you. Make yourself realize the moment—you're starting your erotic history in what will be your new country!"

As I let myself be hypnotized visually by the maze of streets in the spectacular medieval vista before me and by Jacques's gliding movements, which created a friction that warmed our bodies against the cool March breezes, I felt so totally alive, so daring, so right in the moment. I didn't look around.

Suddenly Jacques turned me to face him and lifted off my dress. He stripped and proceeded to engage us in every conceivable sexual position that a couple with a height difference of a foot could manage while standing up. He arranged my legs in directions I never imagined they would go in and lifted me powerfully against him. His strength, agility, and control astounded me.

"I want you to never leave Belgium. I want you to live with me always," he said between long kisses on my breasts. "Always. Always . . ." he whispered over and over again while penetrating me, moving in to the deepest point and then withdrawing completely, keeping his rhythm and strength steady. I moaned with pleasure.

"Yes," he said. "Yes. I want to hear your responses. Your pleasure. You're always quiet. Too quiet. I think because you're so young. It's exciting for me to hear you. Don't hide your responses from me, *chérie*."

I remembered a recently released French song called "*Je t'aime*," in which the female singer feigns her steadily growing sexual excitement until she seems to reach a powerful orgasm against the wild rhythms of the music. The song embarrassed me; I was far too self-conscious to be vocal like that.

"Darling, the aroused whimpers of the female, the throaty moans, the hot breathing is so natural. Earthy. The timeless sounds of lovers in the heat of rapture. The sound coming from a small hotel with open windows to the street as you pass in the night. The sound coming from somewhere on an isolated beach. The sound is its own poetry.

"Don't be ashamed of your femaleness, your arousal. It excites me to make love to you until I've exhausted both of us." As Jacques brought me to climax that dark night, the sounds of lovers in the heat of rapture, as he called it, echoed over the guildhalls and roofs of the medieval Grand Place.

"When you will live with me in Belgium," he said, "I will promise you an erotic history more rich and satisfying . . . than most women will ever know."

The next morning Jacques took me to the airport to catch the plane to Paris, where I made my connection for New York. I was desperately unhappy to leave, but having met Jacques's mother and part of his family, I felt I had truly entered his life. It was no longer a hidden affair.

Chapter 2

It was our second exciting summer together, the second time we would spend a long, sybaritic month in our fantasy city, St. Tropez. Following the same route south from Paris, traversing France, Jacques and I were cruising the final lap toward the fabled Riviera landmark aboard a friend's yacht. We'd been together for a few days, reveling in being a couple again, when we had a series of discussions about our future.

"If Claudine cooperates, *chérie*, my divorce will be final on September thirtieth," Jacques began, "and then I want you to come to Belgium to live with me."

We were sitting on deck watching the spectacular sunset, sipping champagne. At his words I felt my heart leap. "Jacques," I replied, aghast. "I will only come to live with you as your wife." My words, spoken so forcefully, astonished me. I hadn't given my answer a moment's thought before uttering it.

"Sheri, *ma chérie*, you know it would look better for society's sake for me not to remarry immediately." He tried to calm me, to convince me that it would be more acceptable for him to live with me for a few years before we married.

"Jacques," I replied firmly, now certain my words had been the right ones. "I will live with you only after we are married, only as husband and wife. I won't leave my country, my family, my friends, even my career to come to Belgium as a 'live-in.' "

As I looked out over the calm sea, I was beginning to understand why he had always spoken about "being together forever" and had never mentioned the word "marriage."

"And as for children, you must understand I've decided Philippe and Alain are more than enough responsibility for me. You're so young . . . without children of your own . . . could you agree not to have any?" His eyes, serious, intent, searched mine.

At that time in my life I was ambivalent about the idea of having children, and wanted to postpone even the thought until my career was well under way. I was looking for a happy, active, and interesting life, I told Jacques, which did not necessarily have to include my own children.

"Jacques," I said, smiling, "your children will be just fine. I'd like to get to know them and hope to get close to them."

"But Sheri, there is no purpose for marriage unless we plan to have children. Marriage is just a legal document that doesn't make our love any stronger!"

"Jacques," I laughed, thinking that men worldwide used this same argument and that it didn't sound any better in French. "You're beginning to speak in clichés!"

The conversation about our future was not resolved until later that night. While we danced wildly to the pounding rhythms of "I Will Survive" at the Byblos nightclub, Jacques whispered two words into my ear: "You won." And still while dancing, he flagged the waiter to bring another bottle of champagne to our table. When we sat down, he raised his glass and said, "To the future Baroness de Borchgrave."

St. Tropez felt like our summer home now, and, informally engaged, we went about our scintillating schedule of pleasure-seeking with a stronger sense of being together.

But sparks of conflict erupted, and certain traits of Jacques's that I hadn't noticed the year before emerged during those weeks. Jacques never spoke to people on the beach, and admonished me if I, being naturally friendly, began a conversation or continued one beyond a certain point. "In my circles, Sheri, we never disclose personal details about profession or family to strangers or mere acquaintances. It is a major breach of etiquette. Our lives are private. Please, Sheri, understand this. And when people ask me what I do, I say I am in business. I don't volunteer any more information than that to strangers. If they continue asking me personal questions, I simply don't answer them."

I slowly began to understand that he truly believed that friendships could not exist between classes; the nobles associated only with each other. I accepted his thoughts and feelings and didn't resent his lectures because I realized that he was preparing me to fit into his circle. I must admit, though, that a tiny question slipped into my consciousness. Why, then, was Jacques associating with me? How had he ever fallen in love with me? But perhaps that was the answer. We were in love.

Our easy rapport soon returned as the glorious days stretched endlessly before us. We had fun shopping for the latest dresses, the year's "in" bathing suit. Made of less than six inches of fabric, it covered only the pubic area with a small V, with a string going between the cheeks. A small tuft of pubic hair showing at the top of the V was considered sexy, and this style was especially favored by true blonds and redheads to prove they were genuine. Of course, others remedied the problem by dying their pubic hair!

When one wore the tiny creation, the pubic hair had to be styled and shaved meticulously. Jacques insisted upon shaving me each morning to fit the V, as naturally as if he were applying suntan oil to my back. I found this gesture sexy and endearing.

One day on the beach, while watching the parade of perfect women's bodies in the skimpy bathing suits, I asked a most regrettable question. "Jacques, how is it possible that all these women have such large, perfectly rounded breasts?"

"Sheri, my little innocent, these women all have had the operation! You see, I know you have a complex about yours. You're self-conscious, my darling. I could always feel that. Am I right?" he asked.

"Yes, but I've gotten used to the idea of not having much on top. I like my body!"

If only he had known what I went through before accepting that big breasts were not destined to bloom on me. During my teenage years, I always wore padded bras and padding in my bikini tops. Once, while I was waterskiing, the padding fell out of my top. For the next year, it became the famous story that none of the kids would let me forget. I then sent away for several devices promising to increase my breast size through exercise, but finally went back to padded and push-up bras. Although I remained self-conscious about my breasts, I found a way to play up my good features and kept a good figure.

Suddenly Jacques turned to me. "I'm going to take you to a doctor in Paris."

I was shocked. I never thought that normal people, or at least those outside show business, had such an operation.

Just the thought of any operation filled me with dread, but I managed to say, "I'll give it some thought, Jacques. And I'll research the risks! I know you'd want me to do that."

"You Americans are so paranoid about health! Do you think all these girls on the beach would have done it if there were health risks? Sheri, will you come with me to Paris and see the doctor? He'll tell you there are no such silly risks!"

"Yes, I'll come," I said, knowing that I shouldn't agree. Yet one part of me was not totally convinced that I shouldn't look into it—take his idea seriously. Since puberty I had always dreamed of having beautiful, full breasts. I'd admired my friends and relatives who had ample bosoms.

I remembered how embarrassed I was in high school when, during the inevitable make-out sessions in cars parked along the dark streets near our town's lake, the teenage boy's hands ventured onto my breasts, only to fondle rubber foam. I'd quickly push his hands away, hoping he hadn't realized that what he'd squeezed wasn't me. It might be nice to have breasts, even silicone breasts, that Jacques could savor.

"Good!" Jacques said triumphantly. "In fact, you can have the operation this winter, so you'll be healed by the wedding date. Let's plan the wedding for April."

"Wait, Jacques. I only agreed to talk it over with a doctor. Please don't start planning the wedding around it."

"No, no, no. Of course not. But why are you frowning, *chérie*?"

"It is just that I never thought you had such strong feelings about that part of the body," I said. And then to lighten the mood I added, "I always thought you preferred the other half of me, since you seem to always concentrate your attention there."

"*Chérie*, I love every inch of you. But after you have the operation, you'll have the most pampered breasts in Belgium. And when you make your debut at all the important social events, you'll have endless precious gems dangling between them. Magnificent jewels between magnificent breasts."

Seeing that Jacques's imagination was triggered and that he was increasing the pressure to convince me, I changed the subject abruptly. But he brought the topic up with intense enthusiasm at every opportunity. And I watched the operation develop into an issue of ever-increasing importance, one that ultimately, by trip's end, was distorted into the deed that would prove my love for Jacques. My breasts had become an obsession! Why was Jacques finding this external adjustment so important? Didn't he love me for myself? Finally I decided to give him the benefit of the doubt, rationalizing that Europeans were very different and there was no way to understand their vanities. In his society, summers were lived nude or topless on yachts and on beaches, so having perfect breasts, always on view, was important.

Instead of flying home out of Paris, I decided to leave from the Brussels airport in order to spend the last days and night at Jacques's mansion. He wanted me to see the property in its summer beauty.

As we drove up the long graveled driveway I gasped at the sight of the massive white-brick mansion with its several wings. A red-clay-tiled roof mounted steeply toward several chimneys; on the upper levels paned windows protruded like small shadow boxes from the roof. There was a circular walled area of four-foot-thick stucco, with heavy wooden gates leading into the property. Except for roof restoration, repairs, and whitewashing of bricks, the outside of this four-hundred-year-old mansion was in its original state, Jacques told me.

He took my hand as he rushed me through the house and out through the French doors leading to the formal garden, then down several flights of steps to the magnificently planted pool area. There, in the charming pool house, with the scents of roses and lilies and lilacs in the air, he opened a bottle of champagne and ceremoniously toasted the arrival of his future wife. "To you, *ma belle chérie*," he said softly, "my baroness, and to our life together." Tears came to my eyes as he spoke the words so filled with emotion. Was this a dream? After endless years of men who wanted sex but not a relationship, who didn't want to commit to marriage, here was a man who offered me everything.

"I love you, Jacques," I whispered, and then to make myself believe I was really going to become a Belgian baroness, I toasted the Belgian King and Queen. "To King Baudouin and Queen Fabiola. Long live the King and Queen!"

Jacques found my toast so surprising that he burst into laughter.

The large pool with its adjoining house was on a lower level of the property and was completely private. Perfect, Jacques told me, for nude summer living.

I had never seen him so animated and talkative as he was while showing me his estate. The property was surrounded by trees. In one section there was an orchard of fruit trees, plum, pear, cherry, and apple; in another, a shooting range.

After we took a walk around the hilly, expansive property, Jacques brought me back into the house. Throughout the first floor there were high wood-beamed ceilings and red tiled floors in large squares of clay. Antique carpets lay in the living and dining areas, which were combined into one enormous room. A huge gray stone fireplace with one massive wood beam as a mantel dominated the living room, and from this room five floor-to-ceiling French doors opened out into the gardens.

All the furniture was massive, in carved dark brown woods, and had been brought from the family castle. A floor-to-ceiling antique black wood cabinet that held rare books and family memorabilia, an imposing writing table, and two treasure chests in a gold leaf pattern stood along the walls, supporting splendid arrangements of dried forest flowers in wrought-iron bowls.

It was a very masculine house. In one corner of the living room was a sizable walk-in bar, its top constructed of two heavy wood beams. Throughout the room hung old master paintings from the sixteenth and seventeenth centuries, all framed in orange-gold wood. A few were austere-looking portraits of noblemen. All were lighted from above with hooded lamps. And throughout the room, along the walls, hung sconces holding electrified candle lights.

A five-foot-high antique confessional made of white-painted wood with pure gold inlay stood against a wall beneath a portrait of a man in a red cardinal's robe. Several eighteenth-century string instruments hung on walls, and a crown with eight balls atop the spokes hung above the fireplace; the eight balls, Jacques explained, represented the baronial title.

The dining room contained a long, oversized antique wooden table with twelve wooden chairs, and two heavy buffets. Two four-foot angels carved out of dark wood, left unpainted, protruded from one wall. A Flemish seventeenth-century pastoral scene dominated another. There was also an imposing antique grandfather clock which chimed the hours.

Through a swinging door we entered the large country kitchen. It had a sizable center work counter made of butcher block. All the cooking utensils hung from the ceiling beams, along with strings of garlic, salamis, hams, and bags of shallots. On the windowsills were small flowerpots containing a variety of herbs. In one corner stood a ceramic barrel with a spout, which contained vinegar. Jacques told me the vinegar was naturally fermented by pouring red wine over the mother vinegar bacteria. This growth was a rare find in nature and could produce vinegar forever if never allowed to dry out. The kitchen was very well equipped and had all modern appliances.

A door opened from the kitchen into a playroom, which was in total chaos and contained a number of ancient-looking toys—disabled rocking horses, troops of fallen wooden soldiers, broken trains and tracks, and rusty trucks. This had been his sons' game room, and looked as if it hadn't been touched in years.

Another door led from the kitchen to the servants' quarters, which had separate entrances from the outside. All the walls in the house were of white stucco. The dark wood doors, with intricately designed metal handles throughout, were closed. There were doors everywhere, some leading to closed-off wings, others to a woodworking studio, an electronics workshop, a photography darkroom, a restorer's work studio, a disco. The house seemed to be a complete little world.

"Now, *ma chérie*, let's go upstairs," Jacques said, grasping my hand. A handsome wooden staircase, with a carved banister, led upward, its walls hung with Flemish oil paintings.

Jacques's bedroom, unlike the formal, grand rooms in the rest of the house, seemed beautiful, warm and airy. There were shadow-box windows protruding outward, again with many small panes and with dark brown wooden shutters that opened on the inside. The white stucco walls were poured in such a way as to create a round effect. And the built-in arched closets were designed with heavy, ornately carved wooden floor-to-ceiling doors. An oversized, perfectly square bed was covered with a luxurious white goatskin throw. Over the bed hung a painting of two women entwined in a sensuous embrace. In an open alcove, several steps led up to a sunken tub in emerald-green marble, set on a carpeted platform. The toilet and bidet were in the same open alcove, with no enclosure for privacy around them, as were the double sinks built into the long marble counter.

The view from the bedroom, overlooking the many levels of the property and the pool, was spectacular. One French door opened onto a small balcony above the garden.

Other furnishings in the bedroom were an antique desk, a mirrored dressing table, a green velvet chaise longue, and an armoire. Above the armoire hung several hunting guns, and on the desk lay two ornate pistols.

The upstairs hallway had many closed doors, and Jacques took me into only a few of the rooms: the guest rooms and the two austere barracks-like rooms which were the boys'.

Outside the master bedroom in the hall was a giant chest of drawers with a peculiar medieval painting, framed in black, over it. The picture had a gloomy look. Jacques said it was the family's painting, brought out during funerals. It was still hanging because a member of the family had recently died. It showed the family crest—a medieval tower and the crown with eight balls.

Since I had shown great interest in Jacques's family heirlooms, he brought me back to the first floor and opened one of the chests containing records of the Borchgraves. The chest was in Jacques's possession because he was the head of the family.

He showed me documents from the Belgian King bestowing on his ancestors the title of baron, the family seal, and other official documents given to them by the Royal Belgian Court. There were letters and documents dating to the twelfth century.

I was fascinated, almost awed by the ancient papers, seals, and leather-bound documents. I was standing in this magnificent mansion, standing in history, seeing, reading, almost feeling history on the yellowing pages before me. The history of my husband-to-be, the history of a noble European family that reached back through the ages. Although I was getting tired, Jacques couldn't resist finishing his historical introduction to his family, and then put on sixteenth-century hunting music, which he analyzed in detail.

The evening was eventful, and the perfectionist Jacques was determined to create an unforgettable, nonstop loving ritual to commemorate the last night of our summer together. Wilhelm Reich, the philosopher and psychologist whose idea that man's achievement of happiness was based on the orgasm, could have risen from his grave that night to witness our total dedication to his theories.

A formal dinner, served by the maid, was the start. Jacques put on Renaissance flute music and poured a very old and special wine to celebrate our engagement. At poolside we had our after-dinner liqueur, a pear liqueur with, oddly enough, a small snake in the bottle. "The most effective aphrodisiac," Jacques said, smiling.

Jacques illumined all the property with powerful floodlights and we walked around nude in the balmy summer night, the slight breezes caressing our bodies. As we strolled hand in hand, pictures of the future flashed in my mind. Jacques's beautiful mansion and property made the perfect romantic enclave for lovers and seemed to be designed expressly for sensuous living. With swimming pool, Jacuzzis, tanning room, fireplaces, and private gardens with small sculptured waterfalls, I imagined how inventive we could be once we lived together here as husband and wife.

When Jacques led me up to his bedroom, he surprised me by opening a closet filled with exquisite nightclothes—

gleaming silk robes, ostrich-feathered night jackets, hand-embroidered and lace-trimmed satin, taffeta, and organza gowns, drifts of silk and lace teddies. "A present for you, Sheri. I thought you'd like a few new gowns to wear. And now that you'll soon come to live in Belgium, I'll keep them here, waiting for you." Then he took my hand and brought me over to the vanity table, where there was a small wrapped box. "Open it, darling."

A dazzling diamond and emerald necklace, with the gems arranged in alternating rows and short, centered strands hanging directly from the front, glowed on its antique velvet bed.

"This piece has been in the family since the early eighteen hundreds. The gold setting is from Great-grandfather's gold mine in South Africa. Grandmother gave it to Claudine at the birth of our first son. But I took it back from her when we decided to divorce. After all, it is part of our family history. It is now yours, and you'll wear it for the first important event at court after we are married. It will be here, awaiting your return.

"Now, darling, choose a new gown and put it on for me." He buzzed the maid and through the intercom asked her to bring up Mumm Crème de Crémant champagne.

I stood out on the balcony overlooking the breathtakingly beautiful property, still lighted, with the gardens in full, fragrant bloom. I was wearing a tissue-thin pink organza floor-length gown, my legs exposed through long slits at each side. Jacques handed me a glass of champagne.

"You look ravishing in that gown, Sheri. I knew you would. I desire you, my treasured beauty, at every waking hour."

I melted at his words, feeling so feminine and loved.

What a pity more men didn't realize the effect tenderness and romance had on women, I thought.

He approached me, gently unfastened the many hooks, snaps, and ties of my gown, and let it slide to the floor. He lifted me up, holding me tightly in his arms, and kissed me while slowly twirling us around and around. He got onto his knees and kissed and caressed me.

"Quel chat! Quel chat! Si mignon comme une petite fille," he repeated, sweetly teasing me.

Then he leaned against the balcony and lifted me up to him in the lovers' embrace. "Our first and last time together in this house for a while," he whispered, as he eased himself into me. "I want to fix this moment . . . how you feel . . . in my mind, so I can fantasize about you during our separation." He moved so fluidly, adjusting his position, changing the angle, creating rhythms that brought us to pulsating heat. I'd never imagined how different making love could be with a man with such experience. He could control his timing to climax just moments after me. Once again he asked the mysterious question that sounded like "Are you Jewish?" To which, though finding it strange that he was asking this question, perhaps to further excite himself for some inexplicable reason, I responded, *"Oui, oui."*

Later, when I coyly asked him what he always whispered to me at his final moment, he looked at me questioningly and replied, "Do you mean, *'As-tu joui?'* "

"Yes, that's it," I said, now realizing he spoke in French. "Don't you know the phrase?"

"No."

"It means, 'Did you come?' " he said, a little embarrassed.

"Yes, yes, that's what I thought," I said, trying to hold back a giggle. *"As-tu joui,"* pronounced in French, sounded exactly like, "Are you Jewish?", especially when whispered

in the heat of passion. And I, of course, had always replied,
"Yes, yes!"

The plans had changed, and Jacques and I were off to Paris
to meet the world-renowned plastic surgeon whose specialty
was breast implants. I would leave for home from Paris.

We consulted with the husband-and-wife team, the Doctors Rémy, in their splendid Parisian town house, which was
also their office. Dr. Rémy, the husband, as it turned out,
was an artist as well, and his town house was filled with
paintings. He and I immediately established a fine rapport
and discussed his artwork and the latest trends in art in New
York and Paris.

During our conversation both doctors told me that they
were hesitant to perform a breast implant operation on a
woman who had not yet had children, but after Jacques
assured them that I was not planning to have children, the
doctors discussed the implant method with me. We made an
appointment for February of the next year, giving me ample
time to recuperate before the wedding, which was planned
for April.

I didn't tell Jacques how confused I was about the idea.
I wanted to think it out completely. The doctors' explanations
of the implant operation and the rather gory accompanying
pictures didn't make the whole process look too attractive.
They spoke of the risks of leakage, rupture, and even rejec-
tion, but claimed no real dangers to the health, like cancer
or any other complicated medical condition. Most of their
implant procedures had been very successful, they said unequivocally. After questioning them on every imaginable aspect, I found myself still very much on the fence—sometimes
liking the idea of having a newly sculpted body and other
times thinking of it as dangerous folly. But I always pushed
the most nagging question to the back of my mind: why was

the operation so important to Jacques? I didn't even want to think about it; I didn't want to disrupt my happiness.

At the airport our parting was a down-to-earth exchange of plans rather than the usual endlessly yearning kisses. Jacques would now face the uneasy final months of keeping good relations with Claudine so that she would sign the third and final divorce paper. I told him I'd probably be away at Fire Island or the Hamptons during August, but that I'd write to him daily.

"*Ma chérie*, even if she doesn't give me the divorce, I promise I'll find some way. Then it will only take another year or so," he said, trying to be reassuring.

No, I thought, not me. Please do everything you can! I won't wait around indefinitely! Suddenly the warnings of my friends never to get involved with a married man who is awaiting a divorce came rushing into my mind.

As if he read my thoughts, he said, "I'll make it happen by September's end!"

I walked through customs, wondering whether this might be the last of our airport farewell scenes. Then, in our established parting pattern, I looked back at him and waved after every dozen steps, and he did the same. But this time he had tears in his eyes and mine were dry.

Chapter 3

"Think about everything very carefully, Sheri," Mother warned after she'd heard about the breast enlargement issue.

"I'll research it by seeing doctors here and, as you well know, give it a lot of thought," I told her. We discussed the subject often and sadly conceded it was coloring the excitement, the unspoiled romantic perfection of my love affair. We vacillated about what I should do. I knew Jacques's divorce was far from a certainty, but because I loved him I had no desire to begin dating, or to get close to anyone else. Needless to say, this was an agonizing period for me.

On the critical day, early in the morning U.S. time, Jacques called with the news that he had obtained his divorce. I still can't explain it, but a strange emotion came over me. I heard myself telling Jacques that I really hadn't decided whether I wanted to marry him, and asked that he give me a month to think it over. He was astounded and said he would call me in a few days to see whether I had come back to my senses.

Did I mean what I had said? The distance, the separation from him, almost certainly caused my cold feet. Separation from a loved one does cut some kind of psychic cord. The operation and my indecision loomed over me. Then, too, until his call I had never really believed it would happen and so I had never thought out what it would be like to leave my world. My life had begun to take shape for me, and now I wondered, did I want to give up an exciting career in the art world, my friends, to enter a world that was foreign in every sense—the Old World of the nobility, customs and codes, tradition—light-years away from the thoroughly contemporary and unconventional lifestyle I had grown to like? But that foreign world went with the man I loved.

The next morning a florist delivered enough breathtaking bouquets and long-stemmed roses to turn my apartment into a magical garden. "Please marry me," Jacques's message read.

And the very next afternoon, when the doorman buzzed and said there was a Baron de Borchgrave to see me, I was overwhelmed.

Over a three-day period of discussions, wining and dining, he succeeded in convincing me that our married future would be richly rewarding. He took pains to assure me that Dr. Rémy's breast operation was entirely safe; he even yielded to my wish that the operation be done after the wedding so that I wouldn't be alone during the recuperation period, though he did insist that we hide the fact of my surgery from his family. And, finally, he conceded that he would be open to the possibility of having one child together after we had been married a few years.

As part of an unforgettable day of celebration, Jacques took me on a fabulous shopping spree in Manhattan's finest shops and boutiques: St. Laurent and Chanel for clothes, Cartier and Bulgari for glorious jewels. All for my new life. The excitement of these days swelled to ecstasy, and Jacques and I were back to the soaring romantic highs of our St. Tropez summers, when we were the golden couple in the golden coast. I remember thinking over and over, "This could only happen in a movie!"

The last evening, as we sipped champagne at the private club in the Pierre Hotel, Jacques took my left hand and slipped a magnificent ring on my finger. A three-and-a-half-carat dark-red ruby was surrounded by teardrop diamonds, set asymmetrically to accent their brilliance. He said he had commissioned an artist-jeweler to design it, using gems that had been in his family for generations. Then, as the song "The Last Dance" came on, he led me to the tiny dance floor and we slowly swayed together, lost in the depth of our feelings, realizing, finally, our commitment to each other.

He asked me to come to Belgium as soon as I could, to arrange for the legal aspect of the marriage and for the planning of the wedding party. He also wanted me to meet his sons, Philippe and Alain. I promised to come after Thanksgiving.

It was finally real. I was going to Belgium and this time could enter Jacques's home through the front door. My family held Thanksgiving dinner early and I left for Belgium on Thanksgiving Eve.

When I arrived, Jacques's house was overflowing with flowers—birds of paradise by the dozen, orchids, and other exotic arrangements.

Jacques had organized a schedule of steps we would have

to take in the next few weeks to obtain the marriage license. Within several days we had to present all the papers to the Belgian marriage court, which would have the formalities completed in six weeks. Our names and parents' names had to be posted at the City Hall for two weeks before the marriage date. For days we went from one city office to another in a web of formalities.

Jacques was more romantic than ever before, bursting with plans for our future life. He didn't even want me to return to the United States before our April wedding date and urged me to have my mother ship all my personal belongings.

Midweek we went to his notary-lawyer to sign a marriage contract. Jacques claimed it had become a standard document in Belgium, and was to protect both of us.

We arrived at the notary's impressive suite of offices and were ushered into a large conference room with eight people already present—lawyers, witnesses, and translators—for a formal ceremony, lasting forty-five minutes.

The translator interpreted the long document, which outlined how property would be divided in case of divorce and prevented each of us from touching any of the other's property or money that was not earned or amassed while we were married. The contract stated that I had the right to live in the conjugal home for my lifetime in case of divorce or death. Other long provisions dealt with the baronial title and the family castles, with foreign bank accounts and property overseas in case of death; when they were translated from legal French, I couldn't completely follow them. I was asked whether I fully understood. Yes, I understood. But I started to think I was about to sign my life away.

After signing about ten copies of the document, everyone present congratulated Jacques and me so profusely that

I thought perhaps I had misunderstood and instead had been made a partner in the "barony."

Now Jacques seemed especially solicitous, happy that this hurdle had been leaped. I could see that without my signature the marriage would probably have been off. As a lawyer's daughter, I experienced more than a little anxiety over my neglecting to consult my own lawyer before signing such a document, but again, since Jacques had presented the whole matter in such a casual way, I thought it was only the usual procedure before marriage.

That same evening, Jacques's mother took us for dinner at the most famous restaurant in Brussels, Villa Lorraine, in the forest in the middle of the city. She told us she was leaving that week for Marbella, Spain, and seemed happy that all the documents had been signed. I realized that she was referring specifically to the marriage contract. As drinks were being served, she conversed with Jacques, and I watched her eyes—cold, pitiless—boring into his. Even talking with her son, she seemed removed and distant. The conversation then focused on business and investments she had in America, IBM, Honeywell, Sperry Rand, Westinghouse, and land investments in Florida. She asked my opinion of her holdings, and was interested in what I had to say, complimenting me on my knowledge of investments.

She then asked that we meet for lunch to discuss plans for the wedding reception, along with several other issues she wanted to talk over with me. It seemed that she had not yet accepted the idea of a wedding so soon after Jacques's divorce. The dinner was endless, and there was a tension throughout, yet after dinner, the baroness invited us back to her apartment for liqueurs.

The simple word "apartment" did not seem right for

Baroness Adriane's splendidly opulent residence. A private elevator opened directly into it, and there were balconies with exposures in all four directions. The interior was furnished entirely in antiques, and every wall featured paintings with hooded lights above them. The baroness was obviously an avid collector of sixteenth-, seventeenth-, and eighteenth-century European old masters. Once we arrived, the mood changed to celebration and anticipation of the coming marriage.

The next morning Jacques had arranged a meeting for me with his ninety-three-year-old paternal grandmother, who was at present the highest-ranking baroness of the family. She and I would be the two baronesses in the family who held the most important titles, he said. Only women married to the firstborn son holding the title of baron can use the title Baroness de Borchgrave. Among those in the know, there is a big distinction between the people who must use their first names with the title and those who need not. And there are all types of differentiations. For instance, the small *de* identifies the aristocratic families, whereas the capitalized *De* means nothing. Jacques said that later in the evening he would explain more and give me a book to read on the proper use of titles.

Jacques's grandmother lived in an Old World–style apartment. She too had chosen to move out of her family castle, preferring the comforts of a city apartment to drafty stone rooms.

Since Jacques hadn't described his grandmother, I expected to meet an ancient dowager. Instead, I was greeted by a pretty, gracefully aged, slim woman who appeared to be not more than seventy. She had silver-gray hair, perfectly styled, which framed a soft, expressive, barely wrinkled face with animated green eyes. She was dressed to perfection in a gray wool skirt, ivory silk blouse, and gray cashmere cardigan, worn with a long strand of pearls and other precious jewelry. To my delight she spoke English, and she charmed me completely with her easy flow of conversation and humor.

"Only two weeks ago, Jacques surprised me with the overwhelming news that he planned to marry a beautiful young American girl," she said, graciously adding, "Jacques has not sufficiently described you. You are lovely beyond words and I am full of joy that you will soon enter the family. Now, come sit beside me and tell me a little bit about yourself while we have our afternoon tea. Where were you born in that big country of yours?"

"I was born and grew up in Massachusetts, Baroness."

"Please, Sheri, call me Mémé. That is what the family calls me. Now tell me all about your family, *ma petite*. Give me a little picture of your life in America."

I told her about growing up in a small historic town. She liked my stories about my large family of uncles, aunts, and cousins and our summers together at my parents' vacation home on a large lake in the beautiful New England countryside.

"Well, *mon petit chou*, how can you leave all this family in America and live in Europe so far away?"

"Mémé, I love your grandson, Jacques, and I would live anywhere in the world with him."

"Do you have brothers? Sisters?" she asked.

I felt comfortable enough with her to tell her of the death of my older brother, which happened when I was very young, and the more recent death of my father. Speaking about this, I started to get choked up.

"*Ma petite* Sheri, this is all so emotional for you. First, meeting our family, leaving your life behind . . . facing your new life . . . enough for today. Visit me often for afternoon tea and tell me more about your family, and I will tell you all about the family history and background." She kissed me on both cheeks as we parted, and I was overwhelmed by her graciousness, suddenly realizing that she was the first in the family who had inquired about my background.

"Jacques," I exclaimed on the drive home, "your grandmother is remarkable! I adore her and can't wait to visit her again."

"Now, Sheri," Jacques warned, "don't become too friendly with her. She likes to tell too many tales and causes trouble. For example, for a long time she had been living with a man twenty-five years younger than she who was bisexual. He wanted to marry her but the family prevented the marriage. He was quite a gigolo and a fortune hunter, and caused great harm to the family. She has had quite an adventurous life and I do not approve of some of her conduct." Jacques stopped with that provocative comment, and said he would explain further one day.

We had been invited back to the castle of Uncle Gérard and Aunt Hélène for a formal dinner the next evening. Jacques said this time it would be correct form for them to greet us at the front door, since he was now divorced.

Throughout the evening there were congratulatory toasts and I was treated as if I were already a member of the family. As the dinner ended, Aunt Hélène retired to the bedroom wing and Uncle Gérard, Jacques, and I continued discussions of philosophy and politics over brandy until after 3:00 A.M. We talked about German philosophers, especially about the philosophy of Friedrich Nietzsche, on whom I had written my senior thesis at Columbia University.

At one point, when Jacques left the room, Uncle Gérard took the opportunity to warn me that Jacques's mother would soon summon me for a serious discussion. "The baroness wants to discuss her religious convictions with you because she feels obligated to make a statement of her religious principles. As a Catholic, she cannot officially recognize divorce or a second marriage. Jacques's first marriage will always be the marriage of the Church to her. Yet, as a mother, she will approve of your marriage and accept you as Jacques's wife. I think she is silly to even bring this subject up to you, since it doesn't serve any purpose. But she likes to feel that she is righteous and a good Catholic. Well, anyway, be ready for her speech. Good luck to the new baroness!" And he raised his glass.

"I respect you, Sheri," he said then. "I will enjoy many evenings like this one, with stimulating discussions. Unfortunately you will not meet many in these aristocratic circles of ours who can discuss more than food and hunting. I am hard pressed to find people who care to discuss anything but those boring topics, and of course gossip. Yes, we excel in circulating trivial gossip. Sheri, you'll be the favorite subject of these gossip-mongers for months to come. They'll be analyzing your every move—everything you wear, say, or do. But I'll tell them that a very bright and personable young woman has entered our circle."

Just as Jacques returned to the room, Uncle Gérard was on a roll and ready to tell me some juicy gossip himself. I left the castle pleased that Uncle Gérard had confided in me, happy that he had provided me with some insight into this family. Jacques had not yet given me a real indication of his mother's feelings, and by now I knew she was the power figure in the family. The next meeting with her would be a strenuous test and perhaps another probing into my character and background. Although Uncle Gérard had told me that she approved of the marriage, I knew that until I heard it from her directly, nothing was definite.

When the baroness called and asked Jacques to bring me to a certain Belgian farmhouse restaurant where we would have lunch alone, I presumed that this was to be the serious discussion Gérard had warned me about. Since she would soon leave for Marbella and would later meet Jacques's sister Isabelle for Christmas in Provence, where a relative had a château, it would be our last meeting before the wedding in April.

There was no small talk. Over aperitifs, she immediately started a serious conversation. She discussed her religious convictions and told me verbatim what Gérard had forewarned me about, then asked me whether I planned to practice my religion in Belgium. I answered that I observed only the more important Jewish holidays and would perhaps want to be home each year for the major ones. Once the religious issue was out of the way, she posed other probing questions, wanting to know whether Americans believed in short-term marriages. She said she wanted this to be Jacques's last marriage and inquired whether I felt this would be my only time. She was persistent, worried that my American outlook on life and marriage might be different from that of the Belgians, but my answers seemed to satisfy her and erase her doubts.

Then she started telling me about her life. She had been widowed when she was only thirty-three and had to raise four children alone. She confided that Isabelle had caused her the most problems and that Jacques also had been a difficult and demanding child, and that to this day he was often silent and moody. The best approach with him, she suggested, was never to let an argument get out of proportion. I told her that I had already experienced some of Jacques's moods but felt confident that I could handle them. He was mostly even-tempered with me, I said. She replied that there had been a remarkable change in Jacques since he had met me. I was uneasy about her use of the word "remarkable." What did she mean?

"How will you deal with living so far apart from your mother?" she asked.

"Well," I replied, "we will try to see each other several times a year, and will call each other regularly."

She promised to take me to meet various family members and help me learn the customs of the Belgian aristocracy, adding that she would send her cook, who was an expert, to instruct me in French cuisine, and that she herself would teach me how to entertain in the Belgian style.

She questioned whether I was ready to face and accept a new way of life. She said that since I liked the excitement of New York City, perhaps I would be bored with life in Belgium. I assured her that, on the contrary, entering a new society and perfecting my knowledge of another language would never be boring for me, and that I hoped to work in Jacques's business with him, which certainly would be interesting.

Then she asked the testing question. Why had I fallen in love with Jacques, and, more specifically, what did I love about him?

In slow French, pronouncing each word clearly, I explained, "Throughout our long romance I have grown to love him. First it was infatuation. His elegant manner and his presence really struck me. I felt we were physically well suited. I liked the fact that he is a very successful businessman. Now, more and more, I find that his silent strength and his calm personality complement my exuberant style. I especially like his sensitivity to me and his reverence of femininity. I like that he is such a romantic. And I am sure we can make each other happy."

"I feel Jacques is too much of a romantic and you are a good balance for him," she said forcefully. "You are practical, realistic, and optimistic. He is prone to be a pessimist about many aspects of life, and he has a strict personal code of honor and rigidly adheres to it. I like your sunny optimistic nature. It is so refreshing. Yes, Sheri, I feel strongly that you are the right woman for Jacques."

At that she abruptly got up, and kissed and embraced me with tears in her eyes. "You have my permission to make your wedding plans as you wished, but I would prefer you wait the three months as planned, for society's sake. I find it appropriate, since this is a second marriage for Jacques, to hold a small wedding reception at my home. I will arrange it as soon as you and Jacques choose the exact wedding date. Only close friends and family will be invited. Who will be coming from America from your family?"

I told her that my mother and perhaps an uncle and aunt would come. As I said that, I had an amusing thought: I envisioned my whole family arriving at the wedding party, forming into a circle, and breaking out into an ebullient hora danced to "Hava Nagila." As I left I thanked her for offering to give the wedding party.

As I walked out, exhausted yet exhilarated, I had to marvel at myself for carrying off a complex conversation in French with my indomitable future mother-in-law, who had scrutinized me throughout with her cold, critical expression.

It had been a trying two and a half hours of giving the right and well-thought-out answers, and I was relieved that the session was over. Bringing our romance to the conclusion of marriage took more energy than I ever could have imagined!

That night Jacques said he had a surprise for me, a reward for doing such a good job with his mother. She had called and told him she was now ready to accept the idea of this quick remarriage and said she had been quite impressed with me.

Jacques brought me upstairs and we walked down a long

corridor. He opened a door at the end. "Your private room," he said proudly. I was amazed to see that he had converted a large room into a professional ballet studio. He had mirrored two walls completely, floor to ceiling, and had installed ballet bars and a stereo. He had told me to be sure to bring all my leotards, tutus, and ballet slippers, but I had never suspected he would create a personal dance studio for me.

"Do you want to try it out, darling? Put on your tights and a tutu and later I'll come and watch you."

I did my warm-up exercises for almost an hour, and toward the end of the session Jacques came and, after watching me for a while, slowly approached me and removed my tutu, pulled off my tights, and lifted me onto the dance bar. A dance studio is a place for perfecting art, where men and women ready their bodies for greater feats—always sexually charged, because it is forbidden to break out of professional roles and give in to sexual feelings.

Watching in the mirror as Jacques made love to me drove me wild with excitement. From the bar he lifted me up and danced me around the room, delighting me by spinning us around over and over again and then doing some adventurous lifts and movements to the expressionistic music of Stravinsky and Bartók. Then he placed me back on the bar and slowly moved with me in rhythm. We watched our movements in the mirror until the quickened pace accelerated us toward a climax almost in unison. We had fired each other so strongly that we both shivered with waves of tingling sensation and repeated spasms.

My personal dance studio, I suspected, would prove to be a favorite place for sexual play.

I was finally to meet Jacques's sons. The boys would come for dinner and stay overnight. I immediately suggested that I sleep in the guest room that night to ease the boys' psychological adjustment to having a new woman in the house, but Jacques dismissed the idea. He felt we should make no attempt to hide our love affair from them.

But tension filled the air between us once the boys arrived. Philippe was about fifteen years old and bore a remarkable resemblance to Jacques. Alain was a boyish thirteen. Both looked like young aristocrats, very handsome, slim, and rather tall for their ages. They were markedly formal and polite.

Jacques had the bright idea of loosening them up by serving them champagne, and it worked. They soon let down their guard. Both tried out their school English on me, and I encouraged their efforts. After a simple dinner, Jacques gave them the electronic submarine war game I had brought along as a present, and this proved to be the final icebreaker. It took all four of us a long time to figure out the instructions, written, of course, in English, before starting to play the game, which they continued to play for hours on Saturday. A few times throughout the day they politely approached me and asked me questions in French. They wanted me to translate many American rock and disco songs. At that time Donna Summers's *Hot Stuff* album was popular in Europe, and Jacques laughed as I struggled to translate the words to the most popular songs. It was quite impossible to explain to the boys what "I want hot stuff this evening; I want hot stuff tonight. Give me hot stuff . . . I need hot stuff . . ." meant. I finally told them their father could surely explain it. I loved their questions about whether the American cowboy movie stories were true.

Their calm, polite, and correct manner throughout the day was unlike any behavior I had ever seen in American teenagers. Although we had had what I thought was a successful first meeting, when the boys were about to leave I noticed that they stiffened up completely, became formal, and thanked me for the gift with a cool handshake and a ringing, "*J'étais très heureux d'avoir faire votre connaissance, Mademoiselle Sheri.*"

With that trial behind me, I hoped that I had finished the toughest assignment. Jacques had planned to take me to meet his brother, Marc, at the monastery, but a letter arrived which changed that idea.

It was a long and philosophic letter, he said. In essence it said that Marc could not meet me because that gesture would signify his approval of the forthcoming marriage. If he had met me it would have been his religious duty to discourage his brother from remarrying. Marc wrote that he would meet me only after the marriage took place, since at that time the marriage would be a fact. It would be undertaken without his interference or encouragement. Marc would then be guiltless of influencing his brother either way. He wrote that he had heard many favorable comments about me and that only his religious convictions kept him from meeting me.

Although Jacques was furious at his brother's attitude, I was fully able to understand Marc's rationale and was not insulted or resentful.

Having accomplished all the essential formalities and arrangements for our wedding, Jacques took me to Paris for our last romantic prewedding fling, and then I was off to New York.

With less than two months remaining before the wedding, I began to wind up my life in New York. I resigned from the Sonnabend Gallery and sublet my apartment to a friend, since I still had a year on my lease. I made calls to friends and family all over the country to tell them of my forthcoming marriage, and soon congratulatory messages, letters, and calls began pouring in from everywhere, wishing me well in my new life. Mother then began to receive discreet calls, asking about the proper wedding gift for a baron and baroness. I moved in with Mother for the remaining time, and started shopping for my trousseau. An experienced fashion expert at Henri Bendel worked with me for days and pulled together an entire wardrobe, from designer suits for daytime and evening to cocktail dresses.

The only thing that dampened the mood of this period was my indecision about the breast operation, my fears. I finally decided to research it thoroughly once and for all. If it was safe, I'd do it, I decided.

Immediately, I scheduled appointments with four doctors: my family physician, my gynecologist, and two plastic surgeons. With all appointments completed, the prognosis was resoundingly negative. My gynecologist and family doctor did not even want to speak about it and advised me to reconsider marrying a man who could request such unnecessary and dangerous surgery. Even the plastic surgeons discouraged me. They suggested the operation might increase the risks of breast cancer, mostly because the implants blocked breast X rays, and told me more about the hardening which frequently occurred after implant operations.

I was able to research the operation further by contacting a friend of a friend who had had the implants. We spoke at length on the phone, and she detailed the long and painful recuperation process. She said her breasts were now as hard as baseballs. She also told of the necessity to change sex habits permanently—the missionary position was no longer possible, she explained, because the weight of the man was too heavy against the fragile breasts. She was always afraid of rupture. Clearly, she regretted her decision to have the implants.

After these discoveries, I called Jacques and told him of

the doctors' objections and of my conversation with the woman. He insisted that the doctors' warning applied only to the American method of performing this surgery and that the European method was far more advanced and safer. As to the change of sexual habits, he responded that it wasn't true and then joked, "We are inventive enough to find many new sexual positions."

When I told him to take my fear of the operation seriously and said that the doctors warned me that it might increase the risks of cancer, he dismissed my fears as unfounded and again remarked, "You Americans believe that everything causes cancer."

By the end of the call, he had managed to convince me that the European method was really far advanced and shouldn't even be compared to the American one, and pointed out the many movie stars and models who had had the implants done in Europe. He became exceedingly tender, reassuring me that he would never suggest anything in the world that would harm me. His love for me was all-encompassing, he said, and he had chosen the top surgeon—an artist—to ensure that the results would be exquisite. I was reassured and even excited at the prospect of being reshaped by an artist.

Two weeks before I was to leave for Belgium, Jacques called, and after a short conversation about wedding plans, asked, "How is your mother planning to pay for your operation, Sheri? Will she send the checks directly to the hospital and doctor or to my account?" When he quoted the staggering amount for the doctor, hospital, and hotel, I was stunned. Not really knowing how to respond, I blurted out that Mother would send the check directly to the doctor.

"Please do this immediately," he urged, "since the doctor must be paid before the operation. And I've made hotel reservations in Paris for your recuperation week. I think your mother should stay with you while you recover. Then she can leave Paris for New York, and I'll pick you up by car. I don't want you flying so soon after the operation. And *chérie*, I realize Dr. Rémy is a bit expensive, but he's the best. When my wife Claudine had her first operation I made the mistake of taking her to a Brussels surgeon. It was an awful mess. It took several operations but Dr. Rémy corrected the other doctor's work and now her breasts are perfect. Just perfect! Anyway, I miss you, *ma chérie*, and I'll love caring for you."

After his call, Mother and I just sat together, in a state of confusion and disbelief. Not only was Jacques insisting on my having the operation, he expected me to pay for it. I regretted saying that Mother would send the check, but having never paid for anything during all my travels with him, I wasn't prepared to discuss any money matters. His generosity had been overwhelming. Why this change? He had never mentioned my paying for the procedure before. Try as we might, Mother and I just couldn't fathom the mystery and could only assume that some custom or code dictated that before marriage it was the wife-to-be's responsibility to take care of health costs.

But his sudden announcement that his first wife had not only had the operation but had then undergone additional correcting operations really shook me. It scared me back into a state of indecision. Ever since the age of six, when I had seen my nine-year-old brother in a hospital, where he died, I had been terrified of hospitals and hated even the talk of sickness or medical procedures.

But then I began to wonder why Jacques had fixed the surgery for three days after the wedding. Although we'd already had sufficient romantic "honeymoons" together during the past summers and wouldn't be traveling until the coming summer, I couldn't begin to understand his timing.

And how would he explain my sudden disappearance three days after the wedding? Followed then by a month of seclusion? What a rude first impression I would make on my new circle!

Day- and nightmares followed. I knew I couldn't go through with the operation so soon after our wedding, and decided to ask him to postpone it for at least six months. Since overseas telephone calls, with their echo-delay, can cause confusion, I decided I'd wait until I arrived in Belgium to plead my case. I knew he loved me so much that he'd immediately understand my hesitancy to become a mystery woman to his family so soon after our marriage. Mother agreed with me, offering the opinion that he hadn't thought things through.

Loaded with three trunks, skis, and other luggage, Mother and I arrived in Belgium the weekend before the Tuesday wedding. Jacques awaited us at the airport with two cars and drivers, one just to transport all the luggage to my new home.

Chapter 4

$\mathcal{A}$t Nivelles City Hall we were ushered into an impressive chamber, where the mayor, wearing a colorful official sash emblazoned with his medal of office, rose to meet us. Jacques and his mother exchanged formal greetings with him. My mother and the baroness were then directed to sit on a bench on a dais to the right of the mayor. The baroness gazed at Mother coldly.

From his high podium the mayor began the ceremony, reading several lengthy French documents. I understood only the names, which flowed in an endless chain: "Baron Jacques Jean-Pierre Guy Bernard de Borchgrave, residing in Nivelles, Belgium, son of Baron Paul Henri Albert, Jean-Pierre Guy Marc de Borchgrave, and son of Baroness Adriane Marie Jeanne Isabelle Magdelaine de Borchgrave, born as Countess Adriane Marie Jeanne Isabelle Magdelaine von Huart," he read, taking few breaths. When my parents' four-syllable names were read they sounded like simple staccato by comparison. I glanced at the baroness, wondering at the pained expression on her face.

The mayor stood up suddenly, asking us to stand and take our vows. *"Oui,"* I said confidently, relieved to answer the question after three years of courtship. Jacques's *"oui"* was an almost inaudible, shaky sound. We placed the thin gold bands on each other's fingers, then signed the documents; both mothers signed as witnesses.

Seemingly in a daze, Jacques kissed me; then Baroness Adriane, unable to disguise her discontent, pecked me three times on alternate cheeks, the Belgian kiss, and murmured a congratulation in English.

Why was the baroness so upset? I wondered. Because the wedding hadn't taken place in a church? Jacques hadn't appealed to the Vatican to annul his first marriage—a procedure he had always felt was hypocritical. Or had it dawned on her that the new baroness was a Jewish girl, the very first in the family, who would be written into the purest of family trees? Or did she simply not like Americans, or anyone, for that matter, not from within her closed circle? After all, Jacques was her eldest son, the one who carried the title until his death, and his wife would carry it until hers.

The questions continued to tumble through my mind as we walked out of the chamber. A cold Belgian drizzle fell as the four of us left City Hall for the wedding luncheon in a quaint farmhouse restaurant. The somber mood lifted somewhat after the second bottle of champagne, yet there was still an undeniable strain among us.

The wedding party, a small affair with only the close family invited, was to take place that evening at Baroness Adriane's apartment. The baroness had thought it inappropriate to invite *"toute Belgique,"* "all of Belgium," the small, tight circle of the country's titled royal, noble, and aristocratic families.

After all, as she had explained, the wedding must be kept discreet. The formal announcement would be made to the larger circle in time, after Jacques's sons became adjusted to the idea of the marriage.

While dressing for the evening's elegant events, Mother and I anxiously analyzed how we would act with this alien noble group. Jacques had prepared me, telling me that I must try to speak only in French, greeting each guest individually with the phrase *"Je suis très heureuse de faire votre connaissance"*—meaning "I am very happy to make your acquaintance." I could vary the phrase by replacing "very happy" with "delighted" or "enchanted," but he insisted I keep to the whole long tongue-twisting statement, which was the polite form. Mother, who understood some French but didn't speak it easily, would be correct if she spoke in English. We would translate for her. Jacques had also urged that we refrain from asking anyone personal questions, and instead make polite conversation on general topics such as life and customs in America versus those in Belgium, and travel. The family members would all be introduced to us with their full titles, and later Jacques would privately explain who was an aunt, uncle, or cousin.

He also remarked to Mother, "Madame, as I already told Sheri, I would prefer if you not mention to the guests tonight that you are from New York. I have told certain people you come from Boston. You see, here it is hard for us to believe that anyone would want to live in New York City. It is too uncivilized a place. Most of my relatives like the city of Boston, or the idea of it, that is. Boston, to them . . . Well, they feel it is closer to the European style of life. Since you both have lived most of your life there and only recently moved to New York, I don't think it would be dishonest to say that you are from Boston. Madame, please don't feel this is unusual; it is just that my family has such fixed ideas."

Of course I knew that his request went deeper, but that he didn't want to say more in front of Mother. He didn't want New York mentioned because, as he once told me, his circles thought of New York City as "brash" and "Jewish."

As we had discussed privately, only his mother and brother had been told I was Jewish. He felt that there was no reason for the entire family to know at the beginning of our marriage, that it would only cause problems if "all of Belgium" knew. And, since no one would dare ask about my religion if he didn't offer the information himself, it could be kept confidential until after I had been accepted by the circle. I was very secure with who I was and didn't feel I must blatantly take a stand in front of "all of Belgium," so I acceded to his wishes because I believed it was only a temporary measure.

During the past three years, as we had gotten to know each other, Jacques had thoroughly explained his codes and customs to me, and while the formality and pomp seemed arcane by American standards, I was challenged. Formality was integral to Jacques's life, no more limiting, perhaps, than it would be in a family of politicians, where even more public posturing and social restrictions are involved. Here, I was to live as the lofty baroness in a place where nothing had changed for centuries. And I was determined to learn the customs.

"Je suis très heureuse de faire votre connaissance," I managed to say over and over again through the long reception.

Mother and I stood in a long receiving line at the wedding party, where the counts and countesses, marquises, and barons and baronesses were out in force to greet us. And to each I clearly repeated my phrase, followed by a gentle handshake and a sweet smile. Their response was quite consistent. A cool, formal acknowledgment was followed by a scrutinizing gaze. Baroness Adriane was at Mother's side facilitating her introductions.

The men were dressed elegantly. Many women wore an almost uniform-like combination of a long evening skirt, dressy silk or satin blouse, a velvet blazer or vest, and impressive heirloom jewelry. Others wore understated floor-length gowns in muted colors. Almost all wore rings with a large central gem surrounded by diamonds, similar in design to my engagement ring. I surmised that this was an inner circle symbol. Mother wore a sea-green silk chiffon gown with an embossed pattern on the transparent flowing overlayer, and I an ice-pink tissue silk taffeta strapless gown with a subtle design in gold and silver threads. We felt appropriately festive, and our gowns fascinated many of the women, apparently used to their never-changing, conservative evening clothes.

The Roederer Cristal champagne flowed, and foie gras on toast squares was served endlessly by butlers. The party was given in the formal living room, which opened into the vaulted dining room. Both were dazzlingly decorated with massive spring flower arrangements and large candelabra. The tall, glowing candles illuminated the rich earth tones of the many seventeenth-century Flemish paintings that hung on the walls. A single pianist played Mozart and Chopin on a baby grand piano. During this long predinner champagne fest, Uncle Gérard took Mother and me to a private corner. Grinning, he said in a conspiratorial tone, "This little noble circle is the most self-involved and superficially educated group you'll ever meet. Excuse my frankness, Madame. Sheri, don't make the mistake of being impressed by all of this! I hope you'll be able to stand living among us!"

"Uncle Gérard, it is kind of you to warn me," I said, winking at Mother.

"As Jacques has probably told you, Sheri, I didn't come from this circle. I married the marquise some twenty or so years ago. That is why I can tell you—it is not easy to be a part of all this pretentious nonsense. I never have felt part of it and never will. Be warned. They will test you continually. You will not be accepted for years. If ever! But pay no mind to this. You are here only to be Jacques's wife, you have no need to go along with—" He stopped speaking as he saw Jacques approaching.

"Sheri, Madame, Gérard, please come to the table," Jacques said, smiling. "I hope Mother's choice of menu will please you. Madame, please sit over there with Grandmother de Borchgrave."

During dinner, Jacques, surprisingly open with his family, revealed some "personal details" about me and our courtship. Everyone appeared to be scandalized on hearing that Jacques and I had been seeing each other for three years, since they had been told of the marriage plans just the month before, the first time they'd heard of "the American."

"Sheri comes from Boston. Her father was a prominent attorney there. He was up for a judgeship. He died several years ago, just before the appointment was given. Sheri graduated an important American university, one on the level of Harvard in Cambridge, with a degree in philosophy," he proudly pointed out to several aunts and uncles and his brother and sister at our table. Since it was rare in these circles that young women sought higher education, everyone seemed impressed.

"She had been involved with art—painting—when I met her, in an art gallery," Jacques continued.

"Old European paintings—restoring?" an uncle asked.

I knew that dealing in old master paintings was an acceptable endeavor; women in these circles generally did not work, and the few who did were strictly limited to certain fields—teaching elementary school, restoring antiques, working in certain areas of the arts.

"No," Jacques said quickly, explaining for me. "In America there is an interest in paintings created today. She's involved with helping 'living' artists develop an influence. You could call them modern sorts of works."

"Maybe now, though, I will become interested in Flemish painting," I offered, to the smiles and nods of those seated near me.

Jacques then diverted the discussion, back to a safe favorite—what Americans eat—and an animated food discussion continued for some time. How amusing that during this very first meeting with me, the family, though curious about "the American," restricted their conversation to the safest, most impersonal topics!

After the dessert—a splendid artwork, a horn of plenty overflowing with ices and sorbets in a rainbow of colors—was brought out on several platters and presented around the room, telegrams from America were read. There were stacks of them but I stopped the reading almost immediately when I noticed the blank expressions on the faces of most of the guests, who probably didn't understand a word of English. Later, Marc, Jacques's handsome, bearded younger brother, the Jesuit monk, offered a toast in both French and English.

The party broke up early, since the family had long trips back to various parts of Belgium—long by Belgian standards, which meant an hour at most. Those who had come from France, from the north in Normandy and from the south along the Côte d'Azur, would stay the night at the family château. The guests left, each saying a cool goodbye with a curious smile, each formally distant. Strangely, no one wished Jacques and me good luck or expressed any other cordial wish. I wondered why they didn't, and I became more uneasy with each chilly departure.

During the trip home, Jacques, acting unusually formal and stiff, commented to Mother, "Madame, I spoke with some of my family and they all thought you were a dignified lady. Pretty and younger than they had expected. I believe they liked you."

"Thank you. Your family was very kind, Jacques," Mother responded. "The wedding party was beautifully arranged. Please, Jacques, thank your mother and tell her how lovely the evening was and how grateful I am to her for all her efforts in arranging it. I said this to her in English and I hope she understood me. And your grandmother, at ninety-three, is remarkable."

"Sheri, everyone agreed that you were beautiful and unusually poised. My family marveled; they thought you carried yourself like a European girl. Both my sisters, Isabelle and Catherine, said they thought you were sweet and natural. Of course that's a big compliment coming from Catherine, who's so natural herself, but perhaps not from Isabelle, who is quite a manipulative woman. You must stay away from her. I'll tell you why in time. Anyway, the dinner was excellent and I'm sure everyone approved of the evening!" I was intrigued by his description of Isabelle, and I was determined to find out more later.

Finally, when we had bid Mother good night and were alone in our bedroom, Jacques was formally distant. When he didn't observe the symbolic wedding-night ritual, I was stunned. I couldn't sleep, thinking, as I lay beside my sleeping husband, that for a romantic to omit this presaged deep trouble. I realized that Jacques's behavior had been so markedly out of character since I had arrived that it must mean he had suspicions about the operation. I shivered at this prospect, which I'd soon have to face.

The next morning, over breakfast, Jacques announced that his mother expected Mother and me at twelve o'clock sharp to join her for lunch. "I'll see to it that Roland drives you there. Please be ready by eleven-thirty," he said in an upbeat tone. "Madame, you and my mother will have a lot to discuss and since it is private business for mothers I will not be joining you. Sheri, you must be there only because they'll need an interpreter. I think Mother's cook has prepared one of her very best; you'll be having baby quail with her most delectable walnut sauce and roasted endives. And certainly her rich chocolate mousse cake. Madame, you see that we might have the most dreadful rainy weather here in Belgium but we certainly keep our spirits up with our superior cuisine. Oh yes, and Mother will take out a rare Burgundy, perfect for game, for the occasion. Anyway, good luck on your discussion. I'll see you at six."

"Mother, what does he mean by saying that you two will have a lot to discuss?" I asked after Jacques left. "This all sounds a bit mysterious. What do you think? Some ritualistic initiation for mothers? Maybe you'll become an honorary baroness yourself, since your daughter is one. The Baroness-Mother or something," I added teasingly.

"Perhaps she wishes to discuss religion, Sheri. That must be it. How you'll both handle your religious practices. Maybe she wants you to convert," Mother said, laughing. "A little too late for that."

Baroness Adriane did not greet us at the door. Instead, a maid brought us through the two entrance chambers and into the living room, where the baroness sat. She gestured for us to sit across from her, and asked us what aperitif we preferred.

Once the maid had poured us each a dry sherry, the

baroness asked that we get right to the point of our meeting.
I translated this and eyed Mother apprehensively. "Madame,
you may call me Adriane, if with your permission I may—
since we are now related—call you Lilly?"

Mother nodded her approval.

"Well, good," the baroness said. "So, Lilly, the purpose
for this talk is to discuss *what you are prepared to give the couple*."

I translated and exchanged a look of confusion with
Mother.

"Adriane, I don't understand what you mean by this
question," Mother said.

"I am referring to *la dot*, as you must know," the baroness
responded.

I couldn't translate *dot*, since I had never encountered
the French word, and I asked her to explain. After being
given her precise explanation, I translated the word for
Mother. "The dowry," I said. Mother looked at me, astounded.

"A dowry?" Mother questioned. "This is the first time
that anyone mentioned such a thing to me. Am I to understand that you expect me to provide a dowry for my
daughter?"

"Yes, I most certainly do."

"Jacques never said anything to me about a dowry!" I
blurted out. "I've read about dowries in marriages many
years ago. But today? Jacques is very well off."

"Sheri, in Belgium, among us, a dowry is always given.
It has nothing to do with whether a husband is well off or
not." The baroness continued suspiciously, "You're not telling me you knew nothing of this? I'm sure in America families provide dowries at the marriages of their daughters!"

After I caught up with the translation to Mother, she
said, "Adriane, in America, parents of a daughter might help
their son-in-law with the purchase of a first home or with

the establishment of a business. But only if there is need. And in Jacques's case I don't see a need. He has a fully established life. In America the children inherit everything and certainly Sheri will one day have everything I have. Surely she'll bring it into her marriage with Jacques; they'll share everything."

"Lilly, Sheri is living in Belgium now and she will be living, I hope, under our customs. Therefore, I would also hope that you'll think this over and provide her with a dowry to bring into her marriage. Did you think Jacques is expected to support her completely? This is unheard of! She must contribute something toward the upkeep of the couple's life."

"I must tell you, Adriane, that I am not a wealthy woman. In America, we would say I was left in a comfortable position at my husband's death. I live from the income on my investments. I cannot reduce my principal on the amount I've invested, or my income will be insufficient for, let us say, the style of life I have set for myself."

While I was translating this into French the baroness glared at Mother.

"I am prepared, however, to give the couple a present in three years," Mother continued, "when certain of my investments come due. Perhaps the money could go toward a summer home in St. Tropez, which I know Jacques has told Sheri he would like."

"Very well, Lilly, in three years then. It is a pity about our misunderstanding, or should we say differences in customs. Now let us have lunch and speak of other concerns!"

When she brought us to the door, Baroness Adriane asked that I call her Mamie as all her children did. I said goodbye using the new name, pronouncing it with a high-pitched emphasis on the last syllable, as she had done. Calling her Mamie felt entirely alien.

———

"Just another centuries-old custom of these circles," Mother whispered to me as we left the baroness's apartment, drained by the encounter.

"Oh Mother, I'm sorry you had to go through this."

On the drive home, we analyzed the encounter and concluded that Jacques might have misrepresented to his mother that I came from a rich family. Perhaps because I had related stories of trips I had taken both with my family while growing up and on my own in high school and college, he estimated that I came from more wealth than I actually did. Since any travel by members of Jacques's family and their circle involved spending beyond any normal person's imagination, he must have assumed that my family had fortunes to spend.

"My darling Sheri." Jacques lifted a glittering wineglass in a toast at dinner that night. He cheerfully said he had spoken on the phone to his mother and she had told him of Mother's intention to contribute toward a summer residence in St. Tropez.

But in the morning his distant and formal mood had returned.

"Sheri," he began solemnly. "I called the clinic in Paris last week, and no one had received your check for the operation. I suspect you didn't send it as you had promised. In fact, I strongly suspect that you might not go through with the operation at all. Am I right?" His tone had become stern and troubled.

"Let's talk about this tonight after you return from work, Jacques," I said. "The morning is not a good time."

"I see, I see! Aha! Then I was right! I knew you were going to deceive me and not have the operation. I knew it even as I was taking the vows! You are surprised? No! You shouldn't be. I am a man of honor. In my family we follow our code of honor. That is why I didn't stop the wedding.

I had promised to marry you and I kept my word. But you—"

"Please stop. Let us not start this now. It is not what you think. I'll explain later. Please don't judge like this," I pleaded.

"Tell me this—are we going to Paris on Friday for the operation or not?" he asked emphatically.

"No. Well, not this Friday," I said. "But I'll tell you everything tonight. Please, Jacques, let's not spoil our days just after our wedding. We've waited so long for this. Please try."

"Yes. I suspected you'd do this to me. I could just feel you would. I should never have trusted you. Americans don't know anything about honor. You all know, well . . . All of you live by the dubious codes of 'power' and 'money.' Yes, anything is justified to attain these. You deceived me. I know it! I should never have married you! Never!"

The sheer force of his anger terrified me. In three years I'd seen him angry only once before, when Marc refused to meet me before the wedding, but that emotion was like a mild breeze compared to this gale. I'd never expected such a reaction, such intolerance and insensitivity to my fears. I knew I had handled this all wrong. I was devastated. It was agony to hear the words, "I should never have married you."

"Take your mother around Bruges today. I'll be back at six," he said, in a soft voice, but barely containing his seething anger. According to the nobles' code, gentlemen never raise their voices to a lady by even a degree!

Chapter 5

Mother and I couldn't stop thinking about the inevitable confrontation with Jacques as we walked around the marvelous medieval canalled city of Bruges and viewed the world-famous Hieronymus Bosch painting, *Heaven and Hell*. Jacques's threatening morning speech haunted us.

When we arrived back at the house, we took our seats in front of the fireplace, already set by the staff with a roaring fire.

Jacques walked in precisely at 6:00 P.M.

"Madame, I'm sorry you must hear this but I prefer you stay since it involves both of you," he firmly announced. His eyes were in a glazed brown, flickering rage. "I went to the family lawyers today. I am going to start the divorce proceedings immediately. I suggest you pack up your belongings and go back to America. My driver, Roland, will take you to the airport for tomorrow's early-afternoon flight."

"Jacques, are you insane?" I exclaimed.

He walked out of the living room; we heard him climbing the stairs. Mother's face had turned white and mine probably a ghostlier white. We looked at each other in utter disbelief.

I ran up to the bedroom after him.

"Jacques, you must hear me," I pleaded. "How can you condemn me without knowing my story?"

"I don't have to hear your story. I know what you will tell me. It will be only your clever self-justifications. Please sleep in the wing where I've placed your mother; there are several more rooms made up there. Choose one. I don't want you in my bed."

"Think of what you are doing! You love me. I love you, you know that. Are you going to expel me as you would one of your servants, because I won't have this vain, ridiculous operation? I can't understand how bigger breasts can be so important to you. Are you going to reject me for this?" I cried out incredulously.

"It is no longer a point of whether you'll have the operation. You deceived me. This is now the only point, don't you see? You have no honor. No code of honor. Yes, I love you but I can no longer accept you or live with you. You never planned to have the surgery, did you?" His voice, hollow, echoed through our bedroom.

"Yes I did, and I will. I will," I said. "Just not now. Not just when I am getting adjusted to life here as your wife. I've wanted to tell you this. Waited for the right time. Be rational. I would be unable to move my arms for three weeks and then be inactive for months afterwards at the very start of our married life if I had this operation now. Can't you see it would be preferable to have it after a year or so? Please give me time."

"No, no, I won't. Go back to New York," he said unyieldingly. "I should never have married you. You are a deceiving woman and I will not accept you as my wife!"

"Jacques, what are you saying? You never spoke to me like this. What has become of your honor? Talking to someone you love like this. I've never seen this side of you! I thought you loved me deeply, loved me enough to understand me—to understand my fear of this unnecessary breast enlargement. You always loved me in bed. How will larger breasts improve this?" I implored. "Am I some sexual object to you? Is that what you need from me? I know it isn't! You could have found many willing sexual partners if you need mountainous curves to excite you. You can—"

"I will not discuss this anymore, since you know it is now a question of honor, not size. I will not change my mind. I will say goodbye to you tomorrow before I leave for work," he said as he led me out the door.

I rejoined Mother at the fireplace.

"He won't even discuss it," I said. "He said he's made his decision. What madness! This is a nightmare!"

"Sheri, my darling, we will not go until we try to work this all out. He'll calm down by tomorrow morning. Crises are always different in the morning. We'll both speak with him and his mother, too. And we could call Dr. Rémy in Paris, and see if he can offer another solution. Maybe he'll find a medical reason why you can't have the operation now," Mother said, calming both me and herself with sober advice.

"It is too late for that, Mother. I'm really afraid it is just too late. I never expected such a reaction," I said. "Something must be very mixed up in his mind. Something else must be going on! If he is like this . . . God! How could I live with such a man? At any problem he could turn into a monster. He was never like this before. Never!"

"I know you thought he'd accept this simple delay," Mother said. "You've known him for three years. Maybe he still will be reasonable. I agree it must be something more. The pressures he feels from his family about a second marriage must have brought him to this state."

"Can he have the marriage annulled? No! What a thought! For what reason? That I didn't go through with promised cosmetic surgery? But who knows? In this strange country, anything is possible!" I paced the living room desperately. All the severe-looking portraits of the family, caught in the light from the fireplace, seemed to scowl at me.

"He's too gentle a man to reject you, Sheri. Let's just calm down. We'll call Dr. Rémy and then the American Embassy, for their advice, first thing tomorrow. And then hope this all blows over," Mother said reassuringly. And we went up to bed.

In the morning the maid brought breakfast to our rooms, saying that the baron had asked her to do this. When we came downstairs, Jacques was on the phone with his mother. "Yes, yes, yes, Mamie. I am going to be there at noon. Yes. Both lawyers. No, we'll discuss that over lunch."

He hung up and announced to us calmly, "Roland will take you to the airport at eleven. I called Sabena. There are ample places on the one o'clock flight. Madame, I'm sorry for you. And Sheri, to you I have nothing to say. My lawyers will contact you in New York. I'll ship back all your trunks. Goodbye." And he walked toward the door.

"Jacques, you are being crazy! Must I speak in French for you to come to your senses? *Tu es fou et monstrueux!*" I screamed.

"I understand English. Speak quietly."

"We are not leaving," I said. "I will not move from this house. I am your wife. I have a right to be here. And we will work this madness out! I want to meet with your mother and with any other family member who can mediate and talk to you! Bring you back to your senses!"

Without answering, he stormed out.

To regain a sense of reality, Mother and I began making phone calls. First to the Embassy. After hearing my story a lawyer there advised, "There is no annulment in Belgium. Only divorce, and only for very specific grounds. Not having a breast operation is not one, I'm quite sure. Just stay in the house. Do not leave. If you take your things out, even for as little as three nights, your husband could have the definite ground of abandonment by law in Belgium. Please stay there and call me tomorrow."

Somewhat relieved, I called Dr. Rémy in Paris. After I gave him a heart-wrenching explanation of my predicament, his response stunned me.

"Medical confidentiality and ethics prevent me usually from giving out any information," he began, "and you must not use it in any way or I will deny saying it to you. Promise me this. I am making an exception now because I liked you and felt for you when we met.

"Baroness de Borchgrave, your husband, I'm sad to tell you, has a strong psychological problem. I don't know how deep it goes, I'm not a licensed psychiatrist, but I believe he has a medically recognized condition—an obsession—with physically changing women to create his ideal form. And in his case it has been specifically to create large, full breasts.

"He has brought many women to me for breast implant surgery over the years. Most of the girls were very willing. Unlike you. I saw your hesitation, your fears. You asked me so many questions about the risks, I knew you were being forced into it.

"Now, Baroness, I don't know what to advise you. Perhaps you should just return to America and not expose yourself to more serious problems. The baron is probably not going to let up on his demand. If you decide to stay with him after what I have told you, then perhaps you could visit me in Paris and together we will all try to find another solution. I don't know what, but appease him by saying you'll both come and talk to me. Please, I don't want anything mentioned about the other women! Just say you called me to cancel the appointment and tried to reschedule one later.

"Baroness, I only know for certain your husband has an unusual obsession with breasts. He might be normal in every other way. Anyway, good luck to you. Goodbye," Dr. Rémy finished solemnly.

This discovery shook Mother and me into a deeper state of desperation. We panicked. "He might be normal in every other way"; what did he mean? How many women had gone under the knife to realize Jacques's fantasy of voluptuous breasts? I wondered. Dr. Rémy's direct revelation was so thoroughly frightening that neither Mother nor I wanted to face its full impact.

A telephone call from Baroness Adriane came within the hour.

"Sheri, please come immediately to my apartment in Brussels. We will discuss this whole matter over lunch. Jacques is in quite a state and I don't know if anything can be done to save your situation. But we shall try. Although I must warn you. I know my son. Once his code of honor and his trust have been broken I don't know if there is much hope. Please come with your mother at once," she said with cold authority.

Jacques was stunned when he saw Mother and me enter Mamie's apartment. He looked at his mother furiously and started toward the door, but she demanded that he stay and discuss the problem. I looked at the bookcase, where two framed photographs of me stood along with all the other family photos. My photographs had been turned around in their frames, displaying the white backs of the pictures. A very eerie sight!

For the next four exhaustive and anguishing hours, we all argued our positions. The baroness sided with her son in his view that I had deliberately deceived him by agreeing to the operation before the marriage and refusing it afterward, and that in doing so, I had severed his trust in me, a condition which created an infertile ground for the start of a marriage. Both Mother and I tried to balance their decree of my dishonesty by focusing on the superficiality of his demand. After all, I hadn't brought family "ghosts" to the marriage, or hidden physical frailties, Mother explained. My only crime had been fear of the operation and the greater fear of admitting it to Jacques. I added then that if I had foreseen what Jacques's reaction would be, I would never have consented to marry him. The discussion was frustrating and macabre.

By sundown, the decision was made that Jacques would give the marriage a few months' trial, during which time the breast operation would never be mentioned. If he then felt his trust in me was steadily being rebuilt, he would consent to continuing our life together. He warned me that if any occurrence, overt or surreptitious, punctured his trust for the second time, he would immediately terminate the marriage. These were his terms.

Only because I loved Jacques and had given such energy to the relationship, and had already given up my life in the United States to marry him, did I agree to his terms. It was achingly painful to submit to this trial period when it was he who should have been submitting to my conditions. There was a shocking irony in my being judged by an obsessed man to determine whether I deserved his trust. I wondered whether Mamie knew of her son's repeated pattern of sending young women to undergo Dr. Rémy's famous implant surgery. But that didn't matter now, since I had agreed to the terms.

I sadly conceded that I must muster all my courage and give the marriage a try. If Jacques was normal in all other respects, he could continue being the loving man whom I had known throughout our years of courtship.

Mother, who had undeniably always been my very best friend in the whole world, left for New York after several more days. She felt somewhat reassured after she saw that Jacques's behavior had suddenly changed; he now behaved lovingly toward me, as if the crisis had never occurred. We spent the final afternoon before she left pacing the medieval Grand Place deep in discussion. Mother said that Jacques's fit of irrationality and his capacity to get so out of control disturbed her greatly. She admitted that she felt unequipped to advise me definitively because she had never experienced such an extreme reaction before. Her father had been a gentleman of integrity and consistency, and her husband, my father, a rock of stability and rational thought and action.

"I can only leave you here because I have a good impression of the various people I met in Jacques's family," Mother said. "And of course, I know you and your ability to adjust and get along well. They'll all be loving you in no time at all, I'm sure. And Jacques will realize his folly for creating this crisis over your breasts . . . when you have such potential for a happy life together. He'll realize soon, I hope."

With a heavy heart but with Jacques's promise to behave correctly, Mother left on a characteristically drizzly Belgian day. As her Sabena jet took off, I felt a streak of anxiety tear through me. It was as painful as the first day she had left me off in first grade.

Chapter 6

*A*s if the rocky start had never occurred, our first married weeks were idyllic, a honeymoon of sensuous evenings right at Ginal. We were not invited to dinners at family members' homes at first, since they chose to give us total privacy for our so-called honeymoon period. We dressed every night for dinner. Jacques asked me to wear my sexiest St. Tropez dresses—sometimes the long, see-through chiffon ones, other times the short and seductive ones. Candles and the best china and silver service were used at dinner. Jacques too always changed from his business suit to elegant casual clothes.

Jacques orchestrated the agendas for these evenings down to minute detail. One particularly sensual formula became a standard routine for us. Jacques would call me at six and ask me not to dress before he arrived home from his office, asking me instead to start filling the huge round sunken tub for a bubble bath. When he arrived I would be luxuriating in the bath, and drinks and hors d'oeuvres would be ready at the side of the tub. On those nights Jacques asked that I dismiss the maid early so that we could be alone and do our own cooking.

He would undress immediately and join me in the tub, and soon we would be involved in our sensuous, acrobatic lovemaking. Jacques used every inch of the enormous tub for sexual creativity. He usually chose jazz or Brazilian music for these sessions. Then, before dressing for dinner, we relaxed for a brief time under the tanning lamp of a large tanning bed.

Jacques would light a fire in the fireplace, since the house always had a slight chill in the evening. The maid would have prepared an easy dinner, and we simply put the finishing touches to the sauces. Then we ate in front of the fireplace while listening to Charles Aznavour's romantic ballads or other French music. The outside world seemed far away during these evenings of pure sybaritic pleasure. After dinner, followed by espresso and a fruit liqueur called marc de Bourgogne, we made love again, this time in front of the fireplace.

His sexual prowess and appetite seemed infinite. We were making love three to four times a day with endless variation. During these weeks of continual lovemaking, I felt as happy as I had ever been. I had never dreamed that marriage would be so ecstatic. Even the mornings after our evenings of hedonism were an event. Every morning I served Jacques breakfast in bed. The maid prepared the tray and brought it up to our bedroom, leaving it outside the door at precisely nine o'clock each morning. It was served on an ornate silver tray with silver coffeepot, sugar, and creamer. There were an assortment of fresh country jams and a selection of sweet rolls. I placed the silver tray between us atop a specially designed bed tray. Then I chose one of a variety of flimsy, sexy bed jackets. We breakfasted while listening to the morning news and afterward discussed the day's plans, whether Jacques planned to be home for lunch or where we would meet. After the radio news report was over we made love. This started the day off right, and Jacques often joked that I had come a long way since the time when I didn't care for morning sex.

On Saturday and Sunday mornings I would get up before Jacques and drive to the village, joining the hundreds of people waiting at the bakery for the croissants to come out of the ovens.

After Jacques left in the morning, I filled my days with getting to know my new environment—the boutiques, food shops, and other facilities—and also with the study of French. I acquainted myself with the art galleries and museums in Brussels and met some gallery owners and artists.

Learning to shop for food Belgian-style proved somewhat tricky and sometimes humorous. Since there was a national debate raging over which chocolate was better for mousse, whether Godiva was the preferred shop for its chocolate truffles or Neuhaus for its chocolate pralines, and whether Wittamer's at the Sablon or Nihoul on swank Avenue Louise made the best hand-dipped chocolates, I was in a quandary where to go. And not only did I have problems with the metric system, but unusual and unfamiliar products abounded. One day I picked out luscious-looking red, juicy steaks for dinner. Marie-Louise agitatedly called "Monsieur le Baron" into the kitchen, and when Jacques spotted my purchase, he burst into laughter and told me he had no intention of dining on horsemeat that evening.

One by one I became acquainted with the members of Jacques's family. The noblesse were a highly eccentric group, and Jacques's family had its wild, flamboyant personalities.

Jacques's sister Catherine was the first relative to visit Ginal during the wedding week. Jacques had told me that Catherine had been the perfect child whom everyone admired—the girl who had excelled in everything and who had taken the right direction at every juncture in her life. And from his stories I could see that Catherine was clearly their mother's favorite, pushing Jacques and Isabelle, and even Isabelle's twin, Marc, into the far shadows.

After talking to Catherine for a short while, I liked and admired her too. She perfectly fit my image of what nobility should be like. She lived in a castle with her husband and two children and kept up the life that the nobles had followed throughout centuries. And in her natural, direct way she eagerly explained to me what her life was like.

"It's a pity we live so far from each other, Sheri. I'd like you to visit but I think Jacques will insist that you wait until summer. The castle stays cold and quite damp until we get a few months of warm, dryer weather. Maybe you can come in July and stay for a few days."

"Jacques tells me you work very hard to keep up the castle and property and that you don't get to see each other too often," I said.

"Yes. Jean-Pierre and I spend all our time just keeping everything running. You see, it is not possible to have a large staff at the castle. We have only four people working with us. Two of them on the grounds and farm. We have animals—not many. Sheep, cows, chickens. But I also have my horses to keep up. I train and show them. This is my only real pleasure; all the other responsibilities are never-ending work."

"What do you mean?"

"Jacques might have told you that Jean-Pierre and I not

only keep up our property but in a sense we have the responsibility for the whole village. People come to us with their marital disputes, all their conflicts, and we act as arbitrators to help them work out their problems. Not easy, I must tell you. They also come for food. We welcome anyone at the castle and give them the basics they need. Not many come, but we are always ready to help. It is in Jean-Pierre's family tradition to be kind to the needy. But, needless to say, all this is a full-time activity."

I was amazed. "Catherine, it sounds so generous of you to give of your life like that. Do other friends of yours do this?"

She looked at Jacques as if to acknowledge a sensitive topic.

"I wouldn't live that life," he said. "It is too much of the past. But you want to keep up the tradition, which too few of us have chosen to do. My sister is quite a woman!" he said, turning to me. "But it is often too much for her. I know. Even with her energy. She always makes us think that it is all manageable."

"You know, I really hope that times will get a little easier," Catherine said. "Sheri, after Jean-Pierre's father dies, and he's very old, then we will have many more people to help us. He doesn't approve of large staffs, and likes us to do mostly everything ourselves. He believes it builds character!

"But I can't support all the work demands; I really can't say I like the dampness. For nine months of the year, it is always cold in the castle. We set fires in the fireplaces throughout all the rooms in the main wing where we live, but nothing takes the chill off. Jacques, you were smart not to agree, as Mamie wanted, to live at our Loiroi-le-château. It can be ghastly. My children never take off heavy sweaters all through the nine or so months. Getting them to bathe has always been a struggle."

"But it sounds sort of adventurous that you still live as you might have centuries ago," I said, trying to keep her talking. Her lifestyle, needless to say, fascinated me.

"That's quite funny, Sheri," she said engagingly. "Because, you see, I never lived any other way, so I don't see it as an adventure. It is my life. As you have undoubtedly heard, Jacques and I and my older brother and sister grew up at Loiroi. That was uncomfortable too, but not so damp. Jacques probably forgets since it seems so long ago, and then I married Jean-Pierre and moved into his castle. I never had a time in my life, like Jacques, where I lived the so-called modern life. As Jacques knows, I'd really like to change. Just to see what, let's say, living in a city like Brussels would be like. Yes, in a tiny, warm apartment. It would be a dream! Of course I'd miss the horses. But you see, Jean-Pierre's father stipulates in his will that we must continue living in his castle or the properties will go into the hands of his other brothers, along with other holdings. We need this inheritance because—"

Jacques cut her off, unable to resist teasing her.

"Oh, Catherine, you know the old man has a tremendous fortune. You're just praying that he doesn't hang on too long. Then you can just make appearances at the castle and perhaps move into a warm, cozy farm estate like mine. Then let the old baron try to control that from his grave!"

"Jacques, can we please keep a few personal views from Sheri at the beginning?" she said seriously. "Sheri, I'm sure you'll hear everything about all the family in time, but I don't want to bother you with these boring family situations so soon."

Discreetly I agreed with her, though I was very willing

to probe the web of personal situations right now, so that I would get to know my new family.

Jacques's younger sister, Isabelle, a vivid character with manic energy, was the second relative to visit Ginal during the wedding week. I could immediately see the complete contrast between Isabelle and Catherine. Isabelle was beautiful and sensual, in her early thirties, with the look of a seventeenth-century courtesan. She wore her hair in a grand upswept mass, pinned neatly into a centered chignon. Her eyes were dramatically made up, her face a delicately powdered white. She wore an eye-dazzling array of antique jewels on a tight silk print dress. The overall impression she made was one of a seethingly sexual beauty.

"So my new sweet sister-in-law, Sheri! Since *chérie* means 'dear' in French, I must call you my *chérie* Sheri," Isabelle gaily spun out in high-pitched, rapid French. "I've been so anxious to talk with you—to get to know my American sister-in-law—desperately anxious! Jacques didn't let me come to visit until tonight. He's so protective of you. I think he is a little afraid that I will corrupt you, his innocent, sweet American love. Right, Jacques?"

"Isabelle, I don't think that statement was necessary. Take it easy on her," Jacques said, grimacing. "I know you too well. You're here to get all the material you need for your gossip mill. Keeping our relationship a secret for years was a feat for you. But now—Sheri, be careful what you tell dear Isabelle; she'll spread the word to everyone just what you are like. So why not tell her how you couldn't resist me because I am a torrid, merciless lover? Isn't that what you want to hear, Isabelle?" he said teasingly.

"Jacques, you are being unfair! Sheri, you see how he treats me. Oh, he's ghastly! You'll see. He's a nasty big boy," she said in a breathy, sexy voice. "No, Jacques darling, I didn't come here to hear how devastatingly manly you are in bed. I already know," Isabelle said, with a mysterious smile. "I am here to teach my sister-in-law all the things that you can't teach her. What women teach each other!"

"Oh no you won't!" he warned.

"Well, let me see . . . yes . . . I will teach Sheri how to seat your dinner guests, according to their position, their titles. And yes . . . how to serve them properly. Go away, brother. This will be girl talk." She dramatically motioned him toward the other room.

"All right, but keep it to all your nice little lessons of etiquette," Jacques cautioned. "We don't want Sheri overwhelmed by your other lessons, do we, Isabelle?"

I'd heard banter between brothers and sisters, but this sexual teasing went quite beyond the usual. Other lessons? I wondered what he was telling me. Was this some kind of brother-sister secret talk?

"So, Sheri," she went on, ignoring his comment as he left the room. "I've heard about you for years. Jacques tells me some of his secrets. He told no one else. I'm his favorite sister. You've had quite a time together—those summers in St. Tropez! Oh, I'm so jealous. And now you're here, poor girl! No, I'm joking. I'm sure you'll like it. It's an extremely amusing life, you'll see. Well, if Jacques doesn't keep you hidden away. He probably will, though, he's very jealous. He won't want any of his friends to get sight of you because of course they'll want you too. But you and I can go out together. I'll introduce you to 'all of Belgium.' He won't have to know where we'll go."

"Isabelle, I can hear you from in here and that's enough!" Jacques called angrily through the door. "Sheri will never go out with you alone. I won't let that happen! Now be useful. Keep your talk on the subject of our customs."

"Oh, Jacques is such a tyrant! But I'm not afraid of him.

Anyway, let's begin with some pointers on entertaining. Now, Sheri, you realize that absolutely everything here is quite formal, and Jacques must keep all this up, being the baron of the family. I'm much more modern," she said proudly. "Now, if you have a group of people for dinner, you must be very precise as to how you seat them or you'll create real insults. Everyone must be placed in position at the table according to his title. You know, of course, that a marquis is higher than a baron. I'm sure Jacques explained all the titles to you. So the host or hostess, you and Jacques, will be seated across from each other at the center of the table. And on your right are the next-highest-titled guests, and to your left the next. And it goes out from there. You'll have the marquis and marquise, then count and countess, then baron and baroness. Now, let us say there are two couples with the title baron. Then the ones from the more important family are seated closer to you at the center."

"How will I know who's from a more important family?" I asked.

"You'll learn. Jacques or my mother can always tell you," she said. "The head of the table is the least important place-ment. Everyone knows his or her place. It is part of life here. No one is insulted, if you keep the right form. You'll see the maid serve everyone in the same pattern. You and Jacques will be served first. Then she'll go back around the table to Jacques's right, then back to your side and to your right, and so on. It's lots of movement but it is natural to us. You'll get used to it," she said. As Isabelle went on to explain more and more of the precise etiquette, I began feeling over-whelmed by all the formal conventions I'd have to live by; it really sounded like outmoded nonsense. I wondered whether I would disgrace my dear husband if I made a mis-take, and later I found out that indeed I caused quite a stir by deviating from the prescribed form, by doing something as simple as serving an old red wine in a glass meant for a younger red wine.

Isabelle then taught me about table settings and which glasses were the correct ones for the different wines. She showed me the four wineglasses from the blue, red, and clear crystal sets that had to be set at each place—the one for the first course, the one for the main course, the one for the cheese course, and last, the one for dessert. She pointed out the various sets of china and explained which ones were used on different occasions.

Isabelle then showed me how to prepare an oil and vinegar solution to clean the carved wood angels which protruded from the wall in the dining room. "These are precious. The best antique treasures here. You must clean them yourself. Never let Marie-Louise touch them," she said, while carefully applying the solution to the angel on one side. "They've been in the family a very long time. Jacques brought them here from our family château."

Suddenly two gunshots rang out. Isabelle and I jumped. We heard Jacques running down the stairs, a very unusual sound because Jacques never ran; he always moved gracefully and slowly, with a deliberate gait.

"Ladies, I've shot a pheasant, just at the side of the wood," he said triumphantly, and rushed out of the house, his shotgun still in his hands.

We followed, and after looking for it for some time, found the pheasant, still alive, in the brush. Jacques took it by the legs and together we inspected the colorfully feathered bird.

"Now I have a lesson for you, Sheri. We are going to teach you how to age and clean pheasant. In ten days or so, Isabelle, perhaps you would agree to come back here and teach Sheri how to cook it. We'll show her how we remove the feathers. If she will be able to stand the stench," Jacques said, laughing.

"She'll never be able to stand it," Isabelle said. "You must get used to it slowly over the years. Especially when it is aged in *your* method." She grimaced as if nauseated.

"Oh, I'm not squeamish at all. I'll be able to take the smell."

"Doubtful! But we'll see," said Jacques with a smile.

After Isabelle left, Jacques took a bottle of Taittinger champagne from behind the bar in the living room, uncorked it, and poured us our usual cocktail-hour drink.

"There is much you don't know about us and our style of life in Belgium," he said with a look that told me there was no limit to what I didn't know. "It's time you were aware of my brother and sisters and what you can expect from them. I wanted you to ease into our life gradually, and never really wanted to tell you too much because I was afraid you might not understand.

"Isabelle is an embarrassment to me and my mother and my family. Marc and Catherine are not like her. I certainly am not and don't approve of her life. She was married young and had two children. From the very beginning of her marriage she started an affair with Uncle Gérard. It is a big open secret here. She has a definite attraction to older men, much older. Gérard, her uncle, is thirty-five years older than she. Isabelle is crazy about him—for years now. About six years into her marriage, her husband discovered the two of them in bed together. In his own house! There was an immediate divorce and he got the kids. Don't look so shocked."

"I'm just surprised. Go on." I was more surprised that he was finally opening up about his family. He had never spoken before with such frankness.

"And she really likes the good life, loves clothes, jewels,

and cars. And our mother never gives her enough money to indulge her insatiable habits. So she has been in a sense a paid companion to several old men. She seduces them into buying her many gifts for her affections. And they do. Then she sets up all these intrigues and jealousies among her entourage of old lovers, and they fight for her. It's really sometimes quite amusing to hear about all of them recapturing their youth and competing like young knights to win the attention of my temptress sister. She loves to tell about it. And I must admit I do relish her odd tales. In fact, she managed to persuade one old man, whose deceased wife had left him childless, to 'adopt' her and thus leave her his entire fortune. And he's one of the richest men in Brussels! All she does in return is stay with him once a week. Many times she doesn't even show up."

"Why do you think she is attracted to older men? For the money?" I asked.

"The *gifts*," he said, "are secondary, I'm sure. She really is excited *only* by old men. Maybe it is because we lost our father when she was only six or so, perhaps she needs the father image. But grandfather image? I never understood it. I believe she has a need to conquer, to prove to herself she can attract everyone. Women too."

"Women!" I must have looked shocked.

Jacques chuckled. "Sheri, you're really cute. Why does this surprise you?" He gave me a lustful look. "I'm sure you've had women. All the girls here do."

"No, I haven't. I really never had any thought of that."

"Oh, no? It's hard to believe. Not just once?" Jacques teased. "Well, anyway, that's why I am warning you about Isabelle. She will undoubtedly try to start with you. I could see her eyeing you hungrily all over."

Isabelle's visit had been very illuminating. I had quite a sister-in-law. I couldn't wait to get to know more about the rest of the family. And through them, to get to know the man I had just married.

The introduction to my new life was proceeding fast and furious. On the weekend I would finally see the castle where Jacques had grown up. "You can now be greeted officially at the front door," Jacques said. Aunt Martine, Jacques's maternal aunt, lived there alone with her cook and butler.

During the hourlong drive along progressively narrower country roads, Jacques was more forthcoming with advice and a preview of what I was about to see. As he talked, I suddenly and vividly sensed how unreal my experiences of Belgium were to me. I had been going through the motions of learning how to live each day in a new society with a new way of thinking, and I was almost forced to re-create myself as "the baroness."

Castles had been places I'd visited with my parents as a teenager on trips to Europe. I had thought of them as museums of the far distant past. And here I was married to someone who had actually grown up in one. "Please don't dare say to Aunt Martine or the others that the castle is beautiful," he warned. "Everyone in the family is quite aware that it is not. You see, it was not a historic Belgian castle built in the traditional classical design of the period. Rather its design is a bit awkward, unbalanced, you might say, on the exterior as well as the interior. The corner towers were placed without regard to any formula of classical proportion, but at random. You might call it an eclectic mergence of styles or simply bad taste on the part of the overzealous designer."

We entered the grounds through an immense, ornate wrought-iron gate and proceeded along the half-mile-long road, with statues on either side, which ended in a full circle at the front of the château. An impressive spraying fountain with many standing sculpted figures, several of children in the traditional peeing stance made so famous by *Mannequin Pis*, a small landmark statue of a boy on a street near the Grand Place, adorned the front entrance. The huge fortress-like structure, built of red brick and covered with ivy in certain sections, was six stories high, with several towers soaring even higher. Lovely gardens were dotted with sculptures and fountains, and ponds, fields, and forests stretched in every direction as far as the eye could see.

After we were greeted at the front entrance by Aunt Martine, her butler at her side, Jacques gave me a full tour of the castle and grounds. Unlike Gérard's family castle with its resplendent entrance halls and reception rooms, the interior of Loiroi-le-château was not awe-inspiring; rather it was a huge residence with high ceilings and countless cavernous rooms filled with antiques and paintings. Aunt Martine had placed exquisite flower arrangements on mantels and central tables in every room, which gave the interior a grand formal feeling—though upon close inspection, the rooms had a slightly faded look of past glory caught in another age.

But the interior had an undeniable charm and warmth, with its clutter of patterned sofas, sculptures, clocks on the mantels, and collections of all descriptions, and in the wonderland of hidden stairways to the upper floors and towers. A huge attic contained a great assortment of articles: old rocking chairs, wooden cradles, antique washbasins, dollhouses, mirrors of all shapes and sizes, chests and iron bed frames.

Twelve neglected-looking servants' rooms were on an upper floor, and a fascinating children's quarters, looking like a large boarding school, on another. The maze of rooms was still full of toys and children's furniture. They must have been a paradise for the children who learned and played there. We walked up the winding cobwebbed staircase within the highest tower to the belfry, where we rang the corroded bell. From here, with an open view of the spectacular grounds, Jacques pointed out the stable, now overgrown with ivy and weeds, where he said he'd spent endless hours with the horses.

Family members started arriving. Isabelle came with her children. Another elderly aunt and several cousins soon joined us in the salon. In the smallest of the three dining rooms (the informal dining room, I was told), lunch was served by the butler, starting with country pâtés, then roast pork with all the vegetables from the garden, and afterward cheese from the region and berry pies. Since the castle had never been modernized, the kitchen was still in the cellar and everything had to be brought up on a dumbwaiter. The cook filled it below and the butler brought the food to the table. It was fascinating to hear and watch the process—a bell alarm, a grinding sound, and then the sudden appearance of another platter of food or bottle of wine.

After lunch I was taken on an outdoor tour: a walk through Aunt Martine's beloved gardens, ponds, and woods, with the family pointing out the many sculptures and telling me the stories of the artists commissioned by the Borchgraves to create them. We saw four neglected tennis courts, which I was told had been the site of years of fierce intra-family matches.

Listening to Aunt Martine and other family members speak, I realized that I was learning a very distinct conversational French, the speech of the nobles. Their talk was punctuated with dramatic adjectives: "dreadful," "ghastly," "dismal," "unbearable," "sublime," "superb," "most charming," and "enchanting." After the walk, the family photo albums were brought out and I was treated to an intimate glimpse of the family's years at Loiroi—photographs of their first automobiles, horseback riding and shooting competitions on the grounds. This gesture of opening the albums to me was the very first indication that I might be on my way to being accepted as a member of the family, and Jacques looked truly surprised when his mother suggested the showing. I was delighted to get a glimpse of a young Jacques, a giant for his age at every stage, fat Isabelle, and young, always-victorious Catherine receiving awards at riding competitions.

As we drove home, Jacques spoke animatedly about the day. "The Loiroi was a wonderful place to grow up, Sheri. It was always filled with guests and lots of children. You know, I sometimes question my decision to move out, but as I've told you, it is not a physically comfortable existence. And the number in help that I would have needed, well . . . would have been extremely costly. Perhaps, though, if you'd like, we might try living there a month in the summer. Maybe next year. We could fix up the tennis courts and perhaps get a few horses. I think it might be quite amusing for you. I'm sure you would take to it. We would spend July in the South of France and then August at Loiroi. Yes, perhaps an idea."

"I'd love that," I assured him.

"Aunt Martine goes away most summers to visit an aunt, Aunt Gislaine, in Cannes. We'll visit often, *chérie*. After all, it belongs to me, not Aunt Martine. We'll spend our weekends there in late spring and I'll teach you how to shoot."

I visited Mémé; we later arranged that I would come bimonthly. Although she wanted to hear all about me, I insisted that on this first visit she take the stage and tell me about her life and her family. For the next two hours, I was treated to her detailed stories of a noble life.

Her grandfather owned vast sugar plantations in Java. Her father was an adventurer and at a young age went to

South Africa, where he discovered a gold mine, then took in five partners to help develop the mine. The family became tremendously wealthy and lived in a huge castle in Belgium, built so that central rooms could be opened up to create a giant ballroom. "Oh, it was all so glorious," she said, smiling. "My two sisters and I were brought up in the most lavish style. We had a household staff of eleven at the castle, and there were two other châteaus at the Belgian seaside, and two hunting lodges. My father gave each of us two coming-out parties; he bought crystal, china, and silver services for two hundred fifty settings, which were used for the six balls. The two hundred fifty guests were entertained at full sit-down dinners; scores of servants were brought in to graciously serve the guests. All the ballgowns for these occasions were designed in Paris, where Mother's parents lived." She described how delightful the balls were, with music, dancing, and flowing champagne.

"And, you know, *mon petit chou*, Father loved to spoil his women. He was ever so generous with us, giving us the finest gifts. In our summer residences, when we invited guests, they were given full living quarters and a personal maid for each family. My father even gave the guests an envelope with money to use to tip the servants!

"All summer our days were filled with tennis and horseback riding, and at night everyone had to dress for dinner: the men in dinner jackets, the women in evening dresses. Each night dinner was set for at least thirty people, followed by dancing. The family loved music and we often entertained with concerts at our châteaus."

During the hunting season the whole family and their guests moved into the smaller hunting residences. They kept a stable of horses for the hunt and specially bred English hunting dogs. Everyone dressed in traditional British "hunting pinks," and carried hunting horns. During these hunts they had to use all the old French terms created by Louis XIV. Mémé said that she had a hard time remembering this difficult French and everyone teased her.

She became very excited while telling a story about a day of deer hunting. Her father kept a full-time *maître de la chasse*, or master of the hunt, who trained the dogs and led the hunt. She described the different sounds of the hunting horns which meant specific commands to the dogs. Only one deer was killed each day. At the end of the day the animal's head was cut off and carefully preserved, and one hunter who had done especially well during the hunt was honored: the *Maître de la Chasse*, in a ceremony with horns blowing, presented the feet of the deer to the honored person. Mémé said these strict customs were followed throughout the hunt; it was as it had been in the time of Louis XIV.

Later, when she married, she led a similar spoiled life. She never thought she could live without at least a *maître d'hotel* (head butler), head housekeeper, cook, maid, nurse for the babies, and English nannies for the older children.

Just after she was married her father died. The five partners he had taken into his mining business offered her mother a large sum of money, but very cleverly did not offer a share in the gold mine. Having no business sense, her mother accepted the large sum and lost her husband's share in the mine.

As the years passed, her mother had to sell the two châteaus at the seaside. She continued to live in her castle, in a less lavish style, until the war.

Then Mémé explained how her father had handled the marriages of his daughters. He paid each husband a monthly sum. The girls never knew how much. When he died, the monthly stipends stopped, which soured all the husbands on marriage. Mémé said that in those days women had no part in or consciousness of money affairs.

I cringed when I heard this.

"My father was tremendously honorable," she went on proudly. "Codes of honor were rigorously followed in our house. Someday I'll explain them all to you. Many people in my family were diplomats, accredited to the various Belgian colonies, and they upheld their code of honor strictly as part of their loyalty to the King."

I asked her whether she ever went to the court.

"I was presented at the court of Leopold II, at my coming-out ball. My son was very close to King Leopold III. For a while he was in charge of appointing the King's diplomats to the missions. My family was often entertained at the court. I loved those functions; there don't seem to be so many now, or let us say, not so many organized in the same exquisite style."

I could see she was finally getting tired after her animated and articulate presentation of her history, and I called an end to a most fascinating afternoon. Jacques's paternal grandmother was certainly a remarkable ninety-three-year-old with a storybook life.

The next morning at breakfast, I was surprised when Jacques announced authoritatively, "Tonight you will meet Claudine."

He said that he had made reservations at a restaurant in Brussels and we'd pick Claudine up at the new home awarded to her as part of their divorce settlement. Although I found the idea of dinner with Claudine, just the three of us, a rather uncomfortable prospect, I must admit that I was curious about the famous first wife.

We arrived at Claudine's Brussels home, which had a side studio where she did her antique restoration work, and from the moment she opened the door, I was aware of her nervousness. A strikingly sexy young woman, Claudine wore a transparent blouse and no brassiere, showing off her firm, rounded breasts, Dr. Rémy's creation. She had on artistic gold jewelry, tight jeans, and suede boots that came up over the jeans to her thighs. About five feet eight inches tall, very slim and with light-brown hair hanging straight and a bit unkempt to her shoulders, she had a tough, artsy look. Her aristocratic features—the sharp straight nose and sculpted, almost unmoving, eyes and mouth—were quite pronounced. She had come from a noble family in France, though not quite as lofty as Jacques's.

Claudine had set up a bar to serve cocktails in her studio, obviously knowing that the sight of paintings in the process of restoration would provide an icebreaker, and she and I indeed never left the subject of art and art restoration in our rather strained exchange.

At the restaurant Jacques ordered even more courses for dinner than usual, seeming deliberately to extend our time together, wanting the strange dynamic to continue. It clearly excited him. Claudine was aggressively cool and correct, but it was obvious this dinner was against her will. Even the many bottles of wine did little to take the sting out of the tense encounter. Our conversation revolved around safe areas—travel, art, and a bit of European politics. I was never happier to see a check arrive at the table.

As we drove back toward Claudine's house, she suddenly opened the door at a stoplight and jumped out of the car. She ran frantically down the street, Jacques following in the car. She never looked around, just ran as if in a total panic. After taking in the whole scene, I turned to Jacques, who seemed unperturbed. "Do you think this dinner, meeting me, was just too much for her?"

He laughed. "Claudine loves to create scenes of high drama. It's ghastly, but at the same time, quite amusing. In fact, I found the whole evening quite amusing."

"Amusing" would not have been my choice of adjective. The image of Claudine's flight into the dark night spooked me completely. Was she terrified of Jacques? Or somehow still under his control? Or perhaps she was unable to bear another minute of this confrontation and had to burst free from the tension she felt at seeing Jacques and me as a couple. I couldn't figure out why he had arranged such a dinner; yet again, since I would have to meet Claudine as a member of the noble circle, and Jacques would have to deal with her because of their sons, I supposed it was better that we spent some time together, however uncomfortable. But I was alarmed and mystified by the games that still must be going on between them.

He continued following her for about a mile, just watching her run and saying nothing, like a hunter stalking his prey. I felt the oddest sensation, as if we were characters in an episode of *The Twilight Zone*. The dim yellow streetlights of Brussels contributed to the acid, surreal tone. A pang of fear gripped me as I glimpsed what appeared to be a rather sadistic side of Jacques which I'd never seen before.

My first month as Baroness de Borchgrave was filled with learning about my new lifestyle—lessons about how the privileged lived that fascinated me, and lessons that disturbed me because these people's ideas were so completely opposite to the democratic attitudes with which I had been brought up.

Jacques chose to run a formal household. We continued to dress every night for dinner. It was strictly out of the question to wear a robe, even a fancy lounging robe, on the main floor; this went for early in the morning as well as late at night. These rules were just for starters. I learned the subtler ones as the weeks went on. Lunch and dinner were always occasions, never simple affairs; each was preceded by an aperitif and consisted of several courses with wines. Sandwiches were unheard of. In fact, Jacques had never in his life tasted a hamburger until one day I insisted on his trying "cooked steak tartare" on a baguette.

By American standards this life would be considered quite alcoholic. With all the aperitifs (though light ones like pernod, sherry, or kir), the many glasses of wine with lunch and dinner, and the after-dinner drinks, known as *poussecafés*, which often were followed by a final fruit liqueur or *eau de vie*, life took on a rosy haze. Perhaps all this alcoholic indulgence was necessary to fight the "dreadful weather"— as all Jacques's family members referred to the constant rain that chilled us right through the bones.

I was in charge of buying all the wines and liqueurs. When I entered the wine shop, a number of wine consultants often rushed at me, calling forth in loud, clear French, *"Madame la Baronne! Madame la Baronne!"* This address always tickled me, and I was at once thrilled by the unique address applied to me and a little embarrassed, feeling almost as if I must present myself as a formal and distinguished figure, wearing dressy clothing as the rich and titled always did in the old films. I supposed that celebrities had a similar spotlight always on them when in public. But being suddenly a member of the high class, the class set apart by formal address, did something unusual to my sense of self, probably the same confidence-raising boost as becoming successful or famous.

New words seeped into my vocabulary, which brought on new ways of thinking. "Will the party be mixed?" was a question that my mother-in-law would ask before accepting an invitation. This meant, will there be people who are not from the noble circle, not one of us, as she would dryly say, protesting against going to such an event. This not mixing with people not like us went rather deep. I caught myself using the phrase "will it be mixed" when Jacques announced an important white-tie event and afterward couldn't quite believe that I could formulate such a thought.

During these first months in Belgium, my profession once again reverted to student. I went each day to the nearby university, the French branch of the University of Louvain, and studied French in a language lab. I made friends, as one would expect, and was surprised that when I wanted to invite them back to the house for dinner or on a weekend, Jacques simply remarked, "Oh no. We don't mix. I wouldn't have people who are not from our circle to the house. We just don't do this. One day you'll learn." I then knew I had to put off visits from my American girlfriends who had already written that they were dying to visit.

The concept of noblesse oblige also was not easy to accept for an American. Being naturally friendly and appreciative, I could master noblesse oblige without having to take on the attitude that underlay its reasoning, that is, the *obligation* of those in high rank or status to be honorable, generous, and charitable. Each time I watched Mamie or Jacques praise a wine steward, pastry chef, or owner of an elegant cheese shop for their superior product, I felt the "noblesse oblige" of these ceremonious gestures which bestowed grace upon those who the nobles thought were simply put on this earth to serve them. This was one of the few areas that I didn't have to remake when recreating my personality to blend with the cool nobles.

Chapter 7

*I*t seemed to have rained every day of those first two months, every day of my new marriage. Gray skies and drizzle with intermittent showers. Today it was pouring first thing in the morning. How was it possible that in late spring the sun never peeked out?

The maid brought up our breakfast tray and knocked at the door several times, as was her daily pattern. I went to get the tray and brought it to our bed, pouring coffee and offering Jacques his choice of croissant or *pain au chocolat*. But instead of discussing the day's plans, he remained silent. The silence was highly charged. Right after breakfast, when we usually had a quick morning *tendresse*, which started our day with an orgasmic glow, Jacques sprang out of bed and paced the room, opening the French doors leading to the balcony, the sound of thunder crashing through.

"Sheri, I'm going to the acupuncturist again today. I

want you to come with me. I want the doctor to stimulate your breasts to grow through acupuncture methods."

I was taken off guard, so sure that the issue was dead. "Let me think about it, Jacques. I really don't see how that method would work." His idea was so irrational that I decided to ignore it. But it stayed on his mind.

A few days later he said, "Why didn't you come with me to the acupuncturist? I can see you don't even want to improve yourself."

I replied, "You made a promise not to bring up the subject of breasts for at least six months."

"You deceived me. You're a dishonest woman. It has not been easy for me these past months, living with a dishonest woman. We can't go to St. Tropez."

"Why not?" I said, covering up my panic at hearing the words that I dreaded.

"You don't understand," he said sharply.

"It's all right," I said, trying to stay calm. "It is so pleasant here at Ginal." I knew his reasoning—no trip to St. Tropez without the promised breasts.

"You don't understand," he repeated. "You knew before the marriage that you weren't going through with the operation. You tricked me into marrying you. You deceived me!"

"Jacques, you promised my mother that you wouldn't bring this up," I pleaded. "You are breaking your promise. Where is that grand sense of honor that you are so proud of? And how can you turn against me like this after all our closeness, our lovemaking?"

"I couldn't stay silent any longer," he said. "You didn't even try to help yourself by coming to the acupuncturist. It shows me you'll never go through with the breast operation. And you can't win my trust with your sexual talents."

"Sexual talents?" I said. "We're making love. You yourself said that it is a paradise to live with me. I can't discuss this, Jacques. It hurts too much."

"You must discuss this. You must pay for your dishonesty. Tell me how many lovers you had!"

Unable to take any more of his anger, I went to bed. Jacques didn't follow.

In the early morning I found Jacques lying on the sofa in a stupor and saw an empty bottle of vodka and a bottle of Temesta pills open. Temesta pills, I had found out from the village pharmacist, were not a mild sleeping aid, as Jacques had once told me, but a very strong tranquilizer. He seemed to be sleeping restfully, and so I went about my morning routine. I wondered what the maid and butler would do when they found him sleeping on the sofa. He finally got up at noon when I returned from shopping; he had not gone to the office.

I approached him to ask how he felt. He didn't answer but walked to the gardener's shed. I continued my day, studying French, swimming, reading my English and French newspapers, and then shopping for the evening meal.

When I arrived home after six, I found Jacques at the side of the pool working on a life-size puzzle of a *Playboy* Bunny with huge breasts. He didn't answer when I asked him what time we should dine, just continued putting the puzzle together.

The breasts were enormous and rounded. He obviously was back on his breast fixation, and I dreaded the stormy evening ahead. We ate dinner in silence, formally dressed as usual. I tried to start light conversation but got no response. After dinner Jacques drank several cognacs and went upstairs as if to go to bed. I soon followed. When I walked into the bedroom, I saw that all the photographs of me were turned in their frames.

Upon seeing me, he walked out of the room and outside toward the pool and, as I watched him from the window, started drinking at the pool house bar. I stood watching him from the bedroom balcony, undecided what to do, but I knew I must try to force a resolution of this impasse.

I went into the pool house. He poured himself a half glass of cognac, lit a thin brown cigarette, and said, "You are deceiving me with the breast operation. I should never have married you. You are so clever; you think you can trick me. Like your clever avoidance of bringing a dowry. And I know you have a trust fund! And since you made the choice to withhold the trust fund from me, go out and get a job and bring in your share of the household expenses. Yes, find a job and now!"

At this point I knew I must break his increasingly vicious soliloquy and walked away, toward the main house. He followed me, continuing his punishing tirade, repeating all his accusations over and over again, using stronger language but always in a low voice.

After more irrational accusations in which he often blamed me for an imaginary past full of lovers, I went upstairs to sleep. When I awoke, Jacques was not in bed. I looked into the pool house. He was not there. Finally I saw him coming out of one of the guest rooms. He looked frightful. "Go out and get a job!" he burst out when he saw me. After about an hour he joined me at the pool, where I was trying to read. "If you think that your next little deception will be to become pregnant, I will tell you right now, I will not recognize it as my child and I will send you back to America with the child."

After that cruel statement I walked away without another word. I was stunned. Throughout our romance Jacques had given no hint about this side of his nature. He had been the kindest, most loving man. I left for the entire day to try to distract myself with the study of French at my university lab. In midafternoon I called and found that again he had not gone to the office. By this time I was frightened but had no one to call for help. His mother was on one of her trips; Isabelle was with Gérard and Hélène in Lugano. I did not want to upset Mémé, and I did not know how to reach Marc.

I came home late in the afternoon and found Jacques in bed. There was an almost empty bottle of scotch on the night table, with the ever-present pill bottle near it and a large ashtray overflowing with small cigar butts. He was not sleeping; he was moaning and acknowledged my presence by some indistinguishable French phrases. I didn't know what to do. I went downstairs to see whether I could find Marc's telephone number. After a search of Jacques's phone directory I found the number of the abbey. I went to the pool house and used a phone there. When I reached Marc he was amazed that I had managed it; he said times for phone calls were always prearranged. I told him briefly what was happening. His voice dropped and he said that he would be over the next day, Saturday afternoon, as soon as he could make it. He advised me to avoid any confrontations, no matter what Jacques's line of argument. And he urged me to remain as calm as humanly possible. He also told me not to tell Jacques that he was coming.

That Marc was coming to the house relieved me, but the urgency in his voice frightened me. It was the first time I had a sense that I might be in real danger.

As I was hanging up the phone, I looked up and saw Jacques's tall frame hovering near me. "Who did you talk to?" he almost whispered.

"I called my mother," I blurted out.

He asked, "Why? What did you tell her? Did you tell her she has a dishonest daughter?"

"No," I said, "I just wanted to speak to her."

I knew I had to heed Marc's advice not to start any further arguments, so I only asked Jacques what time he wanted dinner. He said he didn't want to eat dinner and was going back to bed. He stayed upstairs while I remained downstairs. At about midnight he came down and started drinking again. Suddenly he broke his silence and became abusive, heaping insult after insult on me. I tried to leave the room but he forced me to stay and listen. I was too afraid to disobey and sat listening while he slowly paced back and forth between the bar and the fireplace.

I kept silent, remembering Marc's advice. "Please, Jacques. I am very tired. I just can't answer any more accusations. I'm going up to bed."

I walked out of the house and went to the pool area, hoping he would not follow me. I slept that night in the cold pool house. I woke up a couple of times during the night and saw that the lights in the main house were still on. The next morning I went into the bedroom to dress and found Jacques sitting up in bed, staring emptily out the window. My photographs had disappeared from the room.

He moaned in French, "Go back to America. I can't live with a dishonest woman."

I said, "I am your wife, Jacques, and I will not leave you."

In a stupefied tone he said, "If you stay, I will make life miserable for you. I love you deeply and will never forget you. And I will never find anyone like you. But go home to America. I will never trust you again."

The man who looked at me had no resemblance to the Jacques I knew. His face was distorted, his eyes completely dull, his voice and manner changed. "Go back to America,

I can't live with a dishonest woman," he began again, and continued with a litany of my sins.

I rushed to the telephone center in the village to call Marc and found that he had left the abbey.

When I came back, Jacques was downstairs, pacing back and forth in front of a blazing fire, drinking pastis, a licorice-flavored aperitif, and smoking his omnipresent thin Cuban cigar. He didn't even look around when I walked in.

Soon after, the doorbell rang, startling Jacques. I rushed to open the door, and Marc followed me into the salon. When Jacques saw him, he turned his back and, without a greeting, rushed to the pool house. Marc and I sat down and he asked me to recount everything that had happened during the last days and nights.

His reaction to the breast story was complete horror. "Jacques forced Claudine to go through that painful operation and she had to have *several* operations to correct the problems caused by the first operation to enlarge her breasts," he said. "But you made a grave mistake in promising Jacques his irrational request.

"Mamie tells me how happy Jacques is with you, Sheri, and what a fine home life you are creating for him. I am sorry you are going through so much."

I told him of Jacques's heavy drinking at all hours of the day and night, and also of his pill-taking. Marc nodded sadly, and said, "A heavy drinking period occurred with Jacques several years ago, but he has not been drinking heavily since. At that time he was very depressed and irrational due to Claudine's unfaithfulness. He had been very unhappy for the last years of his marriage to Claudine. When he met you and over the years of your courtship he changed considerably. He drank moderately and was more outgoing and enjoyed life. Mamie and I saw the favorable changes that came over him because of your influence, Sheri. We became more and more convinced that you were the right partner for Jacques who would be able to keep him stable and happy. I heard all about you for years. Mother especially felt that you had the gift to enrich Jacques's life and have him develop to his full potential. That is why we decided to allow this marriage, even though Mother felt strongly that you should live together for a few years before marriage; of course, I will not give you my personal or religious attitudes on that subject. I cannot.

"Although we did not check into your family background, from your behavior we assumed that you had sufficient refinement and class to assume the role of baroness in our family. So convinced were we that you would be good for Jacques that we took the chance of letting a total stranger into our family."

Had *I* been deceived? Was I only allowed into the family as a potential reformer of Jacques? How many other incidents in Jacques's life were they hiding? The suicide of Jacques's sons' young nanny ran through my mind. I knew then that Jacques's life had to be controlled for some reason, and that thought thoroughly scared me.

I kept my composure as Marc continued earnestly. "Sheri, I've told you all this in confidence, and now let me advise you on how to handle Jacques when a bad situation arises. Just ignore all his comments, even if they are nasty and hurtful. Do not answer with logic; it will only fuel his illogical reasoning. Wait patiently and silently for a few days until the mood passes. He has told me that he loves you deeply, and hopefully you can work this out. And now I must go and talk with him."

Marc came back into the house after another hour and announced that he saw very little hope, saying that his brother would not forgive me for my deception. He advised me to start thinking of leaving for America.

"Marc," I replied, stunned, "Jacques and I have a strong basis of love. I just know that after a longer, happy period with me, he'll forget his breast obsession and find happiness in the real sense. I don't want to give up on our marriage."

I don't know what possessed me to state determinedly and unequivocally that I wouldn't give up. I was confused and numbed both by the behavior I'd seen in the past few days and by Marc's alarming revelations that I was facing more than I had originally thought. I knew now that this was not only about breasts; there was more. But how much more? What were they hiding, the family? How could Marc even suggest ending the marriage?

It was unthinkable for me to leave Jacques after all the good years I had known with him. Perhaps this incident was a freak occurrence and would never happen again. I urged Marc to talk to Jacques again and find a point of reconciliation. He consented.

I watched as Marc and Jacques walked to the orchard and into the woods. It was dark when they returned, and Marc gave me a sign that he had made headway. Jacques looked calmer and actually sat down to dinner, but remained silent. I could feel, though, that the mood had been broken.

After dinner Marc and I walked alone around the property. He would tell me only that he had convinced Jacques to continue the marriage, and he now wished to speak of other subjects. I asked him about his life at Maredsous, the Jesuit monastery, and he readily confided in me.

"I joined the order because I was searching for an extension of my family. I needed a father image all my life and found it in the Monsignor. He and all my Jesuit brothers have become the strong family I always needed. They have strengthened me so that I can now be a strength to my mother and family and to all those I serve."

Marc spoke formally, as if he were giving a speech. Yet his expressions and movements were very relaxed. He didn't look like the type who would choose to become a man of God.

We walked back into the house. Jacques had a huge glass of cognac in his hand. While we listened to music and sat and talked on, Jacques filled his glass several times. Then for the first time since the strange episode had begun, I dared to go upstairs to the bedroom with him. Marc's presence had somehow dissipated the mood of crisis, but the tension was still high.

Watching each other's every movement, we cautiously took off our clothes at either side of the oversized bed. I slipped under the covers quickly, staying close to the edge, and assumed the position of sleep. Soon I felt Jacques move closer to my back, and then suddenly he pounced on me, encircling me with his legs and arms in a tight, clinging embrace. Alarmed at his strength, I tried to shake loose. Soon I heard him give a strange vulnerable cry and knew that his grasp was an act of supplication. After a few minutes, he released his hold as abruptly, rolled to his side of the bed, and fell asleep. It was a strange, final jolt to end the whole frightening episode.

The next morning I went out early to get the Sunday-morning croissants, and prepared breakfast. It was as if a different person had walked into the breakfast room as Jacques watched me set the table and in a cheerful voice told me that he was happy Marc had come. He kissed me tenderly and said, "I love you, Sheri." He looked cheerful and back to his handsome, well-groomed self again. It was bizarre.

After he had one more private talk in the garden with Jacques, Marc left shortly after breakfast, expressing to me his confidence that all was fine and that he felt secure in leaving. This, too, felt strange. Marc believed the storm was over and so he left.

Unbelievably, Jacques and I spent the rest of the day swimming and relaxing at the pool. He now had no resemblance to the person who had been out of control. I almost wondered whether I had imagined the severity of the event. How could this distinguished, gentle man behave so cruelly?

Jacques kissed me naturally and tenderly as we lay next to each other in the sun, as if nothing unusual had happened. There was no mention of the past days. He had undergone a total transformation from cruel monster to loving husband. And I wasn't going to say or do *anything* to trigger a new transformation.

"You know," he said, "since we didn't take a honeymoon in April, I think it's time we took a trip. Get away for a while. We always have such a good time traveling. Would you like that, my *chérie* Sheri?"

"Yes, Jacques."

"Well, good then. We'll go to Japan. I wonder when the cherry blossoms are in bloom. I'll make the plane reservations and we'll be off in a few weeks."

In the evening we had dinner in Brussels at the famous haute cuisine restaurant Comme Chez Soi, and afterward went to a late rock concert featuring Johnny Hallyday, Europe's answer to Elvis Presley. When Monday morning came, Jacques went to his office and I to the university. Amazingly, all was well again in the barony.

Chapter 8

Isabelle and Gérard arrived for dinner and acted like young lovers all evening, kissing and flirting with abandon. It was embarrassing to watch a man in his seventies and a woman who could be his granddaughter, and I really didn't know how to react.

"Look at Isabelle's pure white skin. Isn't it like a china doll's? She never goes out in the sun to mar its purity with even a hint of color," Gérard said, gazing at her. "She does this for me. She wants to be my beautiful little girl."

"Oh Gérard! You are such a tyrant, never letting me lift my face to the sunshine! But I'd do anything for you." Isabelle sighed and then leaned her head on his chest in a gesture that begged his protective embrace. Jacques looked away and suggested we move to the table.

Isabelle and Gérard continued their sexual teasing throughout dinner, only interrupting it for several serious exchanges about food and the new restaurants in Belgium and France. Apparently they often took trips together, driving to the middle of France just to visit three-star restaurants.

When I attempted to lead the conversation into a larger arena and tried to discuss world news, in which I assumed Gérard might be interested, the mention of any country simply opened up the topic of its cuisine or its restaurants. This was at the time when American hostages were being held in Iran, and, like all Americans, I was deeply concerned about their welfare. I read the *International Herald Tribune* avidly. When I brought up the subject of Iran, the conversation turned to "the terrible inconvenience of the interruption of the flow of Iranian caviar and pistachio nuts." I realized that Gérard himself exactly fit his warning at the wedding: "These people here in our little noble circle, you'll find, are the most self-involved and superficial group you'll ever meet. I hope you will be able to stand living among us." I really had thought Gérard would be different.

After dinner, as we were having liqueurs and more very small talk, Isabelle suddenly lured Gérard upstairs with the ridiculous pretext that she wanted to show him a painting.

"I don't approve of such an exhibition in my home, Sheri; I'm sorry you have to be exposed to this distasteful affair," Jacques said in the same protective tone he had used throughout our courtship. It was difficult for me to adjust to hearing a concerned statement like that coming from a man who had exhibited such aberrant behavior just days earlier. Yet he had been a loving husband in every way since the incident. "I'm turning up the volume of the music because they go to the bedroom just above us. Isabelle deliberately shrieks throughout their sessions. I don't want you to hear the soundtrack when she approaches the final minutes before she climaxes. She does it to torment me."

"Why then do you allow it to go on in your home?" Pink Floyd's music now mixed with her aroused moans.

"We made an agreement a long time ago. Isabelle does so much for me, you see. I've needed her kindness many times, and she's always been there for me."

Despite the loud bass rhythms of the disco music to which Jacques had just switched—Kool and The Gang's new album, which had recently arrived in Europe—Isabelle's strange, dramatic moans and shrieks permeated the living room.

"She told me she's never had an orgasm with him. She just loves acting out the scene. She lets him think that he drives her wild and of course that builds up his pride in his brilliant performance. Then she darts in to take advantage of that moment and coyly suggests the next gift she'd like. She has closets full of clothes he's bought her. And the jewels! She always has a plan. And when she tires of one of her old lovers, for a while at least, she often creates a dramatic ending, sometimes with a series of finales to the affair, so they will never forget her. She relishes the grand gesture. It's her way of showing passion. She once took a sack full of jewels given to her by one old man, and threw it into a deep pond. She sent him a note telling him she was angry with him and how she had disposed of his jewels, then said her love couldn't be bought. And told him that because of her love for him she could not bear to wear his jewels except in his company. Of course, through this manipulation, they'll go back to her at any time with even greater willingness to empty their Swiss bank accounts in order to finance her whims."

Just then, Gérard, looking like a knight returning triumphant with the Holy Grail, reappeared in the living room and said he was leaving. Isabelle, following closely behind, announced she'd decided to stay the night with us. She was too weak to drive, she chimed, as Gérard proudly bid us good night.

After uncorking and finishing a final bottle of champagne, listening to Isabelle spin out tales of her lovemaking with Gérard and all the intrigues of their secret love affair, we all walked upstairs to retire.

I found it somewhat odd that Isabelle followed us into the bedroom and stayed there with us while taking off her makeup and jewelry and undressing down to her underwear. The next morning, as we were waking up, she came into our room wearing a sexy nightgown, sat on our bed, and began chatting away. Jacques and I both slept in the nude. My robe was across the room and I didn't want to get out of bed naked, and I wondered how Jacques would maneuver. But no sooner had the thought crossed my mind than he got out of bed and walked into the open bathroom alcove in her plain view.

I was flabbergasted but soon got out of bed, got my robe, and went into the guest bathroom. When I returned, the maid had already brought up breakfast and Jacques and Isabelle were sitting on the bed, eating. I took my place on the bed on the other side of Jacques and the three of us sat there eating together and chatting away as naturally as if this occurred every morning. I was the only one who seemed to feel the dissonance of this cozy morning ménage.

"Your sister is quite a character," I said to Jacques after Isabelle left for Brussels.

"Yes indeed. I can see she really likes you too. But Sheri, please promise me you won't be influenced by her. It is all right to be friendly but I never want you to be alone with her, as I've already warned you. Do you promise me never to call her on your own?"

"Yes, yes, I do." I wondered why he was so emphatic about this. It made me curious. He couldn't think that I was so naive that I couldn't protect myself from her even if there were sexual advances.

———

The next night we were invited to Maurice and Françoise's home for dinner. Maurice was a relative and had been Jacques's business partner for twelve years. On the long drive to his cousin's home, Jacques gave me some background on the couple's relationship and lifestyle. This was the branch of the family that Jacques's mother regarded as several notches below them. Maurice was his paternal grandmother's nephew, the son of her sister. He held the title of chevalier, which was not considered in the same league as baron or count.

We drove along the long cobblestone driveway into the estate. Like Jacques's, the house was a converted ancient farm estate, with stables, meadows, and gardens. The date the house was built—1657—was carved in the massive stone above the entrance.

Maurice was in his late forties, Françoise younger. They were a very attractive couple. Françoise was fashionably dressed and sparkled with jewels.

The imposing house had a number of living rooms, each one grandly decorated. Dinner was served in high style by a butler and two servants; the dishes, crystal, and silverware were beautifully ornate. Expensive wines were brought out with great fanfare for each course. Table discussion was in French, centering around food, wines, and travel, by now, I knew, the Belgians' favorite dinner conversation. We briefly discussed Maurice and Françoise's frequent trips to the Philippines, where the company's yachts were built, and the complicated labor problems they had there.

Artworks collected during their travels, icons and samovars from Russia and jade from the Orient, were displayed throughout the house. Exquisite flower arrangements were placed around the living rooms and dining room, and the numerous fireplaces, all lighted, gave the house a glowing and lavish feeling. I thought the house was designed and decorated beautifully. Jacques, however, found it a travesty. He believed it was a tasteless display of wealth and later pointed out that the furniture and rugs were not antiques but only reproductions.

At one point after dinner, Maurice and Françoise's daughter entered the living room with her two-year-old son. She had been recently divorced and lived on her parents' estate in a smaller house. The grandparents naturally paid attention to her little boy and asked their daughter to join us for coffee and liqueurs. As the evening progressed, Jacques and Maurice spoke about business, while Françoise and I talked about fashion. She suggested that we all go to London together each season on shopping trips, and then invited me to their summer home on the Belgian seacoast.

On the way home, I told Jacques what a special evening it had been for me, and how much I enjoyed Maurice and Françoise. But he thought their behavior was very bourgeois, that they had shown extremely poor taste by letting a child enter the living room when there were guests; a child should not be given such attention in front of company. His remarks surprised me because the child had stayed in the room for only fifteen minutes and had been quiet as a little angel. "Sheri," he continued, "that was one of the differences between that branch of the family and mine. In my family children were never on display. Children were not permitted to sit in the living room or dining room with adults. They had their meals in their own quarters and entered the living room only with their nursemaids or governesses to greet their parents or to say good night. And that is what is proper."

Later that night, he admitted that he had been too critical, and that his cousin's family had gone out of their way to make a special welcome for me. He said that Françoise had taught her cook some excellent dishes and that the meal had been superb. But he criticized Maurice's choice of wines, analyzing each, then pointing out to me what his choice would have been. Once again, Jacques reinforced my impression of his tremendous snobbism.

Lunch at Mamie's had become a Wednesday tradition. This week Marc joined us. We exchanged knowing glances when he arrived, and I gave him a nod as if to indicate that everything was going smoothly. I didn't think he had told his mother of the weekend rescue. We discussed French literary figures during lunch, and afterward Marc and I spoke about American presidential politics while Jacques and Mamie sat on the other side of the room talking about the new house they had recently purchased for Claudine and the boys. Then I overheard Jacques telling his mother that Claudine called him constantly at the office, tormenting him about his sons.

Marc was looking handsome. He wore jeans and a shirt. Though he was shorter than Jacques, only about six feet two inches, he was extremely well built and looked more like a sports star than a monk. We got along famously and now that we had faced a crisis together felt close. He promised to invite me to the abbey.

When Marc left, Mamie, Jacques, and I spent another hour chatting. We discussed her itinerary for her summer travels; she would be going to England on her annual tour of gardens, then to Marbella again, followed by several trips to the South of France to stay at various friends' villas.

At one point during the conversation I mentioned that I would like to order personalized stationery and asked what type of print and layout I should choose. Hearing the question, Mamie and Jacques stiffened and simultaneously made the identical gesture, a sniff with a slight tremor of the head as if a whiff of some unpleasant smell had just wafted in. Hesitantly Mamie showed me her personal note cards. She said she did not use stationery, only personalized note cards for short messages; then she dropped the subject abruptly and my question was left up in the air.

During the drive home Jacques told me that only the bourgeoisie use personal stationery and that instead he would order some cards for me. I was surprised when he suspiciously asked what I needed them for. I answered that I wanted to write thank-you notes to America to people who had sent us wedding presents. Somehow I had the feeling that both he and his mother resented the fact that I wished to use my title. I suspected that if Mamie had said what was really on her mind when we discussed stationery it would have been, "No dowry, no title!" Just as the wealthy always suspect that people want to marry them for their money, apparently the nobility are suspicious of the same for their titles.

The next morning, I tried not to let my mind recall the horrible ordeal Jacques had put me through just days earlier, but his cruel words continually flashed through my mind. Again I marveled at how distorted time was here—days ago felt to me like a month—because everything I experienced was so vivid. I needed to be with someone who had warmth and compassion, a rarity among the people of my new circle. Mémé was the only person who could lift my spirits. I called her and she invited me that day for lunch.

We sat down to a beautifully prepared luncheon served by her maid, and, with a glimmer in her eye, the remarkable ninety-three-year-old Baroness de Borchgrave said she'd tell me stories I'd never forget.

"Let me begin by telling you about my grandson Jacques's father. Paul Henri was a brilliant military man who became the protocol officer and close personal friend to the King. He died in his middle thirties, in a tragic military accident, but I will not tell you about that during this talk. The unfortunate circumstances surrounding his death are a very sensitive subject, and few people in Belgium know the real story. Hasn't Jacques told you how his father died? No? Well. Paul Henri was given a state funeral. I protested that, at nine years old, Jacques was too young to attend, but your mother-in-law Adriane insisted. Young Jacques shed not a tear throughout the entire ceremony. He stood rigidly, then was presented the flag by one of the generals, and, finally, he read a tribute to his father to the assembled dignitaries. A terrifying experience for him."

I tried to picture Jacques, probably a tall, lanky boy, doing this. "How very sad," I said. "Poor Jacques!"

"Yes. Poor Jacques! He became shy and withdrawn after his father's death, and never got any comfort from his mother. Adriane raised her children very strictly. She never kissed or hugged them, believing open displays of affection spoiled children. They ate in their own dining room, and weren't allowed at her table until they were eighteen. Really, nursemaids and governesses brought them up.

"My dear," she continued, "I will never forget this. During a brief period of time she and my grandson stayed in my castle. One day, when she was playing very happily with her little dog on her lap, I asked why she never played so affectionately with her children. She replied, 'This little dog is my pleasure; the children are my duty.' Can you imagine?"

I expressed my amazement and she repeated dramatically, "*This* little dog is my *pleasure; the children are my duty,*" and went on.

"Jacques was sent to boarding school the year his father died. He was a very unhappy child, and when the headmaster called to tell Adriane that Jacques was often found crying, her reaction was to punish him by not allowing him to come home on weekends and holidays! So he spent them secretly with me. Of course, when Adriane found out, we had fierce arguments about child-rearing. Jacques must learn control and not be protected, she said, then forbade me to let him visit. But I found ways to keep our visits secret from her.

"After the obligatory year of mourning, her life became a constant round of parties and balls. She became a real socialite, wanting only to have a gay time."

I could see that Mémé resented Mamie's approach to most things, and wasn't about to hide it!

"Sheri, *mon petit chou*, I am so happy that Jacques now has a wife who will give him all the love he needs," she said, flashing her warm smile. "Yes, I can see you will change his life."

"Mémé, please tell me about Claudine, Jacques's first wife. He never speaks of her."

"Claudine, the youngest of seven children, came from an aristocratic family in France, but a family far below the standing of ours. Her parents were diplomats and often away, leaving their children with nannies and governesses, and, as a teenager, she'd just travel to distant parts of the world for months at a time. She was terribly spoiled. She married Jacques at eighteen and had children immediately. I don't think she ever loved Jacques. She and Jacques quarreled constantly and she'd leave for days at a time. Meals were served shoddily, and the house was in disarray. Why, she didn't even know how to instruct the help to clean or shop correctly!

"She was a very sexy girl with a brash personality, and always embarrassed Jacques in public by flirting with men. Of course, no one in the family liked her, and I'm certain she felt the same way. But she did like being the family's baroness. Oh yes, she loved her title! And took every opportunity to let Adriane know that she had the more important title.

"Poor Jacques suffered so. That, my dear, is why you are so important! He is so confident with you. You are 'the angel that came from across the seas' to make Jacques happy and fulfilled, and in turn make us all happy."

I was very moved by Mémé's statement and promised myself that I would do everything to create a happy and fulfilling life for my new husband. My heart went out to him, and I resolved to change his life and help him find happiness.

Mémé was remarkable, I couldn't help thinking, as she began to discuss Catherine, the youngest of Adriane's four children.

"I never liked Catherine. She is like Adriane. She was bright, pretty, and outgoing, excelling in everything she did, from her studies to sports. So she grew up as the most loved one. She fell in love with a young diplomat and wanted to marry at a young age; but his family was not acceptable, and Adriane broke it up by sending her to boarding school in Switzerland. Soon after, Adriane found a suitable match for Catherine and practically forced her to marry a young man whose family had a substantial fortune and owned one of Belgium's historic castles. Now she puts all her energies into carrying on the tradition of running the castle, being adviser to the villagers, and into her hobby—horseback riding."

I just couldn't believe how frank and aware Mémé was. She gave me the full picture.

"Catherine has very little social contact with her own set and lives a relatively unglamorous life. She rarely comes to Brussels to visit me, which honestly doesn't upset me in the least. She works hard, with few servants, since her husband's father is very miserly. Her husband only works on the land and brings in no money. But once the old father dies, Catherine and her husband will be very rich.

"Now, where was I?" Mémé smiled. "Oh, yes, I'll tell you more about Catherine next time. I want to tell you a little about each of the children. Let me tell you about my favorite.

Well, that's not fair. I think I love Jacques and Isabelle equally. First, though, would you like some more coffee or waffles?"

Mémé had served the most luscious strawberry Belgian waffles, with lots of *crème fraîche*. I was having such fun hearing her unrestrained opinions on everyone and eating this sinful dessert that I resolved to visit her every week.

"Isabelle is my favorite. She is quite a character, though, and I don't approve of all her behavior. She is childlike, without a sense of right and wrong, a little birdie flitting through life seeking only pleasure, with no other thought than her own immediate gratification. She's a twin to Marc and was the least loved of all the children. She was the ugly duckling who could do nothing right. As a child, Isabelle was made to walk behind her mother while Catherine was allowed to walk at her mother's side. In her early teens she became obese, weighing close to two hundred pounds.

"Adriane arranged a marriage for her, when she was quite young, to an older and well-to-do gentleman in her circle. They had two children who are now young teenagers. Right after the marriage, she lost weight and cared very much for her appearance. Under all that fat was an extremely attractive, even beautiful woman.

"Then she began to have indiscriminate affairs, seeking out men old enough to be her grandfather. She was found in bed with a man from our own circle and her husband divorced her, getting custody of the children."

Once again I marveled at her full disclosure of even the sexual details.

Mémé continued, "She received no alimony. She has her inheritance, of course, but Adriane has control of that, otherwise she'd squander every franc on luxuries. Of course she is also often supported by her men friends. She's quite an extravagant girl. Adriane is disgraced by her behavior, but while she had to accept the old lovers from their own society, she abhors Isabelle's forays into the lower classes."

I laughed along in delight as I heard about this unique character, my sister-in-law.

"Isabelle is a woman out of her time," Mémé continued in dramatic earnest. "She should have lived when life at court existed . . . when people spent all day and night being entertained at the king's feasts and had intriguing affairs. She loves gossip and intrigue and relishes scandal. But she is at the same time very good-natured and doesn't deliberately hurt anyone. However, with her childlike mentality she often creates the most complicated situations between people, and her gossip has caused the breakup of several marriages."

Aha, I thought, a key to Jacques's warning me to stay away from her.

"Isabelle gets up at noon and after elaborate makeup and hairdo ceremonies has luncheon dates and rendezvous with her lovers, and each night a dinner appointment. She lives only for dining out and is a connoisseur of food and wine. Her job as a champagne promoter is a total farce; she only works occasionally in order to get free champagne."

Mémé spoke so freely and unabashedly about Isabelle's sex escapades that I felt I was speaking with a girlfriend, not a woman in her nineties. I was amazed by her sharpness and wit.

"She sees her children on some weekends but doesn't really care to play mother. She is close to Jacques because they banded together as children, having been the two unloved ones. In fact, every time Jacques had problems with Claudine he would turn to Isabelle, and on many occasions moved in with her for several days.

"In spite of it all, I really love Isabelle, she's such a fun character. She means no harm. She comes through when she is needed by the family."

"And what about Marc?" I asked, curious to hear Mémé's opinion of Jacques's brother. "He seems so well adjusted and uncomplicated."

"Ah, yes. Marc had always been *my* favorite. He was the least complicated of the four. Handsome, dashing, with a great personality. Everyone loved him. He is also the most educated of the whole family, having graduated from Oxford. He was a wonderful dancer, and went to all the balls and coming-out parties. In fact, he was the most popular bachelor in Belgium! A true *bon vivant*.

"After he returned from Oxford he continued his studies in Belgium and became involved with a circle of young priests. He was very impressionable, and soon informed the family that he was joining the order. Everyone was shocked!

"In a way, Adriane now feels very good about having Marc in the order, since she will not have to share him with a wife. She and Marc travel together all over Europe as often as possible, in the height of luxury, staying at the most elegant hotels, dining at the top restaurants in the world! Adriane doesn't want Marc to miss that pleasure! I must admit that I don't know him well as an adult, and I still cannot understand why he chose such a life. Perhaps some day I shall ask him.

"But he apparently is very fulfilled by his calling, and gave over his inheritance to the monastery. I have heard that he has become a philosopher of his order, and people seek him out to mediate difficult problems. I also hear that he is working on a very important project having to do with computers. You see, he has inherited my son's technical abilities."

Suddenly Mémé just seemed to lose current; she had been talking animatedly for hours, and it was as if someone had pulled out the electrical cord. I announced I must leave and thanked her for a most enjoyable and informative afternoon. She was remarkable, her mental faculties completely intact. She had seemed to relish encapsulating the lives and personalities of her family for me. I never probed; she just talked on and on voluntarily. I suspected that through her I could learn about the new people in my life and how best to deal with them. When she asked me, before I left, to keep everything we discussed between us, and promised she would do the same, I knew I had a real ally.

$\mathcal{C}hapter\ 9$

$\mathcal{I}$mperial residences, Shinto gates and bells, shrines, pagodas, rock gardens, gilded Buddhist temples, Gods of Thunder and Lightning, geisha houses, bonsai trees, intricately carved treasures, tea ceremonies, Mount Fuji. The beauties of Japan and the exhilaration of travel seemed to wind back the clock on my relationship with Jacques to the carefree, untainted love affair we had enjoyed during the St. Tropez summers and the weeks in Paris.

We toured Tokyo, the green city with trees everywhere and the energy and bustle of teeming humanity; strolled the Ginza, the main shopping district, with its multitude of neon character signs; lunched at sushi, tempura, and *shabu shabu* bars; saw endless Japanese gardens with leaning rocks, contemplative fountains, ponds of shimmering orange and gold carp and carved wooden teahouses; went to geisha performances, Kabuki, samurai dancers; to nightspots in Asakusa, to a ceremonial wedding performances with beautiful girls in a scintillating array of colorful silk kimonos; took the sleek futuristic bullet train and saw the Shinto temples at Nara, Nikko, and Kyoto; passed the volcanic black beaches crowded with surfers, saw snow-capped Mount Fuji and rode high through the green-pined mountains, viewing the breathtaking valley below, dotted with pagoda-like houses roofed in blue tile. Kyoto, a city surrounded on three sides by mountains, with eighteen hundred Shinto and Buddhist temples and shrines nestled on their slopes, was our favorite. Rock gardens and waterfalls were everywhere. The city was a network of canals and little bridges connecting tiny islands blanketed with blossoming cherry and gingko trees.

The Japanese people's reaction to toweringly tall Jacques almost bordered on fear. They often stopped in their tracks to look up at this wondrous light-haired Westerner whose upper body and head surfaced far above the crowds of dark-haired Japanese and could be spotted all over the Ginza or Asakusa. We laughed at the sensation we created all through Japan. And, as was the custom, people we encountered in restaurants and at tourist sites were constantly bowing to us and thanking us profusely at every turn.

At the famous Mikado nightclub in Tokyo, a gigantic Las Vegas–style club decorated on one wall with a huge rushing waterfall encased in glass, we saw a show of topless dancers. From our balcony table on the first floor, we looked down onto a unique Japanese scene: hundreds of fancily dressed Japanese girls sat in rows of seats as in a theater. They were "for pay" dance partners and could be taken home as well. The Japanese men, sitting around tables in groups of three to five, eyed them intensely and a brave few ventured out to make their choices even before the show had ended. Immediately after the closing number, props were cleared off the dance floor, there was a mad scramble of men toward the seated women, and within minutes most of the two hundred girls were on the floor with their partners. Jacques of course questioned our bar steward and found out that these high-class call girls received the equivalent of two hundred American dollars for the package deal of dancing, possible massage, and a trick.

"We must try one, bring her back with us to our room. What do you say?" Jacques couldn't resist asking.

I shook my head.

"Oh, come on," he said, flashing his eyes sensuously, as I continued to shake my head. "Okay then, we'll wait until we get to the geisha houses in Kyoto. Remember, I always wanted you to have an experience with a woman, and here, halfway around the world, is a fine place to try it out."

"Jacques, you are totally consumed with sex. It's always on your mind. Right?" I tried to deflect his suggestion. He couldn't really have been serious, I told myself.

"And on yours!"

"We're a healthy couple, no?" I lifted my sake cup and toasted him.

"We will be once you agree to some experimentation. Put aside those puritanical Boston attitudes, then you'll soar!"

"We'll soar. Give me time. I like the idea of it all but prefer to keep my fantasies pure. That is, in the realm of fantasy."

"Your already pretty sophisticated fantasies would be enriched if you turned some into reality. Then you could build more intricate fantasies out of your upgraded adventures. No, *chérie* Sheri?"

"Oh, aren't we getting persuasive?" I said playfully.

"All right, I see you're not willing yet. One day, my baroness, debauchery! Now I must mention something I was thinking about during the show. You'll laugh."

"Oh?"

"You must feel like an absolutely voluptuous girl here. In the show the topless girls were all truly topless. Flat! How does it feel to be the best endowed one of them all?"

"Great!" I said cheerfully, not giving away my surprise that Jacques was able to speak about this sensitive issue in jest. How wonderful, I thought, the breast issue is finally fading. I had hoped it would be just a matter of time, and now I dared to think we might yet have a happy life together.

In Kyoto we stayed at a ryokan, a traditional Japanese inn, in the old and charming Shinmazen Dori section of the city, with its geisha houses, little bridges over streams, and kimonoed women on the streets. Staying in such a unique inn was the most brilliant highlight of a trip with many bright spots: the ever-larger Buddhas (the largest fifty-four feet high), the sacred temples of three thousand lanterns, the Imperial Palace with its Great Hall for Shoguns, and the Temple of One Thousand Blessing Buddhas, all with many sinuous arms and hands in symbolic gestures.

As we drove up to the ryokan we spotted a geisha in full makeup and elaborately embroidered kimono (a guide informed us that the official geisha kimono costs $10,000 or more). We entered through the bamboo gates and left our shoes at the door, to be retrieved only on leaving the hotel, and were led to our rooms through a maze of rectangular chambers with sliding screen walls—shoji—and a series of hallways whose windows looked out on gardens with lovely fountains. Then we were taken into our tiny room with its outer chamber opening onto a garden. The room had the traditional architectural features—sliding multipaned paper walls and tatami mats on the floors. The only furniture was a low bamboo table in the center of the room with a flower arrangement atop it and a large cabinet-closet where the futons were kept. There were calligraphic scrolls on the walls and flower arrangements displayed on shelves against the wall of the *tokonoma* (a niche opening off the room).

After receiving instructions as to the customs of the ryokan, we left for a day of exploring Kyoto's rock gardens and shopping. Jacques got truly carried away with the beautiful clothes, and bought me a half-dozen exquisite silk print kimonos with ornate obis, the belts which are tied in a complicated series of bows at the back. Then, to my amazement, he inquired where we could buy the special geisha kimonos, and soon he chose one of the most elaborately embroidered ones, with gold, bronze, and silver thread and intricate patterns of birds and flowers. It cost more than $15,000 and was truly an artistic treasure. Most kimonos worn by the geishas are made to special order.

Since I now had the true geisha kimono, Jacques of course wanted to create the whole image, probably with future sexual evenings in Belgium in mind. We purchased the special white makeup and eye colors as well as the undergarments and perfumes. Then, with the instruction of one of the merchants, we found a store where we bought Japanese aphrodisiacs and fragrant massage oils for our night at the ryokan.

In fact, I secretly considered Japan our honeymoon trip. The great geographic distance helped to push the misfired start of our marriage into oblivion, and from this long perspective I felt I had a more lucid view of the months in Belgium. The trip served to punctuate the end of the difficult phase. I savored the idea that here in Japan Jacques and I were on equal ground, both entirely out of our element, reacting to an alien universe; no longer was I the only one who struggled to make sense of a strange world. Watching his intense curiosity and enjoyment at being in exotic Asia, I realized that aside from the enormous sexual attraction that raged between us, we also shared a similar capacity to enjoy experiences intensely.

I theorized that our ability to take such thrilling pleasure in experience, and in living the moment, came from our early exposure to death. Having someone "go away forever" when you are a child makes you keenly aware of life's finality. Knowing that my brother was deprived of life beyond the age of ten, I wanted to live every day with a passion. His father's death when he was nine must have given Jacques the same inner compulsion to take joy in life.

I felt an almost conspiratorial link with him in the total pleasure we took in stimulating our senses—seeing new a country, its beauty, its art treasures, tasting its cuisine, feeling that exhilaration that only being in a strange world with different tastes, smells, and sounds can awaken. That is when Jacques became playful and disarming in his sense of fun and daring, ready to try anything, possessing the curiosity of a child, and it was at this point that I felt closest to him, felt the bond that I knew would endure when the erotic passions inevitably eroded with the passing years. Hearing him express his passionate enthusiasm for Japan, I rediscovered the intensity of my love for him.

Jacques's mind was always working, thinking up exciting sexual evenings. It was his personal art form. Before returning to the inn, where a ritual dinner would be served to us in our room in a ceremonial style, we purchased several more items for our sensuous adventure, for this night and many others to come—a small illustrated book showing Japanese lovemaking positions, and tapes of Oriental music.

One of our purchases, the famous Japanese benwa beads, Jacques insisted that I start using immediately, and asked me to insert them in the rest room of the store, to prepare me for the evening. Benwa beads are tiny golden balls connected by a steel thread. They are placed inside the vagina, and as a woman walks the movement of the tiny beads as they rearrange themselves and pull together creates the most stimulating sensation. Jacques thought that if I inserted them before our walk home to the ryokan I'd be very hot for the evening ahead. Since I had refused all of his previous daring ideas, I felt I must oblige him on this harmless one.

We returned to the ryokan at sundown, in time for the first tea ceremony, which was performed for us in our room. Green tea was poured from a heavy iron kettle by a woman dressed in an exquisite kimono. Before she left Jacques used his persuasive powers, supplemented by sufficient yen, to convince her to add a special ingredient to the traditional dinner menu: a potent aphrodisiac called *motsuyagi* (made of animal organs), which we had just purchased. She agreed and left the room, bowing several times and muffling a charming giggle.

We were unaccustomed to the green tea and ordered sake to start the evening off, and then we dressed, I in a beautiful silk kimono and Jacques in a yukata, the unlined cotton robe worn by men. We sat on the floor beside our low table and were served a spectacular array of Japanese dishes by three kimono-clad attendants. The little dishes were brought all together on three huge, ornate trays. Sushi, seaweed, *motsuyagi* soup, nuts, tempura, pickled delicacies, and a number of mystery dishes. We tried each one and had bottle after bottle of hot sake. It rained as we feasted and we listened to the raindrops beating against the thin paper screens.

When the women came back to clear away the dishes they instructed us about the next ritual of the evening, a soaking bath, in Japanese, peppered with a few English words. We were told to put on the yukatas with warm, heavy, woolen outer kimonos. Then we went into the *yokujo*, the communal bath. The *yokujo* had a smoky glass partition which separated the men's and women's sections, but we all went into the same large hot tub. The procedure was to soap oneself lavishly, then rinse off under a shower before easing into the extremely hot water to soak. Then we showered again and reentered the tub for another long soak, with a final rinse under a shower of icy water.

Jacques and I went to our separate chambers but joined each other in the tub, each just against our side of the glass divider. In the strictly Japanese baths, especially in the hot springs regions like Beppu, both sexes are nude together in the same tub, with no division. Only where Westerners and Easterners mix are the dividers installed. Drinks were served us as we soaked in the bath. I shared the tub with several Japanese women and indeed felt voluptuous.

Back in our room, Jacques began directing my performance. I put on the geisha kimono and painted my face with the white makeup and special eye design as indicated in a little book. Jacques then took the snake extract *mamushi* and dropped it into his tea. This, he'd been told, was the strongest aphrodisiac, one which kept a man's "ambassador" (the word used in our Japanese love manual) hard and strong the whole night through. I wondered if combining the two aphrodisiacs *motsuyagi* and *mamushi* would be overkill, but I soon found it was devastating.

When I was in full costume, Jacques ordered more sake while I hid behind the shoji in the outer chamber. The attendant laid out our futons, the puffy, colorful quilts, one atop the other, and transformed our room into a bedroom. She asked that we try to speak quietly, as most guests would retire soon. She explained by performing a complicated charade that the rooms were not soundproof. We nodded that we understood.

When she had left, Jacques picked up *The Erotic Senti-*

ment: In the Paintings of China and Japan, compiled by Nik Douglas and Penny Slinger, and we looked through the Shunga illustrations and read the erotic verse. The positions shown and described had highly humorous names: Shouting Monkey Posture, Turning Dragon, Pair of Swallows, Cranes with Joined Necks, Mountain Goat Facing Tree, Pawing Horse Posture. We chose several daring positions and performed them silently to book precision, right down to the woman's curling her toes in ecstasy after orgasm.

And ecstasy it was! Whether the aphrodisiacs had an extreme psychological effect or a true physical effect, we'd never know. But we vowed to continue Shouting Monkey and Mountain Goat Facing Tree throughout our married life. Jacques planned another trip to the special store to buy a lifetime supply of snake extract.

The next morning the kimonoed ladies entered with trays, bringing us the traditional Japanese breakfast. To our amazement, it was an only slightly changed duplicate of the dinner they had served the night before, little dishes containing the same seaweed, fish soup, pickles, egg and fish, spongy growth, and mystery foods. Along with the undrinkable grassy tea, of course. Though my capacity for adventure was great, facing a Japanese breakfast after such an active night of lovemaking exceeded my limit. We certainly insulted the gracious, soft-spoken maid when we begged her to take it all away at once. Jacques, a European all the way in his love of perfect, strong French coffee, laughed heartily as he and I eagerly consumed the replacement breakfast, watery instant coffee and Rice Krispies with hot water (there was no milk).

The two-week trip brought us back to our premarriage closeness, and when I thought about how different Jacques was when we traveled, I wondered whether that was why I had been blinded to his dark side throughout our courtship.

When he was away from his little world, his circle, he was infused with a positive and open spirit. I hoped our renewed closeness and easy rapport would dissolve our recent problems, and that the aphrodisiacs would have a lasting effect on keeping our erotic life, instead of my breasts, his obsession.

Chapter 10

We came home from Japan in time for our Wednesday luncheon with Mamie, who had just returned from her trip to the English gardens, where she had hobnobbed with the British nobility.

As usual, Mamie looked radiant in her signature outfit: a long-sleeved, cuffed silk blouse and light wool, calf-length skirt with a kick pleat. The skirt and blouse were in matching muted shades, worn with a chain-link belt, simple medium-heeled pumps, flesh-colored silk stockings, and important daytime jewelry—gold chains and pearls, heavy gold bracelets, and clip-on classic earrings, today with inlaid emeralds. Naturally she wore the symbol wedding ring, a precious stone encircled by diamonds, and other rings just as dazzling on her right hand. Her dark-blond hair was perfectly coiffed, her makeup understated, her perfume Yves Saint Laurent; she was a portrait of well-groomed perfection.

Her maid was sick, and since Mamie had never cooked,

Jacques and I lunched with her in less style than usual. The fare was simple, prepared by a gourmet shop. As she had explained previously, she had not been allowed to "enter" the kitchen as a child or young adult. She told us that she had loved the "divine" English gardens but despised the British, mostly because they have such "dreadful cuisine of which they are actually proud."

After she finished telling us that French and Belgian appreciation of food and wines and just about all of life's more refined pleasures were far superior to that of the horrid English, she began talking about the war years and what a difficult time that had been to bring up children. Suddenly a very amusing exchange occurred.

She said that many of the nobles, including her family, had to take Occupation troops into their castles; they didn't have enough staff, and at times unsanitary conditions were unavoidable. Jacques contracted a disease in infancy and the family doctor strongly urged that he be circumcised. At that time Christian babies were not circumcised.

Then she said, "Sheri, aren't you lucky that Jacques was circumcised like your Jewish men? But, although it is good for you, it is not good for Jacques because it made him less sensitive in sex." Jacques wasn't at all shocked by his mother's choice of a luncheon topic, discussed while eating *asperge blanc* with vinaigrette dressing.

Stunned by her frankness, I answered meekly that I didn't know that circumcision made men less sensitive. But I thought to myself that Jacques was having plenty of pleasure without his foreskin! In fact I was finding that the purpose of life here was not simply the pursuit of happiness and pleasure but the pursuit of a state of perpetual arousal. Everything was done to prime the senses for sexual excitement.

Over dinner that evening we joked about it and Jacques

said, "Although my mother speaks very directly about sex, she believes that it is normal for a married couple to have sex once a month; more than that is excessive."

"And what would she say if she knew her very own son had sex three and four times a day, every day?" I laughed.

"She wouldn't approve," he said with a smile, continuing, "Some women of Mother's time and society felt this way because it was customary for their husbands to keep mistresses for sex; the wives' mission was to have children and other lovers."

Although it was only approaching summertime, and the third month of our marriage, I felt as if I had already lived in Belgium for a year. The world I had entered was noble, glamorous, and decadent, different beyond my comprehension.

Because of the consistently good weather I decided to study French only in the mornings so that I would be able to spend the afternoons reading and gardening at poolside. Jacques encouraged me to enjoy the sun and pool; he said the weather could change any day, and there could be many weeks of nonstop rain. I followed his advice faithfully.

On these warm June evenings, Jacques invited groups of either family members or friends for dinners at poolside. Since guests expected these to be casual dinners, we followed an easy formula each time. The gardener helped with setting up tables and umbrellas and started the fire. The maid prepared one of three or four menus: shish kebab with red, green, and yellow peppers; roast leg of lamb on the spit; filets mignons, or baby lamb chops. Each dish was served with a different sauce, which Jacques prepared carefully, since he was the expert. The first course was generally shellfish or fish—mussels in cream sauce, lobster tails, gray shrimp from the North Sea, fish in aspic, or escargot. Summer wines were served with these barbecues—light white wines with the first course, then chilled young rosés. There were always side dishes like tomatoes Provençal, grilled endive, delicious homemade french fries—no meal was complete without those Belgian french fries. Dessert was a display of bowls of blueberries, raspberries, wild strawberries, and black raspberries with *crème fraîche* or a sauce of cream and fruit liqueurs on the side. After the fruit course, espresso, liqueurs, and chocolates were served.

Finally one night, Jacques dared to invite his friends among the young set, those whom Claudine had not influenced with her venomous propaganda.

Six couples arrived, and that evening I had a taste of what life would be like mixing with "all of Belgium." Most of the men were quite tall and handsome. The women were beautifully dressed, but almost as soon as they descended to the pool they removed their clothes and dived naked into the heated water. The men followed. Though Jacques had not thought to warn me of this immediate disrobing procedure, I too slid out of my pink chiffon garden dress and joined our guests, curious to see how this nudist evening would progress. As I looked around, I spotted some of Dr. Rémy's *poitrines*, and also noticed several perfectly sculpted male bodies.

The setting around the pool was idyllic, reminding me of garden restaurants on the Mediterranean. Softly glowing lanterns were suspended from the twisting branches of the exotically shaped fruit trees surrounding the pool, romantically illuminating the surrounding shrubbery. On the two hills rising from the pool area sprawled an untamed rock garden of tangled shrubbery, vines, herbs, and flowers. Lavender was planted around the periphery, and its scent was pervasive. Torches flickered from different levels of the property. Chamber music filled the air.

The maid and butler and an extra servant poured champagne while we all floated on rafts or leaned against the edge of the pool; then, when the barbecue was almost ready, everyone wrapped a pareo around himself or herself and sat down at one of two round umbrella tables.

For a brief time during dinner the conversation focused on me; our guests were curious about life in New York City. Surprisingly, very few of them had visited America; they had traveled mostly to countries in Europe, Monaco, or Zaire, the former Belgian Congo. Very soon the talk turned back to what I was learning were the obsessive favorite topics of this young circle: hunting; who had to sell his castle for lack of maintenance funds; which summer haunt or activity was "in" this year (Ibiza, St. Tropez, cruising the Yugoslavian coast, Portofino, windsurfing on the Moroccan Riviera), and vintage wines. My comprehension of their fast exchanges in French, replete with contemporary expressions and idioms, was not thorough, and occasionally I suffered the embarrassment of answering a question with a response based on the last topic that had just been hashed over. Though the guests seemed understanding about my language difficulty, no one bothered to slow down by one beat; comically, the tendency on everyone's part was to speak more loudly with hand gestures.

After dinner there was much more drinking—champagne corks were being popped as if it were New Year's Eve, and the glasses of *fraise, framboise*, and cognac were constantly refilled. Jacques put on slow music and, like the characters in a late 1930s movie, we all danced under the stars. The ballroom style of dancing felt so wonderfully old-fashioned that I wondered whether this was some new retro-fad in Belgium or just the "in" thing of the moment for this privileged class on a perfumed summer evening.

Very soon, however, the ballroom scene took on some

interesting improvisations when three couples stripped, dived into the pool, and formed a group embrace. Another couple dived in, mounted the raft, and arranged themselves in a *soixante-neuf*. Jacques pulled me into the pool and we joined the three couples, men now kissing the lips and breasts of the women on either side of them. When handsome and very aristocratic-looking Jules picked me up in his arms and held me close to his muscular naked body, I just knew I was going to like living in Belgium.

Jacques smiled at me. "At last! Go with it!" he said and eagerly turned and began passionately kissing the breasts and stomach of blond Béatrice on his right, while pinching the ample bottom of Brigitte on his left.

As Jules became more adventurous, I kept glancing over at Jacques, and when I saw that he was already positioning himself for an invasion of Brigitte, I let Jules's hands wander freely. He asked me to follow him out of the pool to a private nook in the shrubbery. As we tried to sneak away, Jacques caught sight of us and asked us to stay. He wanted to watch.

I swam over to him and asked if he truly approved of my going "all the way" with Jules.

"Proceed," he said, and laughed.

"Only after you," I insisted. "I want it on record that you took the first plunge." I tried to joke about it, because I thought Jacques was kidding.

"Aha! She'll always be a lawyer's daughter. And a clever one," he said, loud enough for the group to hear, and repeated our exchange in French for all to understand. They laughed.

"All right, watch me," he said as he led both Béatrice and Brigitte out of the pool and onto one of the large mats which had mysteriously appeared at the side of the pool. Roland, the butler, must have been trained to efficiently provide all services during these gala evenings. I chuckled to myself as I wondered whether the three servants had positioned themselves at the windows on an upper floor of the main house and were observing the action.

Jacques lay back on the mat while both women simultaneously kissed him, gracefully switching their positions from his mouth to his "ambassador." He then directed the two women to hug and caress each other while he alternately kissed and touched them both.

The group in the pool gradually stopped their own activities and focused their attention on Jacques, Béatrice, and Brigitte as their creative movements, heavy breathing, and moans intensified.

"Brigitte first!" Pierre, her husband, called out.

Jacques pulled Brigitte on top of him and rhythmically moved her up and down until she climaxed. She grasped him with all her strength, rolled off, and with an ecstatic scream dived into the pool. Everyone applauded.

Béatrice, with a rapturous expression, lay on her back with her legs spread wide, enjoying the attention. Jacques mounted her and gyrated in long, exaggerated motions and deep thrusts until she gasped. He pulled out but she forced him back inside her.

The action went on for some time, and finally someone shouted: "We're getting bored. *Allez! Allez*, you two! Let's see the grand finale."

On cue, they seemed to reach orgasm together. After a few moments, exhausted, they rolled off the mat and onto the grass, still joined.

All applauded again and turned back with renewed eagerness to their own partners and little groups.

Feeling like a tourist watching the sexual rituals of an exotic tribe, I'd been attentively taking in all the action from the sidelines with Jules, when through the lightheadedness that came with too much champagne, it suddenly registered that I had just witnessed my husband having animated sexual intercourse with two women. Whether it was the numbing effect of the alcohol or, conversely, the stimulation of sensory overload from all the activity, I felt no jealousy or outrage, but rather detached fascination.

Jacques didn't love these women, after all. It was simply a sport of this circle. I couldn't believe I was feeling so unaffected by his blatant adultery; strangely, seeing him *in flagrante delicto* instead made me understand him and his world. A different set of principles functioned here, and there was no point in judging him according to my system. I wondered whether, finally, I was crossing the first threshold of casting off my so-called American inhibitions and opening up to this wildly amoral pleasure-seeking lifestyle. It was uncanny that instead of being appalled, I was intrigued. A first threshold, maybe, I conceded.

But when Jules urged me to sneak off with him behind the pool house, I knew I couldn't actually participate. I wasn't ready to go that far. Once Jules was convinced this change of mood wasn't a game, we talked easily.

I asked whether this was the usual procedure at Jacques's parties, and he replied that Jacques had toned down the action so that I wouldn't be overwhelmed. When we rejoined the party some couples were sitting with their glasses refilled, watching the others. Jacques was, remarkably, still at it, now with two other women.

Later, when Jacques spotted me sitting alone with Jules, he cautioned, "This is fun and games, remember! We don't take this seriously or form attachments."

"We all know your precise etiquette, *Monsieur le Baron*. But we didn't know that one was allowed to taste all the fruit in one evening. Do you need help?" Jules joked.

"I've already gotten your help in breaking my *chérie* Sheri *acques and I in St. ropez during our engage-ent.*

ABOVE: *Late night at the St. Tropez harbor. I was completely unaware of Jacques's intensity.*

BELOW: *An idyllic moment early in our romance.*

ABOVE: Uncle Gerard's castle, where we had our engagement party.

BELOW: Aunt Helene's castle, built in the 14th century.

ABOVE: *Jacques's castle, where the nightmare began.*

BELOW: *Catherine's castle — one of the most famous in Belgium.*

ABOVE: Jacques and I at our wedding reception.

BELOW, LEFT: Uncle Gerard, Isabelle, and Jacques at the reception.
BELOW, RIGHT: Catherine and I meet for the first time.

My engagement photo — I had no idea what was in store for me at the time this picture was taken.

OPPOSITE, FROM TOP TO BOTTOM: Jacques's brother, his mother, and his sister. My mother, right, with Jacques and his mother. Getting to know Isabelle. ABOVE: With Jacques's mother — I really wanted her to like me! RIGHT: Jacques and I with the wonderful Meme.

out of her unwillingness to experiment. Wasn't she good, my dear Jules?"

"Your new wife is quite the tease, Baron. Perhaps between the two of us we can initiate her to the pleasures of our little circle! I wish you'd import more cute American women to share with your dear friends." He kissed me on the breast as another man walked up and kissed me on the other breast.

"Are you going to be greedy, Jules, or will you allow another gentleman to bring her into a higher state of rapture?" Patrick asked.

I took two steps forward and dived into the pool, emerging to see Patrick and Jules already turning their attentions to another woman.

The party continued into the early hours of morning. But rather than stay the night, though we had several guest rooms, everyone dressed and left an hour before dawn. Clothed, they became the distant, formal, unapproachable nobles again. When Jacques and I finally got into bed, his only comment was, "Well, Sheri, eventually you will learn to enjoy the pleasures of the circle."

As I fell asleep, the reality of what had occurred at the party began to hit me, and my mind drifted into the most disturbing dreams.

Chapter 11

$\mathscr{I}$couldn't concentrate on the French tapes at the language lab the next day, so I went to a coffeeshop on campus and wrote pages and pages in my journal about the previous Dionysian evening, trying to make sense of my mixed feelings.

I felt morning-after remorse; it was so in character for me to get totally caught up in the moment, immersing myself in a new experience. Seeing Jacques having sex with other women brought on a strange gnawing emotion that I really couldn't define. It came as a rude awakening that this went on here, a part of Jacques's lifestyle which he had never mentioned. Anger and jealousy, the normal reactions, I somehow knew would not help me deal with it. I'd just have to live with it.

For the past three months I had written my journal in the form of letters to my mother, so that she could share my impressions of everything in my new life. This system worked

well to ease our separation, and although Mother was contemporary enough to handle my adventures, no matter how
unusual, I decided to write a separate journal describing
the more sexual events. I didn't want to shock Mother. We
both had the misconception that the Belgian nobility would
be stuffy, formal, and very proper. And we thought that
Jacques, although not stuffy, was a very conservative man
with strong morals and a rigid code of honor. We were right
about his code of honor! Our little dinner party had proved
to me that I was frightfully naive.

In fact, coming to terms with the erotically driven lifestyle that Jacques and his circle were leading required constant rationalization; a dialogue always revolved in my head.
I had to admit to myself that in a way I was strangely attracted
by it, even sometimes engrossed by it. Pursuing these fantasies felt safer now that I was far away both in distance and
mentality from my friends and my world; it seemed that word
of these goings-on would never trickle back across the great
ocean. And it also felt safer because the fantasies being played
out were conceived and directed mostly by Jacques. He
wanted me to learn more and more about the forces of sexuality and often spoke about unleashing powerful passions
in me—a concept that intrigued me further. I believed, on
the one hand, that exploring one's own sexuality to its extreme limits was too self-indulgent a goal; yet on the other
hand, it presented an irresistible, if dangerous, challenge
which I had never thought about pursuing before. A great
adventure, a new study, just as certain college courses had
totally absorbed me for a while. But I supposed it was a bit
of a stretch to compare the two, since attaining sexual pleasure didn't exactly lead to constructive ends. Or did it? Was
the preoccupation a part of solidifying the relationship between Jacques and me, making a marriage work, especially
in the context of living in a sexually obsessed circle? Wasn't

it natural to explore this sexual terrain as a couple—even to explore to its dangerous limits, as Jacques had insisted? To me, testing dangerous limits still meant simply letting go with abandon in passion, whereas to Jacques I think these limits were further out than I wanted to imagine, containing and capping a ferocious desire. His threat, "You will be surprised at what you will be capable of doing a few years from now," sometimes tantalized me, sometimes frightened me. I knew it excited him to push me further than I was ready to go; crossing each new threshold seemed to be like conquering another level of my virginity for him.

The sexual soiree had been indeed exciting to watch, somewhat like watching a movie from the first row, larger than life, more vivid than anything I'd surely seen in my life. If these parties went on often, as they undoubtedly would, how long would it be until I dove right into the tangle of bodies? I had been extremely close to yielding with Jules, forgetting, for that hotly charged moment, my marriage vows. But then that voice, the same imploring voice heard throughout childhood, entered my mind: "Just because all the other kids are doing it doesn't give you the right to do it." The voice was getting fainter and my sexual interest was taking over. Yes, it felt naughty, but this was the life here.

A few nights later Jacques invited Françoise and Maurice to an intimate poolside dinner. They were planning to spend the month of July at their villa on the Belgian seacoast at Knokke-het-Zoute, and Jacques wanted to discuss business with Maurice before he left.

Maurice and Jacques had decided to sell the crane division of the company and were looking into other possibilities for expansion. Yacht sales were also down. They discussed dealing in commodities in London. They had also been approached by members of the new ruling coalition in

Zimbabwe Rhodesia, to mine diamonds privately, apart from the De Beers operation. This would be risky, since De Beers was so powerful and controlled at least 90 percent of all diamond mining. Maurice suggested that Jacques and I could live in Zimbabwe Rhodesia part of the year to oversee these operations. Jacques practically fell off his chair when he heard this proposal. He would never consider living outside his little world, I could see.

As the evening ended, Maurice and Françoise told me how much they enjoyed being with us and that they looked forward to our visits to their home on the North Sea coast. They also complimented me profusely on the progress I had made in my spoken French. Since they spoke no English at all, our conversation was all in French.

Although I was exhausted by the hours of speaking French, I enjoyed that evening particularly, and I looked forward to the prospect of working in these business ventures.

I went to visit Mémé and this time took her to lunch at a quaint bistro in the Grand Sablon, the old city of Brussels, a section with antiques shops and art galleries, and ordered a famous Belgian dish—*charbonnade*, a jet-black sausage.

We started our discussion on what I had recently learned was her favorite subject: her adversary, Mamie.

"Your mother-in-law would never associate with anyone who is not in the aristocracy or nobility. And neither would Catherine! She hasn't invited you to her castle yet. Did you ever wonder why?"

"Catherine has told me to wait until August to visit when the castle is warm and not damp."

"Oh child! That's not why. Her father-in-law, the old baron, would never have someone of the Jewish faith enter his castle."

"Really, Mémé?" I said in quiet disappointment.

"But Mamie is the worst," she went on without missing a beat. "She has friends among the highest circles in Belgium and spends all her time traveling from one of their castles to another, visiting her old lady friends. They do nothing but dine and discuss gourmet foods. And they have a merry time finding some of the best old vintages in the wine cellars and drinking heartily. They plan their year of travel and visits to each other's summer residences in Cannes, Monaco, Marbella, or some such place.

"You know, on Adriane's trip to England, she went as part of a society organization that makes trips to oversee the preservation of these castles and gardens. Actually, they do nothing official. It is just society checking in with other society in the next country. Apparently these gardens are the most beautiful in Europe.

"All these castles are partially supported by the English government's preservation programs. So Adriane has a great time smelling the flowers. It is the biggest snob organization you can imagine. Only Count Da Da Dee, Duke Da Da Dum, Baron Tra La La, and Marquis Tra La Lum are present," she said, gesturing as if conducting an orchestra. "Adriane still lives for all these society events and people. She will never attend a party if she hears that it will be 'mixed,' you know.

"My son was a dashing officer," she said. "He had great flair and a great sense of humor. He drove fast sports cars and loved women. Adriane loved him crazily. She suffered a lot when he died. She is a strict Catholic and we are Protestants. The Catholics are so strict and stuffy. The Protestants are so much more open, free, and understanding. She and I have had our differences over religion. You know, Sheri, she can never really fully consider you Jacques's wife because you were not the wife he married in the Church. She likes you, I know. She called me recently and said, 'Sheri is so incredibly endowed with quality. And so good to Jacques. But she is *so* American, unfortunately!' Ha! So I asked your mother-in-law, 'What do you want? We are Belgian and she is American!'

"Oh, Adriane is such a total snob. For instance, Isabelle is having an affair with a French duke. A duke ranks high in the order of titles. There are only a few dukes in all of France. Adriane doesn't mind this affair because it is in *our* circles. She only disapproves of her associating with the bourgeoisie, as I've told you."

Mémé was in rare form, jumping from subject to subject, giving me juicy tidbits on everyone. She retained such a sense of humor, and also a sense of style. As always, she had dressed in the most charming, classic outfit and wore fine daytime jewels. And as on my previous visits, after letting go torrents of words, suddenly she lost the trend of her thoughts and the long session was over. We walked together until late afternoon in the Bois de la Cambre, a section of the beautiful Brussels woods. We exchanged the three-on-each-cheek Belgian kisses and promised frequent meetings. On the next one she'd visit me in Ginal.

I returned home later than planned, and Jacques was already there. He was angry. I was taken off guard, thinking that he might not want me to keep my own schedule.

"And where have you been today? With some lover?" he asked.

"With Mémé," I said. "I just love your Mémé. We took a long walk in the woods."

"I don't know why you love my Mémé so much. She's an old lady. All she wants to do is talk against my mother! I don't want you to visit her alone anymore. We'll go together!"

"Jacques, please, I enjoy visiting her."

Then he blurted out, "Your beloved Mémé is not so lily-white. She has quite a questionable past. My grandfather was a man about town and not faithful to her. But she, in turn, took many lovers and cruised on luxury liners all over the globe. Her favorite spot was Morocco, where the high society really lived it up. And she was one of the high livers. She likes to tell about my mother's fast social life after my father's death, but my mother was a nun compared to her! My mother has always upheld our code of honor, but Mémé knows nothing of this code! So don't always believe her version of the family, since it will often be distorted to put my mother in the worst light!

"Let me tell you a story about Mémé which will show you why Mother and I are resentful of her," he said. "She was the cause of an unfortunate incident. Her elderly playboy friend—who has been away for the past three months gallivanting in the world's capitals—is a questionable character. He uses the title Count but he isn't a real count. He is a slick, doubletalking charmer who preys on old ladies for housing, food, and whatever else he can get. He has been Mémé's friend for years. I think I told you that. Anyway, a few years ago he brought a young male friend out of Morocco and managed with Mémé's help to get him a job as a butler to Catherine in the castle. Soon after, there was a major theft in the castle. Only the best treasures from Jean-Pierre's father, the rich old baron, were taken—lots of valuable antique furniture, paintings, and silver, but just the really top pieces! Well, it's obvious who did it. Mamie and I think that the 'count' is a high-level thief and he has a thing going robbing all the old ladies, getting enough information from them on family treasures to steal the most valuable pieces! Apparently the 'count' and his Moroccan friend cleaned out the baron's top treasures. Now you know one of the reasons for my anti-Mémé sentiment. The 'count' still remains Mémé's friend, since all this cannot be proven. I will never ask Mémé about her friend because I don't want to disturb her. I don't think she wants to give up this friend. He's been a companion to her."

"And now I am a companion to her, Jacques," I broke in. "She tells me about the customs and codes that you have wanted me to learn."

"And stories about all our family scandal, right? Every family has some. But I don't want you hearing it. She probably told you more about the young governess who killed herself in my home."

"No! Jacques, she doesn't speak of scandal."

"Oh, no? I'm sure she does. Well, did she ever tell you about her own daughter?"

"No. She has a daughter?"

"Aha! She'd not tell you that. Her daughter killed herself. Mysterious circumstances. While Mémé was off with lovers in Morocco."

"I won't hear it! Please don't talk like that about Mémé. I don't want to hear bad things about her. I never knew my grandmothers. Mémé makes me feel like I am her granddaughter. I feel good being with her."

At dinner I discovered that the root of Jacques's anger was not my visit to Mémé but rather Maurice's continued pressure on him to travel to Zimbabwe Rhodesia to investigate the diamond mine.

Jacques asked, now calmly, "What is it that you have to discuss with Mémé if it is not family gossip?"

"She explains what I need to know to live in a noble circle. For instance, she explained noblesse oblige to me. The whole concept behind it."

Then, as if not to be outdone by Mémé, he started to educate me on the use of my title. For the first time he told me how and when to use it.

"When you deal in business you may use your title when

introducing yourself, but generally one does *not* use it with anyone *outside* the circle. Within the circle, you don't call yourself by your title. Only when you are introduced by someone else does that person use your title in the introduction. You may use it when making restaurant, hotel, and other reservations, but rarely are titles used during dealings with people who do not know—the other classes, that is. And of course everyone, but everyone, among the aristocracy in Belgium knows each other. So there is no need to be indiscreet by emphasizing your title. They know. And if they don't know who you are, they are not worth telling!" He pushed upward through the air with the back of his hand as if to fling the very thought of those unworthy ones away. I suddenly realized that this was but one of a whole repertoire of gestures executed with precision by all those in the circle to illustrate their dramatic statements.

I almost laughed at his reasoning, and, to bring him off his pompous plane, I instead commented, "Oh, Americans could never bother with all that formality. But someone must keep up the Old World."

At that he softened his tone and abandoned the emphatic "*We* do it this way, while *they*. . . ." He continued, "When people in our circle refer to each other by their family name only, we don't use the *de* or the *von* before the last name. The *de* is understood. Only people outside the circle —who don't know—call us by the *de* or the *von* and then the family name. In other words, one doesn't say the de Borchgraves are coming to dinner, but simply the Borchgraves are coming."

I asked more questions about how to introduce myself to people within the circle.

"Sheri de Borchgrave," he answered, "because you are using your first name, not just your family name alone." And then he tired of the subject and said impatiently, "For these things you just must know. You can't easily learn the nuances and when to use it and when not. You simply know! It is a part of us." Both his hands pushed away the air, flipping back the wrists in a tight V. The female version of this gesture was a graceful, fully opened V. This was not Italian telling-the-story-with-the-hands, but the occasional sweeping movement meant to describe a whole state of mind—disgust, disgrace, disdain, noblesse oblige, or an unbearable travesty of taste. The unbearable travesty was the most frequently used: an exhalation accompanied by a quarter turn of the head to the left, a slow blink, and sometimes a slight pushing out of one hand from the elbow, usually done while sitting at a table—similar to the famous Jack Benny gesture.

He ended the subject there, just as I was anxious to hear more. But I knew Mémé would be glad to instruct me fully before I would have to start actively socializing in the fall.

The next afternoon I called Mother. She was delighted to hear from me, though she realized, as I did, that our weekly phone chat hardly compensated for our previous closeness. I began to tell her about Jacques's pool party and what a wild evening it had been, starting with everyone stripping off his or her clothes on arrival and jumping into the pool. Halfway into the next sentence, I caught myself. I couldn't fathom telling her of Jacques's poolside performance. My report on the mating romps and rituals of the nobles would have to wait for an indefinite future time. I left the subject after mentioning a "nudist party, lots of swimming and lots of champagne."

"Oh my God! How amazing!" she remarked.

I hinted at my fascinating session with Mémé and said Mother could expect a twenty-page letter on the intricacies of this family's relationships and rich gossip. She was delighted that Mémé was giving me insight into the important family members and ways to maneuver more easily through my new life. "I can't tell you how relieved I am that things are going well. The weekend Marc rescued you seems so far away. It sounds like you've gotten through some bad times, but now I think it will be an interesting life . . . certainly a challenging one. You'll never be bored."

Isabelle arrived at Ginal in the late afternoon. Her unannounced visit made me anxious because Jacques had strictly forbidden me to be alone with her. I hoped he would believe her visit was not by my invitation. However, I was delighted to see her and have a real tête-à-tête.

She had a completely different look every time I saw her; this time she wore a simply cut black dress dripping with ornaments—gold belts, chains, and bracelets encircled her and prominent gold loops hung from her ears. She carried the *brillant* pocketbook designed by Belgium's foremost bag designer, Delvaux. She reeked of Madame Rochas perfume and as usual wore heavy makeup. Her hair sat even higher than usual atop her head, in a cross between a fifties bouffant and a Victorian upsweep.

She had come to confide what family members were saying about me and to discuss her favorite subject—herself. She told me that Mémé was my greatest ally and often took my side in talks with Mamie. "Recently Mamie called Mémé and told her she didn't understand why you rushed into marriage with Jacques. She told Mémé that you should have lived with him for a while to see if it would work. So our sweet fast-tongued Mémé shot back, 'Listen, let us take a reverse example. Let us say Catherine met a diplomat in Washington, D.C., and he asked her to leave everything and come to live with him in America for a trial period. Would you let her leave?' Mamie replied that she wouldn't. Mémé continued, 'Sheri is no different. Why should she have been expected to leave her own country to come to Belgium on a trial period?' That quieted Mamie!"

Isabelle went on to explain that for years she and her mother had been almost enemies. She considered her mother "the bank," she said.

"I must confide to you that I heard my mother talk many times about how worried she was to let an 'outsider' into the family. Although she wanted you to be Jacques's wife, and have him start a new life with you, she is afraid to have an outsider share the inheritance.

"My love affair with my dear, dear Gérard infuriates my mother. I started the relationship out of spite, you know. Gérard wanted to marry my mother many years ago. Mother refused outright because he was not titled and not exactly one of us! He was from a bourgeois family of great wealth. Only since he married Hélène, whose title is marquise, has he become a part of the nobility by marriage and now associates with the top circle. When I got into an affair with him, it absolutely killed my mother. You know, Gérard has some Jewish blood. We all know, but I'm not sure if it is through a great-grandmother or whom."

When she talked about "some Jewish blood," I thought to myself that the family really must be scandalized that I have nothing but Jewish blood.

"Oh Sheri, you are so different than Claudine," she went on, switching subjects abruptly. "Not only was Claudine uninterested in being a housekeeper or hostess, she wasn't even the greatest lover. Jacques told me all about her. Everything. She did have the art of working Jacques up sexually over a whole evening, either at home or out with people, and made him crazy to have her. She had that effect on him."

Isabelle advised me to be tender with Jacques. She said he really needed tenderness. "I love my brother deeply. You must be sweet to him always. Never criticize him and he'll show you the same affection and give you the happiest life. You know, Sheri, I've been thinking, Jacques was so calm when he had a dog. You should get a dog. Another Great Dane. He was so happy with his Great Dane, Oona. My brother sometimes has a tendency to get moody, drink a little much, but when he had the dog, he was much more even-tempered."

Funny, Jacques actually resembled a Great Dane, so tall, so aristocratic, so gentle. I wondered whether the Great Dane also had a ferocious side. Isabelle's suggestion seemed like a good one, but unfortunately Jacques had already vetoed the idea a while ago, saying that he would never replace his beloved Oona. She would be the last dog in his life. At the time, I remember thinking how wonderfully sentimental and devoted that sounded, just as a loving spouse would never replace a partner.

Before she left, Isabelle told me not to tell Jacques of her visit, and I agreed. "We must have our secret talks in the fall." She finished her glass of Mumm champagne, the champagne she sometimes promoted—by dining at top restaurants and running up a big check and afterward insisting they stock Mumm. She poured another half glass, toasted me with a high-pitched "chin-chin," and rushed out.

Mamie came to dinner the next evening, and once again I prepared energetically for her visit. I presented a many-course meal of her favorite delicacies. I made sure this time to have a wide-mouthed glass for the wine accompanying the cheese course, correcting a mistake I'd made at the last dinner which I'd heard about repeatedly.

As the evening progressed she became quite high on the many wines and was unusually complimentary to me, repeating over and over again that she was absolutely astounded at the progress I had made in speaking French. She did, naturally, have one criticism; it was about a difference between American and Belgian etiquette. "Sheri, you say 'thank you' too much. You thank often. When I say you are progressing in the French language you say 'thank you.' Why? You see, we don't say 'thank you' much here. I noticed you always say 'thank you' to me after every lunch at my house. Of course I want to have you as my guest. And after a compliment on your dress or hair, don't say 'thank you.' In Belgium, among us, that means you regard the compliment as obvious. You must simply say, 'Oh, do you really think so?' or some such social phrase, or nothing, but not 'thank you' all the time. It is so American! You must abandon your American 'thank-yous'! Only our servants thank us all the time."

I could see that both Jacques and his mother were determined to have me abandon most of my American attitudes. Lately Jacques had been pushing me hard to agree to more sexual experimentation, specifically, to have a one-on-one affair with a woman. I protested such an idea, but he was determined to persuade me. He felt that making love with another woman was the ultimate in sensuality and a necessary step in becoming an experienced and thoroughly exciting woman. Through intimacy with a woman he claimed that I would discover a new freedom from inhibitions and would fully satiate my passions. He described the unique arousal females can bring each other and told of one of his friend's descriptions of the intense pleasures she had found with women, her different climaxes, and her transformed sexual persona.

But this was just one of the many ideas Jacques had either hinted at or had begun to discuss, part of the sexual odyssey that he thought was natural for a couple to embark upon. Until I had seen the drama at the pool party, I had honestly thought that Jacques simply enjoyed speaking out his fantasies and sexual ideas, but now the pressure was growing to actualize them. I was confused as to whether I wanted such an odyssey; was it in a sense part of my marriage vows when marrying into the young noble circle? "I promise not to be faithful" seemed to be the pledge. I feared that if I gave in to even one request at an adventurous foray, soon I'd find myself living like the Emanuelle character in the French movie with multiple sequels, pursuing and realizing one sexual fantasy after another—a true *coquine*, a girl who goes out lustily seducing men and women, creating a devastating sizzle around her; a character considered a legendary femme fatale in French circles.

It was impossible to fathom how far Jacques planned to take this idea of increasing my sexual awareness—certainly not into the kinkier directions, for which he never expressed a taste, not as far as the torrid *Story of O*–style scenarios— but I knew that once I plunged in an erotic direction, the path was irreversible.

While he prodded me to agree, teasing that I was far from innocent, I had to admit to myself that I was already light-years away from the girl who needed dimmed lamps to feel comfortable naked. After three years with Jacques during our courtship, I had gained a more than respectable erotic repertoire and had already changed drastically—even in a half-sleep, my body automatically could move itself into a graceful array of sexual positions; I was able to fire up Jacques within seconds with a certain touch, pose, or well-placed kiss; and my desire seemed to be growing steadily in strength: "the more you grow accustomed to, the more you need."

Yet having an affair with a woman to further arouse my husband was beyond what I could envision myself doing. Another thought added to my nagging indecision over whether I should live like a young Belgian noblette or like a reluctant American. I had always taken it to be a standard truth that men preferred women without excessive experience and liked at least to imagine that their mates had a feminine innocence about them. I wondered whether this rule applied even to a slight extent here; if it did, I reasoned, and I went along with Jacques's advanced erotic plans, he might later reject me for having lost the very innocent quality he had probably liked about me originally.

Between Jacques's and his mother's lectures, it was obvious that I'd soon have to make some changes in my responses and inclinations. Apparently I must be neither appreciative nor monogamous. What would be next to go? My democracy? Heterosexuality? I wondered. And wondered more.

Chapter 12

The next afternoon, before returning home from the university, I made my usual stops at the *fromagerie* for a full selection of chèvre, Camembert, aged Gouda, and Roquefort, to the wine shop for a selection of house wines, to the *patisserie* for fruit tarts, sorbets, and chocolate creations which were even better than Marie-Louise could create, and to the outdoor market for fresh vegetables. The maid bought most of the staples and meats, but it was the duty of a Belgian housewife to do the specialized shopping herself. Jacques praised me because I had learned to shop like a true Belgian lady, and his mother, in her typically exaggerated language, thought it was "truly remarkable" that in such a short time I could converse with merchants and pick out the correct cheeses and wines. Granted I had come a long way from bringing home the horsemeat, but somehow I was always amused when they lavished me with compliments for these simple duties. To them, these actually seemed to be accomplishments.

I drove home earlier than usual with a car full of packages and got out of the car near the service entrance instead of in the garage, to find Roland and ask him to unload my purchases.

As I got out I heard strange moaning noises coming from the house and recognized Isabelle's soundtrack as she approached a dramatic *faux* climax. What is going on? I thought. Does Jacques allow Isabelle and Gérard to arrange afternoon assignations at our house? No. I couldn't believe that Jacques would condone that kind of behavior. I directed Roland to unpack the car and waited outside, as always, to drive it into the garage. The moaning got louder; then Isabelle cried out: "Oh, oh, *je joui, je joui.*" It wasn't Gérard. Another old man?

I rushed upstairs to the bedroom over the living room but stopped when I realized that the sounds were coming from Jacques's and my bedroom. I was outraged as I listened at the door for a second, now hearing only heavy breathing. Since it was, after all, my bedroom, I swung open the door and burst into the room.

There were Jacques and Isabelle nude on the bed, just tumbling apart.

"What is going on here?" I screamed, horrified by the scene before me.

"Come join us, *ma chérie*," Jacques said, totally at ease. Isabelle, however, had a pained expression. I could see she didn't want me to be exposed to this.

"Sheri!" she gasped.

"I can't believe this! It is impossible!" I said, looking at both of them in disgust. "Is this what your 'noble' life is about?"

Jacques smiled at me, enjoying my shock. I couldn't say more. I was speechless. I ran from the room, rushed downstairs and into my car, and sped off. Eventually I drove back to the university, parked in the lot, and sat in the car, crying. I was in shock. But I realized I didn't know how to handle the situation. It was crazy. Jacques was crazy. How could I go on living with him? Did I have to accept his incest along with his open sexual behavior with other women? He'd said I would never understand his code of honor, and he was right. I could *not* understand this insane code. I felt so alien in his bizarre world, so completely alone, cut off from everything that seemed normal, from every good thing I had grown up with.

After several hours of wandering aimlessly around the university grounds, trying to come to terms with this development, I drove home, calmed, determined to get a full explanation from Jacques.

He sat in a corner of the living room, cleaning his guns. A bottle of cognac and a glass stood on the table. He looked disheveled. The image of him with three shotguns and several pistols was slowly fixed in my mind.

"You're back," he said, looking up at me, his eyes dull, his voice hollow. "Good!"

"I'm back to hear what you have to say for yourself, Jacques! How long have you been sleeping with your sister?"

"Sheri, it doesn't affect my relationship with you. Isabelle and I occasionally have sex. So what? We love each other. No one is hurt," he said defensively.

"Jacques, it's incest. How can you take it lightly? Am I to have my sister-in-law as your mistress?"

"Mistress is a big word. She and I just like each other sexually. She's not a mistress. Do you even know what a mistress is?"

"I really am confused. Terribly confused," I said with tears in my eyes. "The sex party the other night was at least in each other's presence. Everyone was present. And I want to tell you something, Jacques. I didn't have sex with Jules that night. I couldn't. Even after watching you with those two women, I couldn't . . ."

I don't know where that admission came from. I certainly didn't have to defend myself or claim virtuous restraint in the face of Jacques's extremes.

"Well, you certainly are a little actress! I'm not certain I believe you. *But.* I will not be criticized by you. If you can't accept my circle, then leave for the States."

"Jacques, I want to understand you. Help me, please. When did you start this? Or should I ask why?"

Merely asking why was pointless: his answers would hardly get me closer to making sense of what was going on. The emotion I felt was one you reserve for the lowest forms of unacceptable and unforgivable behavior. Incest between brother and sister was certainly in that category.

"I'm not going to explain myself to you," he said angrily.

"Please help me understand. I am not criticizing. I want to understand you . . . your world."

"All right. About eight years ago, when I first had problems with Claudine, I'd stay at Isabelle's apartment for weeks at a time. I was very nervous and sad. She calmed me by making love with me. It really helped. And . . . And, well, you see, now she still calms me as she's done all through the years. Ever since you've been here I've needed her. All hasn't been easy with us."

"I see. So that's why you didn't want me to meet with her alone. You were afraid she'd tell me."

"Yes, that. But also, she might influence you."

"As you've been influencing me?" I said, incredulous.

"You just *won't* understand. This does not affect you. I feel better after I am with her. So the only effect is keeping me in good spirits for you!"

"That is self-justification if I've ever heard it! This is really insane. God! Who else do you sleep with regularly? Claudine? Any other mistresses? Do you see any of those five women of Friday night's party apart from the cozy group?" I demanded.

"The subject is finished. That is all I care to discuss. Come to terms with it or go back to the States."

I poured myself a glass of champagne. "Jacques, this is no small affair. It's so sad! And we were so happy together in Japan."

"Happy? You're happy! I'll be happy after you have the breast operation."

As he said those dreaded words, I saw the final transformation in him. As he spoke in a strangely changed voice, he had completely slipped into his second self. I was suddenly terrified. Was he going out of control again? I ran out of the room and upstairs to the bedroom.

Next morning when I awakened, I realized Jacques had not come up to bed. I went over to the window, and as I looked out over the garden I saw him walking unsteadily around the property in the rain, wearing only a pareo wrapped low on his hips, slit open in front and exposing his penis. Obviously he had been up all night.

I went into the kitchen; Marie-Louise wasn't there. I called for Roland. He wasn't on duty either. I went into their quarters; their doors were locked. They were gone. I was alone! I rushed upstairs, got my purse, and dashed to the garage, but when I looked at the key rack where two sets of my car keys were usually kept, both were gone. And so were the keys to the BMW.

I had to call Mamie! Marc had told me never to criticize Jacques, but how could I not react to what I had seen? I had triggered another episode by responding as a human being, but I could, finally, behave no differently.

I couldn't remember Mamie's telephone number, so I went up to our bedroom to find the address book. I entered quietly, surprised to find Jacques there, dressing.

"I've decided to take you to the family castle for the weekend. Aunt Martine is away, and I've asked her servants to take the weekend off, so we can be there alone. Pack a case and meet me in the car," he said harshly. He collected the rest of his clothes and took them into his dressing room.

When he left I picked up the phone to call Mamie. I dialed her number. No answer. Then I called Isabelle. She answered instantly.

"Isabelle, please listen to me," I whispered. "I need your help."

Jacques was immediately beside me. He grabbed the phone and hung it up.

"I told you never to call Isabelle! You are disobeying me. Pack and be at the car in five minutes!"

His voice, hollow, rang in my ears. This was not Jacques. It was his second self, the self I had come to fear. The self who was not my husband.

I went downstairs and got into the car. I tried to calm Jacques by quietly asking why he was in such a mood, but he didn't answer. We drove the forty minutes in silence, arriving at Loiroi just as the weather cleared.

He opened the castle door with a large antique key that was hidden in a crack in the stone wall, then led me upstairs to one of the main bedrooms.

"You'll sleep in here, alone. I'll be in another wing, the wing I lived in as a child. When I want sex I'll come to you.

Now you can unpack and meet me downstairs in fifteen minutes."

At this point I could do nothing, I rationalized, but quietly obey him, hoping not to trigger his violence. When I came into the main living room, Jacques spoke to me more calmly, but with cold authority.

"I have a good plan for today. We're now going to the stables belonging to friends of mine who live at the next estate, Count Guy de Trouville and his cousin Frédéric. I've called and they'll have horses ready. We'll ride all day. It will take my mind off your deception. Now, come with me."

He brought me back upstairs and into one of the attics, where he found a riding habit close to my size and boots just a bit large but passable. He put on his complete riding costume with jodhpurs and a hat. Even in my anxious state I couldn't help marveling at how devastatingly handsome he looked in his riding clothes. How sad, I thought, tears coming to my eyes. I had found my masculine ideal, only to discover a dark interior that threatened to destroy our marriage. Thoughts, almost incoherent, tumbled through my mind. Was he a split personality? Or had his ritualized games turned into sexual sadism over the years, turned into a pattern so fully integrated that it couldn't be changed?

His friends were not at the stables; the trainer brought out the horses and advised us of their idiosyncrasies. The smallest young horse, which I was to ride, liked to jump and often took her own detours, galloping into the woods. A tight hand on the reins, they suggested, and she'd be gentle as a pony. Jacques's horse seemed wild, rearing and whinnying when Jacques got close. Somehow the horse must have sensed his disturbed mood.

I hadn't ridden for more than ten years, since I'd been thrown and the horse had stepped on my left cheek with his hind leg. Fortunately, I had no scars from that accident. I had been a good rider, had even participated in jumping competitions, so I was only slightly fearful of getting back on a horse. I certainly didn't want to refuse this sportive idea and leave myself open instead for sexual sports.

We rode across the property for five hours, only stopping for minutes to give the horses water at various streams. The ride was like a bad dream. Jacques spoke to me occasionally, always in French, only the most unnerving small talk about hunting, horses, and the woods. As each hour passed I sensed a gradually mounting tension, almost visible in the air. I knew he was planning a punishing program for the night ahead. As the late afternoon approached, I suggested we stop for a while, and he gave me a peculiar smile, saying, "You always pride yourself on being the athletic girl. Are you getting fatigued, little devil? No, this won't do. I want you in perfect tone! Those muscles strong! So that at least you will be a satisfying partner in bed. That's your great talent. Are you going to deprive me of that too? Bringing no dowry to our marriage, you must compensate me in some way. Don't think for one minute I believe your convenient story about a present in three years! It's just like the breast operation. Three years! You won't be here in three years. You didn't keep up your side of the prenuptial agreement, which states, as you will recall, that 'both spouses will contribute to the marriage to the best of their abilities.' You have a trust fund. I know it! And you are denying me any use of it. How unfortunate your choices are. Did you really expect me to pay for everything? I won't! You'll be leaving for America before you know it. I'll see to that. You are no longer my wife!"

"Jacques, why are you saying such things? We have been very happy together!"

"I will not answer your meaningless words. Happy! Happy? Just ride without talking. You excite me with your rhythmic posting. That little ass going up and down against the saddle. You're a good rider. That's your role now. Just excite me."

My entire body trembled with a sudden, psychic fatigue, as I realized I had lost any strength to defend myself against his irrational criticism. I felt alone and powerless.

We brought our horses back as the sun sank low in the sky, its red glow shining through the woods. It was an exceptional sunset.

When we returned to the castle, Jacques ordered: "Shower and change. Then come to the side tower library for a drink. Later we'll go up to the attic and choose an appropriate outfit for you. It's going to be an exciting night. Be quick!" His directions, spoken with frightening precision in a hollow voice, seemed to come from a different being.

Summoning my last ounce of strength and self-respect, I answered, "I will not follow your commands, Jacques. I will spend the night alone. I want to read."

"Oh? I'm sorry to tell you, *chérie* Sheri, that you have no choice."

"What has come over you? What? Why are you torturing the one you love?"

"While you stay in Belgium you will do as I say. Or— are you ready to leave?"

"I will talk to your mother about your treatment of me! She'll stop you! She'll control you!"

"Control? Silly girl. Silly American. I am your husband. For a few more weeks at least, if that. And while I am, you'll deal with me, *not* my mother. You are not the innocent child you pretend to be. Don't you dare involve my mother! I warn you."

"But what do you plan to create for this evening?"

"Rest assured it will be fun. We'll drink a lot of champagne. You like that. We'll dine at a restaurant, since Aunt Martine's maid had no time to prepare a meal for us. Then we'll go to the attic, as I said, and choose a lovely outfit for you. A seductive gown. Befitting the lady of the house. Then I'll let you show your creativity in satisfying my passions— very uniquely. Now, that doesn't sound too bad, does it? Go now, and change."

"Please promise me to be gentle, Jacques, and not drink too much."

"Sheri, I promise you you'll never forget this weekend at the castle."

At the charming farmhouse restaurant the owners greeted Jacques warmly and were very happy to meet his new wife. As we dined, he spoke as normally as he had during other dinners, delivering a pedantic analysis of wines, foods, and manners. I didn't utter one word in response, but he didn't seem to notice.

Even when he was in such a state, I had to concede that watching Jacques eat was fascinating. His expertise and elegance in handling utensils was like great theater. At the end of the meal, when the cheeses were brought out, he sliced perfect wedges of three or four of his choices and with sure strokes deskinned the Camembert and the Brie. He could peel the skin off the accompanying fruit in an unbroken coil, using his fork as an anchor and operating his knife with the precision of a surgeon. Of course he never touched food with his hand—this was an unthinkable breach of etiquette —with the exception of *crevettes* (crawfish) or oysters, whose shells could be properly picked up to drink the juice. Every other food was respectfully maneuvered with impeccable steady, sure strokes of the fork in the left hand and the knife in the right, never switching the fork over to the right. His approach to each course, the slow rhythm of his eating—

stopping to taste, smoothly proceeding to another bite, taking a sip of wine to clear the palate—were signs of his remarkable aristocratic bearing.

Watching his grace in dining, I felt even sadder to realize that a sophisticated man, a man with impeccable style, could disintegrate into such mad, chaotic behavior. The only difference I noticed between his eating style while in this state and normally was that he took longer, deeper sips of wine, drinking with a bacchanalian thirst.

Once at home, he took me up to the attic, where there was a huge armoire full of antique clothes, worthy of the Metropolitan Museum's costume collection. As he took each piece he explained which ancestor had worn which dress or suit on which occasion.

"I want you to try on these six, no, these seven gowns, and then I'll choose the image I want."

There were evening dresses with bustiers, some of lace, some of velvet with fur trimming. I tried on each one and he finally chose a lace dress with many tiers of underslips. He found an old corset and a wired hoopskirt and helped me fit them on. Then he instructed me to fix my hair in an upswept style with tendrils drifting down the back of my neck and beside my cheeks. He searched for and found a photograph of a relative who had worn the dress, inspecting the photo and then me to be sure everything was properly fastened. He then put on tails and white tie and we walked down the grand staircase to the living room, my hand resting on his outstretched arm. By this time I was beside myself, trembling with fear.

"What music do you prefer for tonight? I'm afraid Aunt Martine's collection is limited to the classical. How about some religious music? Some Gregorian chants?"

"As you like."

"Here's Chopin. I'll start with Chopin. Then perhaps a

little Handel, and then Beethoven. Unless you'd prefer a Wagnerian opera?" he said with a wicked laugh.

"I'd prefer Mozart."

"Do you want champagne or shall we go into the wine cellar and pick out a divine dessert wine—perhaps a Château Yquem?"

"Champagne is fine," I said immediately, feeling ashamed at my acquiescence.

He poured the champagne and we sat listening to the music without speaking for a long time. But my mind was working desperately, trying to figure out the emergence of his second self. While he was in a happy mood, as in St. Tropez or in Japan, it seemed normal for him to take an interest and pleasure in dressing me, in elaborate evening dresses or kimonos. I'd thought it was sweet of him, finding it an interesting quality in such a masculine man. But during his bizarre moods I had begun to perceive the true meaning of this desire to dress me. It was another, deeper, darker obsession. He was re-creating me.

I thought back to my college psychology courses, trying to apply theories to his behavior. I remembered a theory about people who can't accept inadequacies in themselves and who project those failings onto another. They are then able to hate the other person, and in that way they themselves feel guiltless. Was Jacques projecting his own deceiving nature onto me? In his mind, was I the dishonest and dishonorable woman? With his deviant interest in "costuming," was he projecting onto me his own desire to dress up and present a multitude of personae? He couldn't accept his inner self and could not find perfection there, so he was creating slick, perfect other surfaces for me! It was becoming clear to me now.

But how far would he go? Would he want to destroy himself, kill himself? Would he project *that* onto me? I shuddered, and I knew that after this weekend I would definitely seek Mamie's help.

I was deep in thought, and suddenly was startled by lights in the driveway as a car pulled up.

"My dear, I forgot to tell you I asked Count Guy and Frédéric for drinks this evening."

What a relief, I thought. Now I won't have to bear being alone for Jacques's games!

Jacques introduced us all and we exchanged a formal "*Je suis très heureux/heureuse de faire votre connaissance.*"

Count Guy was rather heavyset and had the look of an outdoorsman. Frédéric, strangely, looked very much like Jacques, but had a dark mustache and hair, and was a few inches shorter.

"What is this, a costume party?" Guy asked.

"No, no." Jacques laughed. "Sheri just loves to get dressed up in period clothes! Champagne or cognac?" he asked.

"Cognac, of course," said Guy.

"Do you still have the Delamain Daum Crystal?" Guy asked.

"My aunt keeps it all," Jacques responded. "What will you have to drink, Frédéric?"

"The same," Frédéric answered. "How was your day of riding?"

"Sheri loved it. She hadn't been on a horse for years. But she's still quite a rider. One day I'll buy a few horses to keep here."

For the next hour the men all spoke animatedly about horses. The glasses were filled again and again. Jacques seemed to be back in good spirits. His friends were gallant and charming. Soon the distraction lifted my spirits too, and I participated in the discussions, a sense of relief flooding my body, my mind.

During the next hour both Guy and Frédéric became progressively more drunk; some of their joking and banter grew rather vulgar, with a few subtle sexual remarks directed at me, but I ignored them.

Jacques poured me another large cognac and said, "Drink up, dear wife. We're almost ready! Didn't I mention to you that I invited my friends over to help me satisfy you completely? Unselfish, no? I know that one man can get boring, so tonight you'll have three."

"Jacques! Surely you are joking?" I laughed. But I was terrified.

"Joking? Frédéric, Guy—am I joking, do you think?" he asked.

They smiled, more at one another than at me.

I sat, stunned, then drew strength from I don't know where. "Frédéric? Guy? This is not my choice. I beg you not to go along with Jacques."

"Perfect, *ma chérie*. Perfect. She is making it more fun for us! This is her own game. She's being coy," Jacques said. "She loves the idea of being forced. And she'll love the feel of three of us taking our turns. Go on, my little horsewoman, give us a good fight! But first, drink up!"

"Jacques, I am not playing a game. I won't do this!"

"Don't be rude to our guests. I don't want them to feel rejected. They're handsome, no? Your type? And though Frédéric doesn't have a title, I assure you Guy's and his family's is one of the best in Belgium. If that's what you're worried about," Jacques said, smirking at them. "Families are very important to her."

I started to cry. Jacques, Frédéric, and Guy just watched me as they refilled their snifters.

I got up and started to walk out of the room.

"Where are *you* going?" Jacques demanded.

"Do I have to ask for permission to go to the bathroom?"
I said, thinking quickly.

"Oh. Go ahead."

I went out toward the downstairs bathroom, and, remembering that the stairway up to the bell tower was close
by, I rushed up the six flights and hid in a corner of the
tower. It was a beautiful summer night and I sat for what
seemed to be hours, trying to calm myself, praying that perhaps the men had given up, that they were too drunk to look
for me.

A helpless terror enveloped me along with an alarming
awareness of the danger and the absurdity of my situation.
Would my once greatest lover become my rapist and force
a triple rape on me? The castle was completely isolated.
There wasn't even a glimmer of light from a passing car.
Only the lanterns scattered around the grounds faintly cast
their light. I felt myself trembling uncontrollably.

Suddenly a strange thing happened. The sight of those
lanterns brought flashbacks to the romantic years, the real
happiness I had felt when in love with Jacques. I was flooded
with vivid images and sensations from those times. My trembling quieted.

I relived the nights in Paris when we often walked back
to the Left Bank hotel from one of the nightclubs, Maxim's,
Regine's, Castel's, always very high on champagne, kissing
and laughing. As we walked we watched the cafés closing.
Most of the houses along the narrow streets had their shutters
tightly fastened for the night. The streets were silent and on
some nights a light snow fell, covering the street lanterns
and creating a magic feeling on the dimly lit route. When
we arrived back at our hotel we called the guard from his
waiting cabin to open the door and then squeezed into the
tiny elevator. We entered our small, floral-wallpapered room
with its two-story ceiling and drew the heavy wooden shut-

ters, closing out the city for the night. And then we dove into our four-poster bed under the voluminous feather quilt. That was where the lessons in lovemaking began. The nights of abandon, when Jacques taught me how to lose myself in passion, to surrender my body and will to his creative pleasuring; and taught me how to drive him to heightened levels of desire, exploring the sexual limits, by aggressively taking control of his body and his sex and using it to bring us to climax again and again throughout the night.

Then my mind flashed an image of the first summer of St. Tropez, the romantic hilltop restaurant above the harbor, where just a few tables were placed outdoors on the cobblestone alleyway. The street was narrow and dark and lit only by the dim street lanterns and by candlelight. A single saxophone player rang out jazz which echoed through the narrow streets. Couples stunningly dressed in white and other summer shades breezed by on their way to other restaurants, like apparitions illuminating the dimly lit alleyway. The mood and setting bordered on the surreal; I remembered thinking that if one of Salvador Dalí's horses with armored rider, spear in hand, had quietly trotted by at that moment, the fantastic scene would have been complete.

As I was about to doze off in the balmy air, I heard footsteps coming up the staircase. I could not escape.

"Well, well, well! We've found you! What a marvelous hiding place. Very clever, Sheri. You gave us good fun searching the attic and the wings. I suppose I'll never be able to fathom your thinking!" Jacques lifted me in his arms. "Come, let's go into one of the master bedrooms for a little fun."

Guy and Frédéric laughed viciously, the laugh of conquest. Even outside in the open air I could smell the three of them. Guy and Frédéric smelled of horses and sweat; Jacques reeked of cognac and cologne. It was a complex aroma, the body odors mixed with the scent of cologne, the bouquet of rare cognac on soured breath, and horse. I was too numb to fight.

Jacques investigated at least five bedrooms; finally he chose a room with a canopied bed, both canopy and windows draped in rich chintz.

Jacques laid me on the bed and immediately started to undress me. I was frozen with fear. I couldn't find enough breath to cry. He forced off aggressively the wired hoop and flung it to the floor. It rolled away, giving off the strangest creaking sound. He then meticulously and roughly pulled free each tier of my underslips, letting them fly through the air in different directions, creating a frightening chaos. I watched in horror as both Guy and Frédéric unzipped and started to remove their pants. Frédéric stumbled to the floor, obviously too unsteady to accomplish such a maneuver while standing. Guy didn't even notice the fall and, standing close to the bed, had already stripped off his briefs. Never had a penis looked so ugly to me, hanging limply from below his heavy sweater. I felt nauseated and helpless, imagining his imminent attack.

Jacques stopped his concentrated disrobing of me, leaving the antique corset still tied, loosening only the bottom ribbons over my lower abdomen, and then stood back, hovering over me, watching my growing fear. Finally, finding a surge of energy to resist the imminent drunken rape, I started to scream for help in French.

"Au secours! Au secours!" I repeated at piercing volume.

My screams disoriented the three men, seeming to jolt them into a stupor. They all recoiled as if to remove themselves from this game. It was no longer under their control. They stood motionless while I continued to scream at the top of my lungs. Jacques then turned to Guy and Frédéric and mumbled something in French.

"My dear Sheri," he said, putting his hand over my mouth to muffle my cries. "We will leave you now. You are no longer fun. Someday you will appreciate our games!" With these chilling words, he turned and left the bedroom, followed by Guy and Frédéric, carrying their pants, and closed the door behind them.

Welcome to the Belgian nobility, I said to myself, tears running down my cheeks. The memories of the earlier days with Jacques tore through my mind, pulling at my heart. I loved this man! But had I been blind? How had I missed the earlier signs? Was this to be my new life? Did I choose this? Why in God's name did I stay here in this debauched society? How long before I, too, became like them?

Chapter 13

I awoke in the late morning in a nightmarish mental fog. As I came downstairs, I heard noise and activity.

"Good morning, Sheri," all three men greeted me cheerfully.

"Frédéric and Guy have already picked up croissants and I have the coffee ready. Come sit down, darling," Jacques said, smiling. He was himself again, well groomed, in good spirits, his voice melodious. Did he have to take a mood to its extreme to dispel it, break it, and only then come back to normal? Yes, that was the pattern.

"We certainly had a good time last night!" Guy said. "You were great fun! What a time we had looking for you!"

"Yes. I really like you, Sheri," Frédéric added. "You and Jacques must spend more weekends at Loiroi, so we can really have some exciting times together. Next time perhaps I can invite our friends. We'll have dinner at our house. It would be my pleasure to introduce you to our little group. That is, if you don't mind country folk! I know you big-city people can't figure how we amuse ourselves out here without all the fine restaurants and nightclubs of Brussels, but we manage."

"Yes," Jacques said. "We'll come often in the fall. Aunt Martine closes the château for the summer, as you know, and leaves for her villa in Cannes. She'd prefer not to have it used in the summer. So in the fall, then."

"Anyway, we'll be at our summer home on the coast for most of July and in August we'll be going to Deauville for a little gambling and sailing," Guy said.

"Do you know Deauville, Sheri?" Guy asked.

"Well . . . yes. My Parisian aunt spoke about it."

"Ah! Now, that's an idea. Sheri and I won't be going to St. Tropez this summer because I've bought Claudine a new house and I'm going to spend July helping her plan the renovations and direct the team of workers. But perhaps we'll join you for a week in August at Deauville."

"Good! Then we'll call you with our plans. We can make reservations for you at the same hotel," Frédéric said excitedly.

"I don't really like casinos or sailing," I said. "Couldn't we visit them at the coast instead?" I didn't know what I was saying. All this talk was so pointless.

"Oh, *chérie* Sheri, are we being contrary this morning?" Jacques asked. "You mean there is a sport that you don't like?"

"Yes. Sailing has always scared me. It's so easy to tip the boat over."

"Come now. We're talking about large sailboats, not little Sailfish!" he laughed. "I'm sure you'll take to it. What, with three strong men to protect you? We'll not let you get swept away.

"Sheri, do you want to go riding again today?" Jacques asked, seeming almost to want to please me.

"No, I'd prefer to go home," I said. I felt so emotionally spent, so terrified, I knew I couldn't stay another day in Loiroi.

"Very well, *ma chérie,*" Jacques said, leaning over to kiss me lightly on the forehead.

Frédéric and Guy left after breakfast, and, ironically, they kept to the custom of the formal, "I am happy to have made your acquaintance." They seemed to believe my struggle had been purely a game I'd staged for their pleasure. They had not an inkling of the terrible ordeal they had put me through.

Jacques and I drove home. He was cheerful and talkative, but I couldn't dismiss my growing awareness that there was a definite pattern to his behavior. He really didn't remember anything when he entered these strange states. It had to be that. He spoke with the sketchiest recollection of what had really happened. It was not a mood, as Marc had told me. "Just wait a few days until the mood passes," he had said. But this was more than a mood. An evil, a sadism took hold. Something wildly out of control. Very dangerous, very volatile.

I was not prepared to handle this force. It was so far outside my frame of reference. I had always had such a normal family life—the proverbial father, mother, dog, cat, house in small-town Massachusetts. I wasn't prepared for these dramatic scenes—this bizarre behavior. I really didn't know how to deal with it.

"Jacques, what came over you yesterday?" I asked, mustering up courage to broach the subject. I had a growing fear of antagonizing him and setting off the "force."

"Oh, yesterday? You didn't have fun?"

"No, definitely not."

"Oh, well then. That was yesterday. I feel better today. We'll go home and have a relaxed day at the pool. If you like I'll take you to a marvelous new restaurant just outside Brussels for dinner. They have a specialty there that you'd love—fresh eel done in several divine sauces!"

"I'm not in the mood, Jacques. I'd just like to be alone when we get back. I need time to think."

"Well, if you feel that way I'll visit my sons tonight."

"Fine."

During the rest of the trip I was silent, while Jacques chatted on with stories about his friends Guy and Frédéric.

As he talked, my head pounded with confused thoughts. I would come to one conclusion, only to doubt it and change to another. I realized I was slipping into a victim mentality. On an intellectual level I realized what was happening and knew I should just run away. But the emotional weakness of the victim had already taken hold. A voice in my mind kept repeating that I deserved such treatment, and I had a feeling of inexplicable guilt. Jacques had a right to punish me for deceiving him, because I had broken "the codes," even though I wasn't fully versed in them.

This was insanity! To be terrified by my own husband! Dear God, what had come over me? How could I accept these demoralizing acts? I even felt relieved that last night's madness had not been as bad as the first bout of verbal cruelty.

Take the next plane home, I thought. You're free. It's not the nineteenth century. Jacques's sadistic nature was definitely a pattern. It could happen a fourth time, a fifth. It *would* happen.

But I couldn't make a decision. I didn't want to act, just wait. Another voice echoed: I can't leave. I must stay to right a wrong. I did betray Jacques by refusing to have the breast operation. Maybe I deserve his wrath, his punishment. I must win back his trust. Then the marriage will succeed.

My thoughts kept coming very clearly and then reversing themselves. How could my mind function so irrationally? Was I in shock? I knew I needed help. I must seek help from Mamie. Make her my ally and persuade her to talk to Jacques.

When we arrived home, Jacques left immediately to visit his sons, leaving me in the care of Roland.

"Roland, *Madame la Baronne* is not feeling well. Please fix her a good dinner to bring her energy back."

"Yes, *Monsieur le Baron*." Roland smirked as if he knew just *why* I wasn't feeling well.

I was starting to dislike him and Marie-Louise intensely. I believed they had their own sadistic streaks, and liked to watch Jacques's abusive moods unfold for a new lady of the house. Their formal attentiveness to me felt creepy.

I sat alone at the big table while Roland served a five-course dinner. He came back into the room every few minutes to refill my wineglass and ask if I needed anything. I felt alone and lost. I had no one to confide in. I didn't want to frighten Mother by telling her what had happened with Guy and Frédéric or about Jacques's infidelities.

The next morning I called Mamie and asked that she not tell Jacques of our luncheon appointment for that day. Mamie agreed cautiously.

I had barely entered the apartment when Mamie dived straight into our discussion.

"Sheri, you know that Jacques's lack of trust in you is causing his reactions. Not only did you deceive him about the breast operation, but he told me you now refuse to pay your share of the household expenses. You brought no dowry and you expect him to support you totally. He's very upset about that," she said.

"Please, let me tell you what happened while you were away," I interrupted. "Jacques now has twice put me through the most frightening bouts of his bizarre behavior! You once said during one of our talks that he was moody, difficult, and had a tendency to blow certain things out of proportion, but you never warned me that he has two personalities! He becomes a different person over any disagreement—real or imagined—and slips into another self! He's cruel and demands that I perform to his peculiar sexual demands."

She stoically listened as I described the first episode to her, without specific sexual details, and told her how terrified I was until Marc had arrived to help me.

"You lost his trust and he hasn't recovered from his disappointment," she said coldly. "Now you could calm the situation if you at least tried to meet your financial responsibilities."

Trying to control my rage at her insensitivity, I explained once again that he had *never* mentioned a dowry or shared support of the household. Of course my willingness to work in Jacques's business to do my share meant nothing, was not the point—there was no financial need; it was just the principle. It was another attempt on her part to force the dowry issue, "the bigger money."

She explained once again that in Belgium women were expected to bring a dowry. "In America, women squeeze their husbands like a lemon until the men die early of heart attacks or strokes; they take over the fortunes, having contributed nothing! You are living in Europe now and you must adjust to the European ways."

"That is the European view, perhaps, Mamie, and your generalization assumes that there is no love and that marriage is a business," I said. "I came here to create a happy life for Jacques and myself and I will put all my energies into being a loving wife, if he lets me. He never warned me that he expected money and I never told him that I had my own source of income." Silently, though, I wondered how I could ever be a loving wife to Jacques.

"You are so sure of yourself," she answered sarcastically. "You come here and try to live in your American way. Don't you think you should consider Jacques? He has sacrificed for you! You cleverly convinced him to marry you before he was ready! He wanted to live with you first, but you wouldn't consider it. He married you six months after his divorce and that has caused him much criticism in Belgian society."

I realized the incredible absurdity of this conversation, and I yearned to tell Mamie that I knew she had wanted me to marry Jacques and that she was contradicting herself, but I dared not. I had come to her to gain some understanding of her son's behavior, but once again I found myself in the position of defending the fact that I hadn't brought *her* a dowry.

"Well, then, I hope you will at least be more like a Belgian wife and consider marriage forever," she said, her eyes piercing. "I know that young Americans believe that marriage is for a few years. They like to marry many times. Maybe that is why you will not commit dowry money—because you plan to have only a short marriage to Jacques."

"Mamie, I love life in all its adventure and mysteries. I love Jacques. I have loved him for three years!" Suddenly tears filled my eyes. "If he doesn't drive me away with more insane behavior, I plan to stay with Jacques for life."

"Sheri, Sheri. Jacques is difficult. But I believe you can handle him," she replied, now in a more sympathetic tone. "Just don't be too critical of him. Try to discourage his drinking. If he enters another mood, just be quiet for several days and let the mood pass. Don't try to reason with him or he will get worse. Treat him like a child and let him brood. Pamper him. But above all, remember, at the start of a mood swing, try to stop it before it grows; try not to let him blow things out of proportion."

As she spoke I was struck with her speech pattern, her continual use of understatement. Jacques's madness was simply moods, as if he went into a corner and sulked. Understatement was as intregal to the noble's speech as dramatic overstatement. There seemed to be no middle ground or moderate reaction to anything. Inconsequential events were "devastating" or "dreadful," but major events were "unpleasant" or "disagreeable and certainly unfortunate." A catastrophe might be "quite inconvenient," but someone canceling a dinner appointment was "dreadful and horrifying."

"Mamie, please tell me. Has Jacques ever been physically violent during his moods?"

"No, Sheri, never violent; but he was self-destructive. Very self-destructive."

"But he seems to spiral out of control. Could this cause him to commit an act of irrationality? Was he ever violent with Claudine?" The questions tumbled out of me, perhaps because I was so desperate for answers.

She, like Marc, avoided the questions and only said, "If you don't provoke him, he will be fine."

"If, if . . . There are too many ifs, Mamie."

"Sheri, he is not violent. Be assured," she said, exasperated.

"Maybe Jacques should get some psychiatric help to control his moods."

"Nonsense!" she snapped. "You can handle him." And then she added with forceful authority, "Remember! Just remember you promised me you would not leave; you would give it a try! You are strong. I want to hear you reinforce that promise."

I bade her goodbye, after again promising her, hoping it hadn't been the wrong place to seek help. Was it pointless to confide in her? I now just prayed she'd keep her promise not to tell Jacques of our discussion.

Jacques arrived home early, since he worked only a few hours a day in July. Most businesses in Belgium close completely in July, as do those in Paris in August.

"I was at Claudine's in the afternoon and then I passed by Mamie's apartment. Strangely, your car was parked there. Did you visit my mother?"

"Yes. I needed her advice on . . . well, on cooking. I want her maid to give me more lessons."

"Oh? Couldn't you wait to discuss that with her at our Wednesday lunch?"

"Can't I see my mother-in-law alone sometimes? Women like to be alone to chitchat."

"Is that so? And what did you chitchat about?"

"The usual gossip."

"You told her about me, right? Yes! I'm calling her. And if you did, because you remember I warned you not to, you'll be very sorry you did!"

He called Mamie. No answer. I was relieved that perhaps I could get to her before he did.

"I don't have to speak with her to know that you told her about our little games. Well! Before you leave I'll give you plenty of fun and games to tell her about. If you ever dare speak with her again . . . !" he said in fury.

I rushed up to the bedroom.

I didn't reappear on the first floor until dinnertime, and when I entered the living room, I noticed that Jacques had again reversed all the photographs of me in their frames, and only the white backs were exposed. An open bottle of pills spilled over the bar. I peered out the window and Jacques was floating on a raft in the pool.

I can't go through anything more, I thought. I'll go crazy. I felt trapped. Isolated. Again, I had nowhere to go for the evening. No friends. No family to visit. I poured myself a drink at the bar to calm down. I'll become alcoholic, I thought, like everyone around me if I stay here. I turned on the TV at station TF 1, news from France. News, yes, I reasoned, I'll bring myself out of my own problems. There's a world out there. The hostages were still being held in Iran.

Jacques came in. "I'm going to spend the night at Claudine's. She's more fun to be with than you. Look at you with your depressed face. You'd better perk up; I don't like to see frowning faces."

"You are getting so close to Claudine again," I blurted out without thinking.

He smiled at me. "It's not your concern."

"I see," I said, resigned that I had no power to question him. Suddenly, in my mind I made a decision: I'd give this marriage one more month. I'd leave if things didn't change.

"If you want to make yourself useful tonight, you could go over the bills." He laughed. "Yes, do that. And maybe while you have some time alone to think, you'll decide to contribute your half. I think our basic expenses come to about ten or twelve thousand U.S. dollars a month. Of course that doesn't count your clothes. Think about transferring a little money into your account here."

I turned away and walked outside. Six thousand a month! Impossible! To be treated as his slave, and pay for his truffles, caviar, foie gras, and Dom Pérignon champagne? His self-indulgence was mind-boggling. And now he was breaking the taboo code; he had actually used the word "money" without euphemisms! His code was never to talk about money in figures, but his second self did so freely.

In July, only the fourth month of my marriage, I felt myself falling deeper into depression, a frighteningly anxious and helpless state. Jacques spent long days at Claudine's new home, leaving me alone at Ginal—sometimes for a whole evening. The summer session at the university was now taken over by students from African countries, and the few acquaintances I had made left for the summer, so I stopped going to classes.

It had rained every day for four weeks straight. Though it was just the continual summer drizzle, lying near the pool was not possible. I felt that after a few more weeks, Noah might rescue me! All the members of Jacques's family were away at their summer homes; only his grandmother stayed in Brussels. I didn't know what to do with myself during the long days. I sometimes swam in the rain for exercise. I was too anxious to sit for long reading novels or studying French. I lost the will to write positive details in my letters to Mother, and there was little of interest to write in my journal. The isolation, the inactivity, and Jacques's brainwashing were eroding my spirit. I didn't know how to save myself.

The few books I read were on Belgian history and art. I looked in them for clues to the psyches of the people around me, this strange noble group. I decided that fundamental to the forming of their collective way of thinking was their rich and turbulent history in the High Middle Ages, when the cities of Antwerp, Ghent, Bruges, and Brussels thrived.

It was a time of noble houses, flourishing commerce in Northern Europe's key ports, first Bruges, then Antwerp, and the creation of art. The Flemish "Primitives" of the period left the country with its masterpieces. But it was also a time of feudal wars, nightmarish torture, and the Black Plague. The whole period was thought of as the Dark Ages.

I started thinking of Jacques in terms of his history, coming out of Gothic times, his penchant for the dark side of life. His taste seemed rooted in his nation's collective unconscious. Even his preference for art ran to frightening images—severe portraits of noblemen, fierce animals, visions of Heaven and Hell like those in Hieronymus Bosch's creations. I could easily imagine Jacques living in giant drafty fortified castles in the 1300s, protecting his lands from invasions by other noble houses from France, Austria, Germany, and Spain.

His honor code, his pride in the family crests, ancient seals, and stamps, his love of intrigues and conspiracies, were all probably remnants of these times. Even his physiognomy and the faces of his family and friends resembled medieval portraits. But most of all his capacity for fright games, his unique brand of cruelty, could not have been of recent vintage but certainly had its seeds in the slowly evolving genes of his ancestors, who could easily have been among the ruthless Counts of Flanders.

On the nights when Jacques did come home in time for dinner, I was happy to have any companionship at first, but his presence shortly deepened my depression. He drank heavily every night, and by dinner's end he usually had consumed almost two bottles of wine. Then the cognac or marc de Provence came out, and that was when he started his punishing tirades.

He would begin an insane cross-examination and demand I answer his questions and accusations. After this had happened a dozen times, I simply responded with memorized lines, as if I were an actor in a Chekhovian drama. "Please give me time for the breast operation." "I didn't deceive you." "I've come here to make a happy life for us both." "I only had a few boyfriends before you, no lovers." "I have no trust fund." In fact, I convinced myself that I *was* a character in a play so that his frightening attacks of drunken fury were less painful.

Often the first words he blurted were, "Why did you deceive me with the breast operation? I would never have married you. You are so clever; you think you can trick me.

Like your clever avoidance of bringing a dowry. And I know you have a trust fund. And since you made the choice to withhold your trust fund from me, you will regret it until you leave for America."

At that point I'd walk out of the main house to the pool house. He would follow me, repeating his litany over and over again, in stronger language but always in a low voice. I tried to answer some of the questions as he posed them, while always assuring him I had loved him and had had no reason to deceive him. I urged him to forget the past and start our life over, as we had been doing so happily. But all my pleas were to no avail, and he once again repeated all my sins. He said he could never trust me again. Never!

After what seemed like endless hours of this nagging repetition and more irrational accusations, I went upstairs to sleep. Sometimes he would follow me and demand I let him exercise his husband's right, as he called it. Even his disrobing showed the marked difference of his other personality. He undressed with a halting slowness and deliberate precision, first letting his shoes drop loudly to the ground, then undoing his shirt button by button while watching me with an enigmatic expression, removing it and hanging it on the back of a low chair. Next he unzipped his jeans, and the sound reverberated through the room with a palpable sexual aggressiveness. He pulled the skintight jeans off, and the rustling of the denim seemed to merge with the sound of the zipper still hanging in the air like a primary chord. He folded the jeans and laid them neatly on the same chair.

Then he would come crushing down on top of me, spreading my legs with his, moving them apart, thrusting himself into me, gyrating and moaning loudly, and he would come within minutes. He would then demand to know if I had come, and if I said no, he'd say, "Are you trying to humiliate me by claiming I am not man enough to bring you to climax?" "No," I'd reply. "I'm just not in any mood for sex." "This won't do. You must come. While you're here, I want you to have orgasms so you won't seek out anyone else." Then he'd demand that I masturbate to climax. It was sickening to have him watch and not allow me to stop until he thought I had finished. Of course, I faked it.

On other nights he would simply come to bed and announce, "Since I've just been with a woman, I won't be wanting you tonight. But tomorrow morning I'm sure I'll feel differently and I'll give you the opportunity to please me. So good night, my deceptive woman. One day you'll face up to your dishonesty."

The psychological torture of his brainwashing was so debilitating that I had no mental energy left to figure out what I should do. I couldn't think clearly. I didn't want to call Mother and ask her to come to Belgium because I didn't know whether I was capable of describing or admitting to the horrifying degradation. I saw no way out. I just prayed that one day he'd change back into the loving, sweet man I thought I'd married. I had even begun to fantasize that this bizarre treatment would somehow stop and everything would be happy again. My thoughts were so confused that if I went home I wouldn't be able to face anyone. I was horrified by the terrible mistake I had made in marrying him. My stupidity! I'd never recover from this, I thought, and therefore I had better stay, because it was the only life I could have. One of my worst, heartbreaking worries was that he'd already turned me into a whore. There was nothing innocent left about me! It was too late for me!

And Claudine was poisoning him slowly but surely against me. Always when he spent time with her, I faced him at his most venomous.

"I'm giving up my life for you!" he said, arriving back from one visit. "Claudine has had me excluded from the most important hunting weekend in France this fall. I will receive no invitation because of you!"

"Why? What do you mean?"

"She just found out you're Jewish, and now all of Belgium knows. I'll be excluded from everything! All the special events! All the hunts! I'll be cut off from my life!"

"How did she find out?" I asked.

"The banns were posted at the City Hall for two weeks before the wedding. Your mother's maiden name was obviously Jewish! One of her friends saw the banns, but didn't tell her till now. I can't imagine why she waited to give Claudine such pleasure. She's gone to all my friends and told them that they should not have the savage Jewess in their company—nor *me*! You see! You see what I will sacrifice for you? Missing that hunting weekend, the most important social event of the entire year! Give up my position in our circle? And for you? You who have deceived me? No operation, no dowry, no—"

He broke off and paced furiously, but did not raise his voice. Once again his face became tightened and angry, completely changed. His skin had a ghostly pallor, his hair seemed darker, his eyes were dull and hollow.

"Go home to America! You are not my wife. You are a deceiving woman. I will not accept you. Your trial period is over!" He grabbed his suit, shirt, tie, and toiletries and left the room.

I rushed to dress, since it was strictly improper to appear on the first floor in a robe, and ran downstairs to catch him before he left for the office. In minutes, he came down and walked briskly past me into the garage.

"Jacques, please. I am your wife! I will not go to America! This is my home. Please try to calm yourself. Let us meet for lunch and speak to each other."

"I will be home sometime tonight. You could use the time to pack your trunks."

"I won't let you do this. What have *I* done? You've been happy with me. *We've* been happy! We—"

But already he had closed the door of his BMW and was backing out of the garage.

I was in shock. I couldn't get his physical image out of my mind. The hollow eyes and pasty skin haunted me. It was again as though he had assumed a different persona in front of my eyes.

I wanted to call my mother and insist she come, but it was the middle of the night in New York. I decided to wait until afternoon. I had to calm myself somehow, so I drove to the outdoor fruit and vegetable markets in our village and several nearby villages, and even to a faraway bakery famous for its quiche. Still very tense when I arrived home, I decided I had to loosen up, and went into the dance studio I loved. I was choreographing a long modern sequence to some inspiring flute music when Jacques, champagne bottle in hand but with only one glass, appeared at the door.

He said nothing, poured himself a glass of champagne, and drank it in one gulp. "I see you didn't pack your belongings. And here you are happily dancing and admiring yourself in the mirror. Well, I want you to study yourself more closely. I want you to see your interior self. Your true deceptive core!"

He threw the champagne bottle against the mirror. The impact sent sharp spines cracking along its large surface. Then another loud crack as he smashed the side mirror with his champagne glass. I stood frozen in fear.

"Now, my sweet, dance! Dance! Look at yourself in the cracked mirror. Now we'll see the cracked inner self. And your face in a hundred parts. That's your face, not the pretty, smooth covering surface." He laughed, then picked me up roughly and pushed my face closer to the broken mirror.

"Look now. Ha! Didn't your favorite artists, your cubists, present faces like this?"

I looked instead at his face. It had that frighteningly cruel expression, dull fixed eyes, a pinched mouth, a visible quiver to the tight jaw. Dangerous. All my instincts held me back from antagonizing him, pushing him to further anger.

"Stop, Jacques! Stop! What are you doing? Please stop this horrible demonstration!" I implored him, trying to sound calm.

"No! Now that you are no longer my wife, I will treat you as I wish. You will go home to America, I promise you. But first you will satisfy me. I want to take you—not like a loving wife, which you'll never be. I want you to give me pleasure. My way. Until you leave—and you will leave—I will take you any way I choose!"

"Stop! Stop! You're frightening me! Stop! You love me. Try to come back to yourself."

"Ha! Take off your leotard. Now! And dance for me, naked in the prism of your deception. Watch yourself change. There is no hiding behind your beautiful surface with this mirror; it fragments the surface and shows your inner being. Dance!"

"No! Please stop yourself. These are dangerous games. Stop this!" I began to weep, taking huge gulps of air. Once again the man standing before me didn't look like my husband. Didn't sound like my husband. It was vividly clear that his second self had taken possession of his body.

He locked the door, put the key in his pocket, then turned on the *Firebird Suite* at full volume.

"Dance! Take off your suit as I told you!"

Almost afraid to move, I took off my leotard and tights and did a spin and an arabesque.

"Faster! Move! Excite me! Kick and jump high as you always do," he demanded. "Yes! Yes! That's it!"

And he watched while I jumped and twirled to the furious rhythms.

"Good! Now lie down on your back on the mat over there and spread your legs."

"No, Jacques, I won't. Please! You've never been this violent! I will not be raped!"

"You are no longer my lover or my wife. I've restrained myself long enough. You deceived me and now you will be punished! Then you can leave for America. Lie down!"

I obeyed only with the hope of ending this mad scene.

"Jacques, please! Please don't! Can't I satisfy you in some other way? Because—"

He collapsed on top of me and mercilessly forced himself deep inside. I screamed, struggling to push him away.

"Come on, *chérie* Sheri, move with me. Don't just lie there. It's not like you."

"Please, just come, quickly. I can't bear it," I moaned.

"No—no—no! Not so easy. Now, how many lovers have you had before me?"

"Please, Jacques!"

"Answer me! All right. Then I will thrust once into you for each one. When I reach the correct number, tell me to stop." And he lunged again. "One, two—"

"Stop!"

"No. Not two. That is impossible. You've had at least two hundred men. Haven't you?"

"I don't like these games and I won't give you numbers. Now please let me up. You're being cruel."

"We'll try just a few more numbers." And he moved in

quick short gyrations, thrusting rapidly. "That's twenty. Now thirty." Suddenly he cried out: "*Je joui, je joui!*" and pulled out of me and came on my stomach, a symbolic insult. He didn't want to deposit his seed in me. I remembered he had once told me he did this to women before he married.

I lay there weeping bitterly as he rose and started to dress.

"Get dressed!" he said roughly. "We'll have dinner and then we'll count out some more of your lovers after dinner. I need some strength first."

"I don't want dinner. I will go to my room."

"No! Get dressed in one of your prettiest long gowns. The red chiffon strapless. Wear the ruby necklace and put your hair up. Full makeup too! Then we'll dine. You must please me the short time you'll be here. And put on the Rochas perfume for tonight. Remember—all over your *petit chat*, too. You'll have your chance to please me tonight."

I was in such pain I was hardly able to walk through the long corridor back into the main wing of the house and upstairs to our bedroom. I didn't know what to do. There was no one I could call for help. I knew his mother was away again, as usual on a trip to Marbella. Isabelle was visiting Gérard and Hélène in Lugano. Marc was in England. There was Catherine, but she lived so far away. Who else is there? I wondered. I'll wait till tomorrow and call Catherine if Jacques continues to be out of control.

I went down to dinner dressed formally as Jacques had stipulated. We sat down and the butler began serving dinner.

"Drink a lot of wine tonight. It will make you more sexy as it always does. Do you like this wine? I brought it up from the cellar. It's from an Italian vineyard. You know that the Italians don't export their best wines. They keep them for themselves. I bought several cases of this on my last trip to the north of Italy," he said, making easy conversation in an obvious attempt to unnerve me. "I'm so glad you've taken such an interest in wines. Most Americans don't. Oh, maybe in California wines, but they have a long way to go until they are really drinkable. What do you think?"

"I don't want to talk. Unless you want to explain to me what has come over you, explain your violence. You raped me!" I had to challenge him, hold up his behavior to him, finally.

"Violent? No. You thought so? No, my sweet. I'm not violent. I'm just instructive. I am teaching you that women must be punished for their deceptions. Only then will I let you go home. You could have packed your trunks today. But it was your decision to disobey me. You're my destroyer. Because of you I am excluded from society. It is intolerable!"

His voice was strange, hollow. His accent in French, his mannerisms, were all different. We ate the rest of the meal in silence. He filled my wineglass each time even half was gone.

When we rose from the table he asked the maid to finish the dishes and then go directly to her quarters; we wouldn't be needing her further that night, he said. She smirked at him as if she knew something was going on. *"Oui, Monsieur le Baron."*

"Now, Sheri, go upstairs and change into one of your short sexy dresses. I'm already tired of this one. Put on one of the white transparent ones and wear your string bikini under it. No, wait! Take your long ruby necklace and pull it through your ass cleft and attach it in front to the jeweled string bikini, through the front and back loops."

I walked upstairs, too frightened to do anything but obey his cruel orders. How had I ever loved this man? How had I not seen signs that he was capable of such acts? He could be violent, there was no doubt. I was not safe with him.

When I came back into the living room, he was on the

phone talking to Claudine. When he hung up he said, "She will not let our sons enter this house while you are here! Now I must give up having my sons in my own house for you, too."

I didn't answer, afraid to accelerate his madness. To my relief, he stormed out of the house. I heard the garage door open and his car pull out. My whole body was shaking as I heard his car screech down the long drive. The bleak Belgian weather always seemed to provide the perfect movie-set backdrop to our most frightening episodes, and tonight the lightning and thunder were raging. The house was isolated, with many doors and floor-to-ceiling windows. I had an overwhelming sense of fear. Although I didn't think Jacques would return, I couldn't be sure. And I was irrationally afraid of what lurked outside. I looked through the phone book to find the number of the village police. Then I took my car out of the garage and parked it near one of the main entrances.

I lit a fire in the fireplace, took some of the oldest cognac, and put on classical music, trying somehow to still my terror. I felt too vulnerable to think about what I should do. In case he came back, I didn't want him to hear me calling my mother. I was in too much of a panic anyway to tell her why I needed her to come immediately. I'd call her tomorrow. She'd come. We'd figure it out, I kept on repeating to myself. She'd take me home.

Jacques did not come home that night, and I awoke to the knocking at the door signifying that Marie-Louise was back and bringing me breakfast. I felt as if I were a prisoner, under house arrest.

Chapter 14

Not to be overheard by Roland or Marie-Louise, I rushed
to the phone center in Wavre to call my mother. No answer,
though it was six hours earlier, the middle of the night, her
time. She had to be away; it was the middle of summer. I
decided to check in to a Brussels hotel for a few days until
I reached Mother and together we'd decide what to do.

Back in Ginal I went into the luggage room to find a
small valise. I tried to go undetected, but Marie-Louise spotted me. I suspected she'd immediately call Jacques. I proceeded to pack hurriedly, but in my state of throbbing anxiety
I just couldn't get organized or move fast. I searched the
desk to find my credit card, then threw together the absolutely necessary items and ran toward my car. Jacques was
already there, his car's remote control just opening the garage door.

He sprang out of his car and came toward me, deterring
me from opening my car's door. "Don't leave me," he said,

tears streaming down his cheeks, his eyes now human, warm, concerned. "I love you, *chérie*. Please!"

It was frightening, almost nightmarish to see him and hear him in his first self. The good twin was back. The transformation was hellish. I hadn't seen him fully in his first self since June. Now there was no doubt. My mind was not playing tricks. Something was so very wrong, off balance, an undeniable split in personality. It was serious. How had I thought that I was the cause of the anger, my breaking the codes?

"Jacques, I must leave you for a while. Try to figure things out. I want to go home to the U.S."

"Sheri. Sheri. Why? Why do you want to go? Leave me? Let's talk this over!"

I shivered at his questioning why, his apparent lack of memory of the terrible night before. "I want you to come with me right now to the dance studio to see what you did! Will you come?" I said, hoping to bring forth memory and remorse.

"We must talk first. I know a place where we can go, a place that I have wanted to show you for a long time." He opened his car door and urged me in.

"No, Jacques, come with me first to the studio."

Ignoring me, he got into the driver's seat. "I know I was upset, overwrought perhaps, about Claudine's finding out. Dreadful development. Just dreadful! She torments me, Sheri. You must try to understand the pressures I'm under combating her games. She won't stop until she succeeds in having me excluded from society. We will be shunned by everyone. I've tried everything to stop her. A lot goes on that I struggled with, but haven't wanted to tell you." He pulled out of the driveway. "Anyway, I've instructed Roland to clean up the little mess we created in the studio. I feel much calmer today."

I strained to listen to his inner voice, not just his words, trying to determine how much was true and how much he actually remembered. I wanted a real discussion, not the usual ignorance of the occurrence the next day. He had at least remembered that something had gone on in the dance studio; but did he remember the severity—the rape, the counting out of lovers?

We drove to the entrance of the Brussels forest, Forêt de Soignes, which had a long straight walking path flanked by toweringly tall beech trees. A tranquil, beautiful spot. "There's an arboretum just beyond planted by Leopold II, king of the Belgians in the last century, the king who founded the Belgian Congo. In fact the royals and nobles loved this forest. Charles V and the Dukes of Brabant all used to hunt here. Ruysbroeck the Wonderful, the medieval mystical writer, wrote in one of the abbeys in the deep forest not far from here."

I started to worry that we would have another long history lesson and not face the problem. I wasn't going to let that happen. I gave him an anxious look.

"I've often intended to bring you to this enchanted place," he went on with the enthusiasm of someone who is purposely avoiding another subject. "When I was missing you terribly during our engagement, I'd come here to walk in the woods and think about you and dream of what our life would be like together."

"Jacques, those dreams, I want to hear them all. But first tell me why you have the need to punish me. Rape me like last night!"

"Punish you?" he said, genuinely surprised. "I have no desire to punish you. I love you. Yes, I'll admit I'm not always calm. As I said, it is Claudine who has created terrible pressures for me. If I am less tender, less concentrated during our lovemaking, it's the pressure from Claudine that keeps me on edge. This past month I realize I've been very nervous."

"But you've been violent, Jacques!"

"Violent? No. Very upset. In turmoil. Stopping wicked Claudine. Saving us, *chérie*. We'll get over this period. I haven't been as attentive to you. Forgive me. I've spent too much time working on Claudine's house and . . . I'm finished with Claudine's house! I won't be going there anymore, I promise. That's what has made me so nervous."

"Do you remember what you say to me when you are nervous? Last night, do you remember what you said?"

"It's the pressure, tremendous pressure. Not you, darling. I love you. I know I've drunk too much lately in order to calm myself. To forget the ghastly situation. She tells her cunning little lies to all of Belgium. I'll stop drinking so much."

I knew very well that it wasn't the drinking. He had very little memory. And no answers. "Did you ever think of seeing a doctor when you feel pressures like this?"

"Oh, I sometimes talk to Gérard. Or to Isabelle. I don't need any doctors. But Sheri, the thing with Isabelle, it only happened a few times when I was feeling badly and it will *never* happen again."

I shuddered at his mention of Isabelle. "Would you talk to a doctor, a professional adviser? For me. We could go together."

"I don't really see any point to it. No, I'm afraid that in my family, in my circle, we don't expose our lives, our problems, our secrets to such people. How would they ever understand our codes, our lives, anyway?"

I wondered in sad irony whether indeed there were doctors who specialized in this circle's special brand of psychology.

"Why do you act so cruelly, then tell me you love me?

I want a doctor to help you find out why," I said, probing further at this rare moment when he was receptive to discussion.

"Sheri." Tears welled in his eyes. "Understand that I love you so deeply that I want our life . . . our love to be perfect." He suddenly changed from slow English to French, as he often did when speaking of his feelings, his love. "Pressures have not let me give you the happiness you deserve. Soon they will be over. Give me a chance to show you that happiness. We are from such different backgrounds. Different worlds. Don't try to understand me. I often don't understand you. But I don't need to understand. You are forever a part of me. And I'm a part of you. Love is a mystery. Complex passions. It's not always pleasure, but a powerful and marvelous force."

He spoke so sincerely that I felt myself wanting to believe that what was happening between us was all a part of this mysterious force of passion in its turbulent and painful phase. Yet at the same time I knew the insidious nature of Jacques's changes of personality and wondered whether this seductive talk of love and passion was only another of his clever machinations.

"I never thought I'd find the perfect love," he continued in French. "But I found that in you. You are my sweet American beauty. I love you, *chérie*. We have overcome the worst maneuverings. Yes, even conspiracies of Claudine, her friends, and even my mother. All of them against our love. Stay with me always. I'll give you the happiest life, my treasured love. I promise you. And don't ever think of leaving me."

I was still deeply in love with his first self. So much so that I was able to delude myself, almost dividing Jacques in my mind into these two separate selves, convincing myself that his first self was his real essence and that the second, the bad, sadistic Jacques, was not really a part of his being, but an intruder—a spirit that possessed him occasionally and then vanished. My journal entries in July were full of appearances of the complex disturbed character—the second self never really left for the whole month—yet I still refused to accept it as an actual strain of his personality. I wanted to find a way to reclaim the good Jacques for myself and banish the visitor, who had mysteriously never once appeared during our three-year romance. I knew I must try.

"I'll have to think what I want to do. I've been very confused and lonely. No one to confide in. No friends. I want my mother to visit. Can she visit soon?"

"Of course, *ma chérie*. Have her come in September, when my family will all be back from their travels. Late September. Still before the rains."

He pointed out an abbey where Pieter Brueghel the Younger, the last of the Brueghel family, painted, and continued, "You know, darling, if Claudine manages to have us excluded from society for a while, we'll travel. We both love to travel. I want to take you to Patagonia at the tip of Argentina to see the elephant sea lions. We can tour the South Pole, go to the Antarctic station from there. Oh yes, then we must see Madagascar, stay at Nosy Be, a resort just like St. Tropez, except we can go in winter. Then right nearby we can see the most beautiful islands of the Indian Ocean, the Seychelles. And maybe even a long trip around Indonesia; we can take a boat up the coast of Sumatra and also go to Java—we'll visit the sultan's palace. We'll plan at least four trips next year."

As I heard myself agree to come back to him, swayed by his tenderness, his painting another vivid image of the dream life still to come, I knew I was giving in out of weakness, my emotions too raw even to insist on any conditions or concessions. I felt the weakness of a gambler, who has lost repeatedly, already gambled away almost everything she owned, but still has the inexplicable hunch and hope, the irrepressible confidence in her infallibility—so sure she can win it all back!

"Jacques, will you promise me that you never again will do something like last night? I can't bear it and can't go through any more of it. Can you make that promise?"

"I promise you the bad times are over."

"Can you really control your angry passions? Give me your word of honor."

"*Chérie*, you have it."

He kissed me and lifted me high in his arms and swung us both around playfully until we fell to the ground beneath the giant beech trees.

"Good. So you'll come back. And stay forever, *ma belle, belle chérie* Sheri," Jacques said with his disarming romantic cadence. "Tonight I'll open a bottle of Château Lafitte Rothschild, the most precious from my wine cellar for my most precious and beautiful love."

As August approached, the weather finally broke and the sun shone every day. The property was in full bloom, the fruit trees full of apples, pears, plums, and cherries. And with the break in weather came the change of mood. The long, easy days of sunning and swimming at the pool started the healing process and slowly lifted me out of my deep depression.

The day we returned from the woods Jacques turned the pictures of me in their frames and my image was reinstated. His strange, symbolic gesture brought me uncanny joy. But I realized that I was exhibiting the behavior of a hostage, taking delight in my captor's small kindnesses.

Jacques reentered and remained in what I thought of as his first self, the self that was loving, gentle, and generous.

But it was difficult for me to make the leaps of mood with him and respond to his gallant transformation with immediate carefree openness and sweetness. I remained quiet and untrusting of his loving approval, knowing the pattern too well, knowing it could switch off after any tiny incident.

Jacques had finished his project at Claudine's house and now spent more time with me, and during these sunny days we adopted a style of nudist living. We spent hours at the pool, had meals served there, and even spent the night sleeping in the airy pool house. It was very sensual to walk around the property or into the main house free and natural, naked as an infant, and to get a golden tan on every inch of the body. Marie-Louise and Roland were always there serving us, and accepted our nakedness very matter-of-factly.

Only at night did Jacques ask me to dress for dinner and later disrobe for our evening of swimming and sex. He'd spend a few hours at the office in the morning and often come back with sexy transparent gowns in organza or gauzy cotton. His dressing obsession continued, but in its positive form. He bought me dozens of dresses, pareos, and jumpsuits, lots of playful summer jewelry, hats, and all sorts of toys.

While keeping my emotions on guard, I let myself go along with him during these pleasurable days. I tried to justify my actions by telling myself that I would stay until I healed enough to leave him. I had thought through the rainy spring that I would give our marriage until the fall, and if things didn't change, I would have to leave. I still felt that way and hoped that the sun and play would bring me back to myself.

But I couldn't come to terms with the fact that I desired him sexually. Every time he made love to me (and his lovemaking reverted to its most gentle and romantic), I hated that weakness in me that desired him so desperately. We took each other to madly passionate highs and explosive orgasms, four to five times almost every day. My physical attraction to him seemed uncontrollable as I watched him walk nude near the pool, each day tanner and with tighter muscles. But, at the same time, I hated the darkness that I knew existed inside him. I tried to obliterate any thought of his alter ego and only hypnotized myself into enjoying his physical presence, his masculinity and sexual prowess. Of course all the champagne, wines, and aperitifs helped to dull my awareness of my hypocrisy . . . of my acting as if we were a honeymoon couple on a retreat in our private nudist colony.

Then he started a new game that we played incessantly. He was the photographer, I the model, on a full-time assignment to create a complete portfolio of nudes. He shot hundreds of pictures and developed them himself in his photo lab at Ginal. He was particularly creative in setting up the photos and backgrounds. He claimed that I was looking more beautiful, more sensual than ever with my golden full-body tan and long curly hair. He took shots of me under water, in the woods, floating on rafts. Not one of the glorious photographs had even a hint of the pornographic; they were all as gentle and sensitively sensual as Klimt paintings.

One day his sons arrived for a visit. Claudine had allowed them to come to Ginal. It was a monumental breakthrough and a welcome sign to me that life was normalizing. At least I would no longer hear "My sons will never enter this house again while you are here. You've destroyed my life."

I was anxious to make this unexpected turn of events into a permanent positive turn. I instructed the maid to ready the boys' rooms. After a little discussion about menus and food preferences, I went on an extensive food shopping trip. The boys immediately jumped into the pool and seemed right at home.

We all swam and happily played at sports in the afternoon. Dinner was a cookout at the pool, and then more Ping-Pong contests and evening swims.

I made an especially strong effort to help them enjoy themselves and tried to be very natural, presenting an image of friend to them, not stepmother. Jacques had told me that parents in their society speak to their children using the formal *vous* for "you." Therefore, I used the *tu* form to make them feel more at ease, as if I were a friend, not an adult.

Throughout their stay we had a wonderfully carefree time. I gave them some English lessons and they in turn tried to teach me the "in" young people's French expressions. They chuckled at my accent and mistakes.

Jacques praised me and watched me lovingly, at one point asking the boys, "How do you like your big sister?"

They talked about wanting to come often and I encouraged their plans. One afternoon during their stay we spent hours at target practice. Jacques brought out his hunting guns and all three of them practiced shooting apples. Jacques and his older son, Philippe, amazed me with their skill, Jacques explaining that this practice would prepare Philippe to join the hunts soon. They taught me how to shoot and I was scared to death each time the gun exploded. Hundreds of apples were demolished in a few hours.

The boys felt so welcome at Ginal that they asked to come again for a day during the week. This time Jacques urged me to stay nude at the pool during their visit. I thought the idea was preposterous. But Jacques explained, "My sons are so used to nudity at poolside, they found it strange that you chose to wear a bathing suit when they were here the last time. They found you unnatural. They would be much more at ease with you if you were nude."

"Jacques, I would be mortified. I'm trying to build a relationship of mutual respect. Our being nude and natural with each other is one thing. But for me to be nude in front of your sons, that is just too much."

"You are in Belgium now. We are not in America with its rigid attitudes. What do you think—my children have grown up with natural ideas; they've seen plenty of nude bodies and it is no big thing to them. Not only did their mother go nude in front of them all the years but also they've seen many of my friends nude at our weekend parties. They really have been brought up with the idea that the body is not a thing to hide. Please, Sheri. Be more open and live in the way we do in Belgium. You'll see that in a few years you'll laugh at the attitudes you had when you first came here."

"In a few years!" The words echoed in my head. I was stunned that he was now thinking in terms of years with me!

"I understand life is different here, Jacques, but I'll have to adjust at my own pace," I answered, hoping that my answer implied that we still had a future.

That week the boys arrived on a very hot and sunny morning. We spent several hours swimming and playing water games. Jacques remained nude. After lunch, he again strongly insisted that I start being natural in front of the boys and sunbathe nude. I resisted. The older boy, Philippe, left suddenly for Brussels after a phone call from his new girl-friend, asking him to join her. Alain remained and was due to spend the day and evening with us alone.

I decided to yield to Jacques's urging and not chance a potential reversal of his good mood. I came out of the pool house without my bathing suit and lay down next to him in the sun. He was happily surprised, yet amused that I walked out so self-consciously, diving for the mat to lie on my stomach.

Alain stole several long looks at my body, as if to really size up his father's new wife, and then seemed unaffected.

Soon we were diving and swimming together like schoolmates. Alain didn't remove his bathing suit because, as his father had explained earlier, he had recently arrived at the age where he could no longer control his masculine equipment.

I felt reasonably comfortable being nude in front of Alain but I realized it was because he was still a child. I decided I would not go nude in front of the older boy, who was already a young man. I told Jacques that I would not repeat this display in front of both boys and this time he laughed with an intolerant ring. "You'll be surprised what you'll be capable of doing as time goes on, *ma chérie*."

His statement set off another anxiety attack in me and sparked a remembrance of the horrible episodes I had tried so hard to repress. The clock was ticking, I realized sadly. It was only a matter of time before another mood swing would follow as sure as summer follows spring.

One of the important society events of the August season was an evening at Aunt Hélène's family castle, where a Theater of Manners play was staged in the courtyard. It was a white-tie occasion, and Belgium's top society attended. Not "all of Belgium," but only the A list of "all of Belgium."

The castle was one of the most historic in the country, pictured in many books on Belgium's ancient castles. It was among the best-preserved fortified castles in Europe, with a working drawbridge and an impressive entrance flanked by two voluminous towers with turrets. The castle's walls were very high, with perhaps ten towers soaring higher and it stood like an impenetrable fortress. All the rooms looked out onto a huge stone courtyard. The play was staged in the courtyard on a warm, starry night, with about two hundred people in attendance.

After the colorful play, champagne was served in one of the reception halls. Then Hélène took me on a tour of the castle. It was splendid. She introduced me to her nephew, the Marquis de Paternos, who lived alone in this enormous fortress, with only a small staff of servants. He was extremely handsome, charming, and bright. He gave me a brief explanation of the castle's history and spoke about some of the art pieces he treasured.

"You would just love the parties he throws here, *ma chérie*. But it will take years until your inhibitions are dissolved enough to attend one of them. They're unforgettably naughty."

That spectacular evening, when I was introduced to the greater *Who's Who*, gave me my first real taste of the almost unbelievable storybook glamour of these society evenings.

The younger generation of noblettes were also out in force, and I watched their furious circulation and the staged introductions by one family to another. Jacques had told me that everyone was expected to choose a partner from right within the circle. I sensed how convenient and cozy the process was, although I also realized that all this intermarriage among those in the magic circle didn't refresh the pool of genes.

Michelle, one of Jacques's cousins who lived in America, called me one day, to give me regards and love from my mother. She had gotten Mother's telephone number from her mother, who was very close to Baroness Adriane. Michelle told me that she'd liked my mother very much and that in fact she had spent long evenings talking with her. They had developed a real friendship. Their conversations had lasted so late into the night that she had slept over several times. She had never met Jacques because her family was always on diplomatic missions in several countries. She had gone to boarding schools in Switzerland and England and had rarely been with her Belgian family. She had been married and lived in America for three years but was presently separated from her husband. She worked in a New York museum doing restoration of art objects, mostly antiques.

We met for lunch and hit it off instantly. Michelle was a statuesque beauty with silky long black hair. She opened my eyes to many things.

"You know, Sheri, my mother married into the nobility and it took long hard years for people to accept her," she said, seeming to sense my unhappiness. "The aristocracy is really closed-minded and slow to let anyone enter their circle. My mother suffered a lot. She was from a Belgian society family but not the nobility. I can just imagine the resistance to accepting you because you are an American, and Jewish!" She laughed.

"Nothing can change in the nobility," she said. "They never change attitudes. Your husband must have loved you very much to marry you. Eventually you probably will be accepted but it will take time. When you have proven to the immediate family that you are living according to their rules and molding yourself into their ways, then they will accept you. Soon after, the word will get around in the active gossip grapevine that you are acceptable and then the warming-up process will slowly start. But aren't you bored with all these antiquated customs? Have you learned how to seat and serve people according to their titles? How can you, an American, adjust to all these silly rules of etiquette that all of our circle take so seriously?"

"Why, I dress for dinner every night, and most of our dinners are formal."

"What?" She laughed. "I'd never do that. A lot of the younger couples have abandoned this formality, but perhaps since Jacques is forty he just missed the loosening of style."

"Just my luck," I moaned, happy to be able to talk with this new friend, happy to be able to be myself.

Then she told me about herself. She said that she had had a real society wedding and married a playboy. They were both very young and they went to America, where her husband planned to study business. For two years she and her husband lived in complete luxury; he never went to school, and they only played and traveled. After two years they had used up her whole dowry, and they split up. Only then did she realize how childish and irresponsible they had been, and she started studying toward a profession in New York.

"But must all girls bring a dowry when they marry?"

"Yes, of course!" she said emphatically. "Every girl must bring a dowry. Didn't you? I've heard that in America many classes do not follow this custom. American women think that they should be fully taken care of and that the husband should pay for everything. These women squeeze their husbands like a lemon until they die young and they are left rich widows."

When I heard this all too familiar lemon story coming from modern Michelle, I had to laugh inside. This phrase must be memorized by "all of Belgium."

So, in moderate defense of Americans, I said that I believed Belgians had an exaggerated concept of American women's intentions and that customs were different. I told her that I had not brought a dowry but that I planned to work and eventually contribute toward a vacation home.

She was stunned that I had not brought a dowry at the outset of the marriage. Then she turned to giving me advice on how to make the marriage work and said, "Have an accident. They will fully accept you once you have children.

Then they know you are here to stay. You know, my mother was accepted by the time she had her fourth child. She liked the feeling of acceptance so much that she went on to have five more."

She leaned closer. "I must ask you one thing that I've been curious about, Sheri. I've heard from some of our numerous cousins that during his first marriage, Jacques was famous for nude parties at your pool. I heard that those parties were swinging parties . . . you know, sex parties. Has Jacques told you about them? Have *you* had any?"

Not wanting to get into a discussion about sex at Ginal or at Loiroi, I just responded that I hadn't experienced anything of the sort as yet.

We parted, feeling close to each other. She gave me the address of another female cousin of our age and said the cousin could introduce me to a young crowd in Brussels. I really looked forward to developing my own friendships with women so that I wouldn't feel so isolated, I told her. And she agreed.

As the nudist days full of photo sessions, outdoor sex, and play continued, Jacques and I returned to a more natural rapport. I went with him occasionally to the office for the few hours a day he could bear working and handled correspondence in English, mostly to Britain. In August, after Belgium's July vacation, full business activity resumes; but Jacques chose to declare that the vacation would last for at least another month or as long as the sunny weather lasted —beautiful, hot, dry weather being a rarity bordering on miraculous for the Belgians. He suggested that in the fall I might work on any business transactions that required English. I hoped that there would be increased business with English-speaking countries, so that I could work with him regularly and perhaps further normalize our relationship.

I dared hope that his strange second self was gone forever and that I really would have a life with him. Still, I questioned myself on how I could forgive him all his terrifying episodes and wondered what in me clung desperately to the hope of a life with him.

The glamour of our life returned to its seductive high. Almost daily Jacques presented me with gifts of more family jewels to wear to important social functions. We spent a weekend in Deauville on the coast of Normandy; we gambled at the exclusive casino in nearby Trouville, with its private dining club, and danced into the night at Regine's. Once again I was feeling the glow of being the spoiled baroness married to the dashingly handsome baron.

I was not naive enough to really trust that he'd never revert to his other self. Would our recent closeness truly make Jacques forget the fact that he'd been excluded from the top hunting weekend in France? And would I still suffer his reaction later? The choices were never as simple as that. I was living a full-fledged psychodrama, and I didn't dare to project beyond tomorrow.

Chapter 15

$\mathcal{I}$t all started so innocently. Jacques and I were invited for dinner to see the just completed renovation of Gérard and Hélène's new home, and arrived there in the late afternoon in time to walk around their expansive property before dark. Their new house was one of the ancient farmhouses in the village of Hélène's family castle. It used to be occupied by the head overseer of the family estates. The whole village was owned by Hélène's father and his ancestors, and all the people of the village worked for the estate. Before Hélène's father died he sold most of the village houses to the farmers and estate workers for a very low price. He retained the castle and the largest houses for himself and his family. Hélène was still beloved by every villager, although she no longer actively advised or helped them.

Gérard and Hélène had converted the large, ancient farmhouse into a comfortable, luxurious dwelling. They meticulously retained the original architectural features, taking great pains to restore rather than rebuild, and the outcome was a work of art.

The interior design was a sight to behold. They had taken many of the treasures from their castle: paintings, rugs, their clock collection, and some of their smaller pieces of furniture.

As they opened the floor-to-ceiling doors from the living room, which was at the back of the house, a pastoral scene stretched out before us. Their land extended as far as the eye could see. Cows, horses, and sheep grazed on the gently rolling meadows. Farm sounds—cackling hens, crowing roosters, quacking ducks, and whinnying horses—filled the air. This was Belgium's most beautiful farm region.

We had drinks on the terrace overlooking this scene and watched the sunset and the animals being herded toward their barns by farm workers.

Dinner at their home was always a very special occasion. Hélène was one of the best-known hostesses and finest cooks in the Belgian nobility. She always made her own sauces and never trusted anyone with the intricate preparations. The results were spectacular, and she promised me that soon she would start teaching me some of her secrets.

Even though their new home was inspiringly beautiful, they told us they were sad to have left their castle. They had made the decision to leave because for a couple getting on in years it was too damp and cold. Much of the dinner conversation consisted of reminiscences of their long life at the castle.

I felt natural with them; they were the warmest people I had met in Belgium. Hélène was especially sparkling and spry; she had returned recently from a cure in Italy, where she spent a few weeks every year. She talked about meeting all her friends from other European countries at the spa.

To celebrate our first dinner together at their new house,

Gérard chose particularly fine wines to go with each course, which made Jacques ecstatic.

I had brought along a *Town and Country* magazine that Mother had sent which contained an article on the historic castles of Belgium. They were delighted to find both their family castles photographed and described in detail, as well as many of their friends' castles.

After dinner Hélène asked Jacques to help her with her stereo system hookup, and Gérard and I were left alone to talk.

"Now tell me the truth. How is my favorite American baroness?" Gérard said tenderly.

I responded to his warmth. "Gérard, I must tell you in confidence that all hasn't been easy. I'm sure you've heard from Isabelle how many people have excluded us from social events that Jacques finds very important to him, and he hasn't taken these snubs easily. He's very moody."

"Yes, yes, my dear. Jacques, I know, has always been a difficult man. But I'm sure you are bright enough to handle him. You're a remarkable girl."

"Thank you for your confidence in me, Gérard, but I must admit to you that at times I question if I can handle his extreme moods. He blames me for cutting him off from his circle. Please never mention to him we've talked about this."

"Of course! You have kept my little secrets very discreetly. Let me give you some advice. I remember Jacques was very happy with Claudine for a long period while they were bringing up the boys. I trust you know what I am going to suggest?" he said with a gleam in his eyes.

"No, Gérard," I said, even though I did. Funny that Michelle had brought it up only days ago.

"Dear girl, why not have a child with him? Start a bond, a family! He'll then be as gentle as that Great Dane which he loved. Do this soon and I am sure you'll be much happier. Everyone in the family would love it. We haven't had babies around us for some time."

Hélène retired to bed while Jacques, Gérard, and I spent more hours talking. We shared an emotional parting, Jacques saying to Gérard, "You've always been like a father to me."

And Gérard responded, "I love your sweet American wife. We'll all share the best evenings together for years! The years Hélène and I have left."

When Jacques made love to me that night, he was especially tender. I took the moment of closeness afterward as the right time, and mustered my courage to venture the question:

"Jacques, I have a great feeling that I will be very happy with you. Gérard told me he has heard that many of the people in the family and friends in the circle like me very much. I feel we are over the worst hurdles. And with the boys coming regularly . . . Things seem to be going well. I am also calmer and now enjoying my new life."

"Well, good! The boys do like you a lot. They've found a sister. Even Claudine is behaving slightly better."

"Yes . . . but I was thinking. Maybe now is the time for us to have a baby. Our own! Wouldn't it be lovely to have a little girl? A real sister for your boys?"

"No! Definitely not!" he answered vehemently. "I have my boys. I don't want any more children."

"But Jacques, not if you don't want to right now, but you did promise you'd have one child with me."

"Go to sleep. I won't discuss it. It's out of the question."

The next morning he awakened in a silent mood, didn't say a word as we ate our breakfast in bed, and then left for his office. I went in later. We didn't consult on the all-important lunch plan for the day.

Jacques didn't arrive home that night until eleven and

offered no explanation. He went straight to the bottle of cognac and took out several Temesta pills, which he swallowed with a gulp of cognac. Once again he looked angry, and I dared not speak with him. He flipped through *Paris Match* while I read the *Herald Tribune*. Soon I went up to bed. As I left the living room I saw him take another pill with a swig of cognac.

Some time during the night I heard him get up and go downstairs. After what seemed like hours I awakened, and when I saw he was not in bed I went down to the living room, where I found him sitting, dazed, his skin pale, with a glass of liquor in hand, smoking a Havana cigar. The photos of me were again turned around, with just the white backs exposed in their frames. I cringed when I saw the empty bottle of liquor on the bar with the open bottle of Temesta pills and the overflowing ashtray. These were like a leitmotif in my tragic opera. I sat down across from him.

"I'm sorry I upset you. We'll just forget the idea of a child for a long while. I just thought it might bring us closer."

But my words didn't soothe him.

"I will never have a child with you. Never!" he said, his eyes narrow with anger, his voice hollow. "You deceived me and I am not bound to keep any of my promises to you. I am not your husband."

He got up and slowly walked out into the garden. I was too stunned to follow him. My wish for a child had brought out his second self. He came back holding garden shears. He looked at me, held up the shears, and snipped off his gold wedding ring. He picked up the severed ring from the carpet and tossed it at me. "Take this to your mother when you go back to the United States for good. I am no longer your husband." And he walked out of the house, back toward the pool house.

I left the ring on the mantel just under the crown with

the eight balls and went back to bed. After I had slept for what seemed a long while, he awakened me. "I'll always love you and I will never find anyone like you, but I know you want to destroy me," he whispered into my ear. Then he kissed me passionately all over the face and then the breasts, and then below. He kissed me with frighteningly intense emotion. He penetrated me, thrusting in deeply, trying to push in farther and farther, moving with increasing desire and passion until he grasped me in a tight embrace and held me, breathing deeply.

I couldn't understand how he could express such cruel thoughts and violently cut off his own wedding band and still want to take me with such fervor. The French writer Marguerite Duras, whom I had read in college, wrote of *l'amour fou*, or crazed love. She described violent eroticism, destroying one's lover as part of the sexual excitement. Apparently this violent passion was something known among Europeans, if not of French origin. I wondered whether Jacques deliberately created these violent altercations to raise the emotional fever in me and in himself. He seemed to push scenes to their extremity until everything whirled out of control and raw emotions surfaced. I wondered also whether this was another raging obsession of Jacques's—to destroy me, his love object. Or perhaps he wanted me to destroy him with my love.

"Get up. I have something to say," he said in a biting voice. "I've thought about your new idea. Do you want to know what I've thought?"

"Yes, of course."

"All right then. I know you. And I know you will be ready to deceive me again. You have it in mind to get pregnant. Now let me tell you"—he took a long gulp from his cognac glass—"if you get pregnant . . ." I turned away. "Now listen to me! *If you get pregnant* I will throw you down the stairs and you'll abort the baby. So don't dare try to deceive me again! And I am taking you to the gynecologist soon to be sure you haven't already taken out your IUD."

"Jacques, you don't realize what you're saying. I will not hear any more tonight."

"You'll listen to me! I have more to tell you. A woman is not a woman until she has a child! And you! You'll never be a real woman because I'll *never* have a child with you!"

"Stop! Stop! Stop!" I gasped, and put the pillow over my ears.

And he repeated the words: "You'll never be a real woman," and I could hear them even with the pillow covering my ears.

The next morning I couldn't go to the office. Jacques's threat to throw me down the stairs shook me to the core of my being. I *was* in danger living with this man. I called him at the office to tell him I was leaving for Paris for a few days, that while I was away I would decide whether I wanted to continue the marriage. Before I had finished packing, he arrived and burst into the room.

"You will go nowhere! I will not allow it! I have taken your passport, your license and identity card. You will not be able to travel without my permission and company. You realize you must pass the border patrol, customs, and when you drive to Paris without your passport or any ID you will be arrested, my sweet. So unpack. I am going back to the office and I think I'll take your car keys along with me. Until you calm down. À *bientôt*."

This is the end, I thought. I will not be a prisoner. I called Mamie to announce I was leaving for America. I told her what had happened and begged her to get my passport back from Jacques.

"I'll talk with him," Mamie said. "Just don't make any rash decisions. You upset him. He can't deal with having a baby with you. I'll come over tonight and calm you both down. Remember, you promised me you considered this marriage forever. You must give it a chance. Learn to understand him!"

"I'm afraid of him. Afraid!" I said.

"Nonsense! He'll never hurt you. He just tries to frighten you, control you. That's his weakness."

"I know he can be violent!"

"I told you many times he is not violent, he is only self-destructive."

"How can I stay if I am so afraid of him? He dismisses Roland and Marie-Louise and I am alone with him. Then he gets so out of control. You have taken no responsibility for me. You haven't helped me at all. I feel so alone and unprotected."

"I'll tell you what I'll do for you. I will arrange that you will have your own servant. I will personally pay for it. He will be there all the time and listen to only your instructions. Yes, I'll do that. At the same time, he'll do some long-needed repairs on the house."

"Well, I don't know what to say," I said cautiously, feeling relieved that now she had finally become an ally. "You say he's not violent, yet you are providing me with a bodyguard."

"Nonsense! I'm just doing this to reduce your fears. Unfounded fears, to be sure. I'll be there at your house tonight to discuss this further. Do not say a word to Jacques about this. See you around seven o'clock."

"Yes. Please come tonight. I will not sleep here alone with Jacques until this calms down. I am afraid of his sexual games when he is like this."

"Please! That's enough! It's your business. I don't want to be told. You may sleep at my home tonight unless Jacques decides he will leave himself."

I was at the bedroom window watching for Baroness Adriane, and was relieved as I saw her speed up the long drive in her powerful BMW and come to a screeching stop.

Jacques had come home but had not spoken to me. When Roland served us aperitifs, Adriane behaved at first as if she were there on a pleasant social visit. She chatted on and on about certain three-star restaurants she had visited the past summer—Alain Chapel in France, Girardet in Cressier, Switzerland—and also about her trip to the same spa in Italy that Hélène had mentioned. Jacques asked her to describe every course and the wines served with the meals she had chosen. Then she spoke about the hot-air ballooning events throughout Belgium; her friends owned and operated huge, colorful balloons. She said she planned to take me to balloon galas. My anxiety level was so high that had she gone on for another ten minutes I might have exploded.

But at dinner she demanded concessions from both Jacques and me. I was to get my male servant and certainly have no baby for the present. Jacques would behave, she threatened, or she would rearrange some financial instruments that would be very unfavorable to him. I learned that evening that she held all the family money under her complete control. There were bank accounts in Switzerland and Luxembourg, and Jacques could not touch the accounts without her signature.

The male servant, Pierre, arrived as promised just a few days later. He knew he was there to act as a bodyguard. Mamie had a bell installed in the bedroom which rang in his quarters. As the workman installed the bell system, I thought: Am I going crazy? I am surely sinking to a new low. Throughout most of August Jacques had been so calm and our lives so pleasant that I had fantasized that bad times were really over. But here it was happening again. In my vulnerable state of mind, Mamie's gesture to help me seemed like a monumental breakthrough. And with her help I had to believe a new dawn could break.

Jacques's drinking and pill-taking went on nightly. I found out more about Temesta from the pharmacist. A powerful tranquilizer naturally should not be mixed with alcohol, he said. The combination kept Jacques in a strange, almost incoherent state. And my lonely existence kept me in very low and confused spirits. I had plummeted back into a well of despair.

Mother called often and wanted very much to visit. She wondered why Jacques had postponed several of her suggested visits, but I never told her how desperate the situation had become. I knew that if I had, she would have been on the next Sabena flight to bring me home. But I still did not want to give up; I held on to the irrational desire to salvage the marriage. Finally, Jacques agreed to let her visit the next month. He thought it would still avoid the worst of the Belgian rainy season. I wondered whether I could last another month.

But a lingering premonition possessed me. Had I made a great mistake in not leaving the day Mamie came to calm the situation? "You had a chance to leave," a voice inside me kept repeating. "You should have left."

Amid all this turmoil, Jacques planned a large party for the start of the fall season. By now I knew that nothing could stop the nobles' pleasure-seeking. The annual party took precedence over everything. And from the meticulous preparation of the guest list and his elation as he anticipated the event, there was little doubt in my mind that this would be another sexual soiree. I hated the idea of planning this party, but I was too terrified not to.

I had to send out all the invitations in the de rigueur formula:

Baron and Baroness de Borchgrave request
that Count and Countess de Vimont join them
for the opening party of the social season at Ginal.
Their presence is requested for 9:00.
Dinner, dancing and merriment.

Pierre, Marie-Louise, and Roland had been kept busy for weeks buying the food, wines, and flowers, and making the arrangements.

The guests arrived, fifty strong. Our driveway looked like a BMW dealership. Just as there was a custom or code dictating all behavior, owning a BMW was one of the codes of the noblettes. A practical, understated car, but with a reliable, powerful engine. Never a showy car like a Mercedes or a Jaguar.

There was the formal cool exchange of handshakes. A glass of Taittinger Rosé champagne was then placed in each hand, and was refilled moments after it was emptied. Men were in black tie, some in tails; women in spectacular *dernier cri* outfits, many with bare shoulders or daring décolleté, and all with dazzling gems. The family jewels certainly were brought out to launch the new season.

I too wore a spectacularly radiant necklace, a sapphire and diamond six-tier display which Jacques had taken out of the bedroom safe for the occasion. He had also insisted I wear a very racy bejeweled string panty with matching lacy garter, which certainly confirmed my suspicion as to the forthcoming activities. I had warned him while dressing that I was not going to participate in his orgiastic ritual, but he had only snickered derisively. I felt the emotional toll of our distant relationship and was not up to playing the role of scintillating hostess-seductress.

Foie gras on toast squares and black caviar on eggs with

a dash of sour cream were served with the champagne. Dinner, on a *fruits de mer* theme, consisted of bouillabaisse, *moules* (steamers in a spicy cream sauce), octopus, and lobster, along with other sea creatures and colorful salads. The dessert table tempted the weak with all the fruit tarts, sorbets, mousses, chocolate creations, and *crème fraîche* that the Belgians are so famous for.

I was introduced to many guests for the first time, and I felt the cold currents in the air. Many, I'm sure, were friends of Claudine who scrutinized me closely. And though they naturally avoided direct personal questions, their comments were obviously meant to bring forth personal answers from me. Some discussed President Carter and wondered whether he would enact a law that the whole country jog before work. They ridiculed the Americans' jogging and other athletic obsessions, as well as our foolish choices for the presidency. All seemed to canonize ex-President Nixon, stating that he was the greatest American leader of modern times.

When certain people discussed the failed rescue of the hostages from Iran and surprisingly compared it to the "heroic" Israeli rescue in Entebbe, I conveniently slipped out of the room to check the supply of champagne. I didn't want to be the spokesperson for two nations against inevitable currents of anti-Americanism and anti-Semitism. Though I had certain friends in the room, I was struck with the feeling that I did not belong in this group.

When I returned, the group fortunately had veered away from politics and started on the predictable topics of travel and leisure, specifically where everyone would hunt and ski this fall and winter. The consensus for skiing was Courcheval, France, the jet-set winter resort for the young —the St. Tropez of winter. Paul of Chez Paul, the restaurant that was a part of the St. Tropez beach club Voile Rouge, would be opening a restaurant and club in Courcheval this winter, and everyone wanted to be there. Fortunately Jacques, who had been totally absorbed in conversation with a new female interest, rejoined the conversation after the discussion of fall hunting weekends in France, but in time to hear the ski talk and commit to going with the group to the French Alps.

After dinner Jacques asked everyone to go into the disco to dance, and he took his place in the control booth and started his mix. As I began to dance, feeling happy to let loose and have some fun after the recent tense times, I looked over again at the booth and saw Jacques's hand sliding down the deep cleavage of a tall and beautiful female guest. It was at that point that I decided to get drunk. I rarely used such a defense mechanism, but that night I'd face the evening in a haze, coasting along with the action fueled by champagne.

The dancing became wild and sensual. Ironically, as a cooling-off interlude, Jacques screened pornographic films against one wall. The first was a type of *Emanuelle* story. The short film showed mainly heavy lesbian sex, with many beautiful women engaging in the most outrageous acts. A small zoo of animals was a part of the action. My mind drifted back to the time when Jacques had taken me to the sex theater in Paris and had feigned such disgust at witnessing "perverted sexual acts." I remembered how he had insisted we leave immediately; he had not wanted me exposed to such things. I now wondered what had possessed Jacques to go to such great lengths to hide his real nature from me.

The next film was a European version of *Deep Throat* and seemed to be a distinct crowd-pleaser among this group. Europeans seemed far more obsessed with foreplay and stimulation techniques than Americans. As the film ended, to great applause and feigned rapturous moaning, I surmised that the spectator events were over and the participatory events would shortly begin. I was wrong. The disco dancing continued for another hour, and the champagne corks popped along with the grinding American hard-rock beat.

Then, as in a precise script, just after Donna Summers singing "The Last Dance" was fading out, Jacques cut the lights and music and they all followed him out of the disco. About a third of the group went back into the main house and the rest moved toward the south wing.

Strangely, I hadn't revisited that wing since my very first tour of the estate, and I was surprised to find it changed. Apparently the servants had been instructed to prepare the bedrooms for the party. There were exquisite flower arrangements placed on chests and mantels, and many paintings had been hung along the hall. The guests seemed to know their way. They separated into little groups and entered the various bedrooms. Roland and Marie-Louise were right behind, bringing up bottles of cooled champagne. I glared at Marie-Louise and she smiled at me impudently. Apparently they had instructed Pierre to remain downstairs and attend to the guests there.

Jacques and five other men led me and three women guests into one of the larger bedrooms, which had a fireplace and a huge bed with a white fur spread. There were flowers on the tables and bowls of chocolates. Jacques, with the help of one of the men, arranged the logs and lit the fire, while another man chose records and put them on the small stereo set in the room. His first selection was an album of slow love ballads sung by the French Moroccan Enrico Matheus. Jacques then called Roland in to refill all the champagne glasses and asked him to leave a few extra bottles in the room.

I looked around and noticed that the women already were removing their gowns, with the chivalrous assistance of a few men. The sounds of zippers opening, taffeta rustling, and shoes dropping to the floor reminded me of the back-stage scramble at my college plays. Jacques, in characteristic style, took charge.

"Please, Yvonne, Jeanne, Véronique, and Sheri—get on the bed. We want to watch you make love to each other." He turned to his five male friends and said gallantly, "What beautiful girls!"

Still fully clothed, I called Jacques over to a corner and whispered, "I am not going to participate!"

"You will do as I say. If you disobey me . . . embarrass me . . . I will be extremely angry. Remember that. Just play along. You will enjoy it!" He kissed me aggressively and began to take off my gown. "Keep on the string for now. I want Véronique to take it off you. Later!"

The three girls were already on the bed, nude or semi-nude. All three had kept on their sparkling necklaces and bracelets and Jeanne her gold lace bra and bikini panties. The push-up bra flattered her voluptuous breasts. As I ap-proached the bed, Véronique opened her arms to me and pulled me on top of her in an embrace.

"Bravo! *Allez, allez!*" said Jacques. "Véronique, you have a virgin—with women, anyway. Her first time! We're count-ing on you to show her the tender pleasures that you know so well how to administer."

"Jacques, you flatter me. But I'll share her with my friends," Véronique said. She spoke French with a pure Pa-risian accent.

I looked straight into Jacques's intense green eyes and scowled at him. He laughed and said, "My *chérie*, Sheri, be happy. You are in noble company. Véronique is a countess; Jeanne and Yvonne both married men who, upon their fa-thers' deaths, will become barons, and they will become baronesses."

It infuriated me that Jacques put out that same line again, as if to say, "You love the titles, now have some more. It is all right if we keep to our little noble circle. But *never* the common class." He once said, "Sex is too good for them."

As Véronique kissed me passionately on the lips and I felt her body, so soft and different from the male, against mine, I decided not to fight it. I hadn't the will to fight it. I just hoped that the sex wouldn't become too distasteful or go beyond the limits of my already distant line of demarcation.

Véronique was really beautiful. She smelled delicious. I could see she was a natural blond, though her hair had had a little help to achieve its white-blond shade. She was about my height, with a thin, curvy body. Breasts, yes, probably helped a bit as well, but they felt natural. When she removed my string panty and began touching me below, the men drew in for a closer view.

The other two girls soon turned their attention to Véronique and me. I remained passive, praying for it to be over. I could see Véronique was into it for herself, apparently liking sex with girls, while Jeanne and Yvonne were aware of performing for the benefit of the men. They played the aggressors with Véronique and me and tried to satisfy us in many unusual ways.

The men watched silently, transfixed, only moving to bring their champagne glasses up to their lips.

Christian, a friend I knew from past events, broke the spell when he picked up a champagne bottle and sprinkled champagne over the four of us. I could see now that that gesture certainly wasn't unique to Jacques. Then, without being instructed, the three women eagerly licked the champagne off each other's bodies, giggling and rolling around playfully on the bed. Yvonne and Jeanne were both dark-

haired and very tall. Yvonne was so thin that I felt Rubens-
esque lying next to her. She was the kisser of the group, wet
and passionate.

At a certain point, as if on cue, the men all had had
enough of watching and joined the action. Jeanne insisted
she be allowed to undress all the men. She did it so
gracefully—one by one. I had never seen six men being
undressed by an expert disrober. It was as if she were very
carefully unwrapping huge presents marked FRAGILE. They
all stood at attention, as if for their mamas' approval.

Two men, Christian and a new acquaintance named
Yves, lifted me off the bed and held me between them in a
tight embrace. Suddenly, I was angry at myself for being so
passive. Did I really want to have sex with these two relative
strangers? I froze and abruptly collapsed on the carpet, then
rushed out of the room. Roland and Marie-Louise were right
outside in the hallway peering into an adjoining room. They
looked at me, startled.

"*Madame la Baronne*, is she all right?" Marie-Louise
asked.

I didn't answer. I asked Roland to zip up my gown, which
I had snatched up as I ran from the bedroom. As I walked
along the corridor I glanced into a few rooms and saw that
in each the guests were involved in the same furious action.
Fortunately, Jacques did not follow me.

I went back into the living room, thinking I'd join a mild
gathering in conversation. But there, in front of the blazing
fireplace and on couches and chairs, was the rest of the
group, just as intense in their creative postures, both voyeurs
and actors. As I took another long look around, I thought:
All the sex is playful, not sadomasochistic or violent in any
way. Not like what I experienced with Jacques. Over in one
corner, I noticed the only couple present having a gay male

encounter. They naturally were the best-looking men at the party.

Pierre came toward me to pour champagne and asked if I was all right. I told him I had had too much to drink and felt unsteady. I asked that he be alert in case I needed him after the guests left. He offered to take me to the master bedroom and said he would check to see whether it was occupied. I told him I could manage myself.

Several men tried to pull me back into the continuous action, followed later by a series of women, who even more aggressively urged me to join them. I sat alone for a while just watching scene after scene until the rhythms put me to sleep.

When I awakened, hours later, only a few people remained sleeping on the carpet in front of the still smoldering fire. I was curious to see what had evolved in the south wing. The sun had come up and the house was absolutely silent. I tiptoed up the stairs and down the long corridor. I looked into each of the six rooms. In each were curled little groups of embracing nude bodies. Naturally Jacques had two women on either side. All the sleepers' faces looked like those of innocent angels. Clothes were strewn all over. Tipped-over champagne flutes. Bottles floating in watery coolers. Empty chocolate dishes with a few bitten bonbons. Only the beautiful fresh flower arrangements—birds of paradise, orchids, yellow roses, and lilies—were still neatly in place, upright, standing glorious guard.

Before the guests left they were served coffee and croissants. One by one the BMWs pulled out of Ginal. I felt an overwhelming relief that it was over—but also a frightful sense of shame at my complicity and weakness.

Chapter 16

*M*y spirits remained at a nagging low after the party. I couldn't shake my fear of Jacques's volatile moods; the possibility that his violent nature would erupt at any one of my mistakes kept me on edge. I knew he was not over the "breast operation deception" and was still plotting the right time to punish me, even playing complex mind games with me to enforce his deviant control. Sometimes he'd suggest a long future with me, and other times he'd hint that I was still on indefinite trial. He alternately viewed me as either the extraordinary wife capable of bringing him untold happiness and fulfillment, or the devil who was out to destroy him. I realized that, although many couples had elements of the love/hate cycle in their relationships, there was a marked difference here. And I felt an overpowering malaise—a lack of will to do anything. Within Jacques's noble little circle the precedent, throughout the centuries, was to play out these passions with a complete lack of restraint. And Jacques's predilection for staging a lesson with the exaggerated gesture was more developed even than that of Isabelle.

There were times when I truly believed that Jacques had married me as part of a grand scheme to torment and vanquish Claudine, even telling me that Claudine was driven crazy by the idea that an American now held her previous title and had the right to live in the family castle until death.

The ancient code of honor that Jacques lived by was unfathomable to me, and I suspected that I could again make an error there, bringing frightening consequences down upon me.

The Belgian rain began again and was constant for days and nights. I started taking on a North Sea personality—gearing all my activities to staying inside, shopping in the indoor arcades, always sitting close to the fireplace while reading or writing in my journal, feeling more and more like a figure in a painted interior by Jan van Eyck.

One rainy night while we were lying in bed, Jacques said that he wished to share something that had been occupying his thoughts and on which he needed my advice. He held me tenderly in his arms and hesitated for several minutes. "Where do I begin? Ever since my boys were very young I suspected that Claudine had plans to teach them how to perform sexually when they were old enough."

I gasped as Jacques continued, not knowing what to say.

"I've noticed a change in Alain. He looks at me as though he's proud to be my equal, or that he has a secret over me. Lately he has been very protective of Claudine. I've noticed other changes in him too subtle for me to explain. I hate her for it!"

This had to be another case of Jacques's paranoia. I

dared not comment. The subject was too explosive. I only listened sympathetically.

One early morning the next week, Jacques called Claudine and Alain passed the phone to her. When Jacques hung up the phone, he sprang out of bed and furiously paced the room.

"I really suspect something is going on! She's doing this to hurt me for marrying you!"

Again I remained quiet. I was too afraid of saying the wrong thing about his conflicts with Claudine or concerns for his sons, afraid of his way of believing his own fantasies and blowing them way out of proportion.

Of course the thought crossed my mind that Jacques found it entirely acceptable to sleep with his own sister. I suppose a mother's sexually initiating her teenage son, even in this society, was considered taboo. I still struggled to figure out these codes.

"I know," said Jacques with a flash of inspiration. "Oh, yes! It's perfect!"

"What? Tell me."

"You teach Philippe! Yes! Don't you see—in this way we'll have Philippe under our wing." He laughed triumphantly. "She'll have a big surprise. It's the perfect way to trump Claudine. Yes!"

"Jacques, there is another way. A better way," I said, stunned that he could actually entertain such an insane idea.

"What do you mean?" he responded with a raised eyebrow.

"Take Philippe to a prostitute immediately."

"A prostitute? Certainly not. It must be *you*!"

"I could never do such a thing with your son—my stepson. I would be just as bad as Claudine if I did such a thing!"

"Nonsense! You're not my son's mother. So it is surely

preferable for you to teach him. You're such a sexual expert and I want him to learn in the right way from someone who knows him, cares for him, and will take special care with him. Then he'll be able to enjoy sex for the rest of his life."

"Jacques, I understand your wanting him to have a good first experience. But it can't be with me! I could never do that."

"And why? Why not?"

"Sex is such a powerful force and this plan of yours could destroy all of our relationships! It could have terrible consequences. Although it is not directly incestuous on my part, it certainly feels like an incestuous, sinful idea." I almost swallowed the last words, suddenly realizing that Jacques might take this as a criticism of his past relationship with Isabelle.

"Sinful?" he said angrily. "What is sinful about it? You are not his mother!"

"Don't you understand? It could have such an adverse effect on Philippe's mind that his *stepmother* is having sex with him. Jacques, this is outrageous! These types of sexual ideas are not healthy! Not for anyone! They are outside my conception. I can't be a part of them!"

He glared at me and shook his head.

"I really can't, Jacques! I won't be a part of destroying all our relationships! Let's not make this into a Shakespearean tragedy and compound all the wrong deeds. I—"

"We'll speak more about this tonight. I have an appointment this morning in Antwerp and I must leave now."

I prayed that Jacques would realize how outrageous his plan was. But by now I knew that he had to control everyone, and was capable of staging a major scene until he got his way. Oh, how I dreaded the evening.

When he stormed into Ginal at 7:00 P.M., I could see in his tight face the all too familiar signs of his second self.

"I can't understand you!" he said as he poured us aperitifs. "This is the only way to handle Claudine. And Philippe will benefit tremendously."

I didn't answer, just listened to him with a concerned, calm expression.

"Then I'll have the power over Philippe and she won't. We will spoil her plan to take both sons!"

"Don't you see that if you brought Philippe to a prostitute—a good one in the profession—you'd also spoil her plan? Philippe won't be under her control."

"No! It must be you. Only you!"

"I couldn't. Please understand."

"What does it matter to you?" he said with a razor sharpness. "You! You, who have slept with so many men! Why are you trying to be so modest now? Now that you can help *me*, you refuse me this most important request?"

Of course, in a way Jacques was right. What did it matter to me now? I had already rolled around on a bed with three other women. But I had not yet dissolved the guilt of that night, inebriated or not, and had been trying to let up on berating myself—I was, after all, in a circle of debauchery and decadence and had resisted going on a rampage. Although having sex with a minor, a sixteen-year-old, was against the law and against my instincts about what was right, laws and instincts were hardly deterrents from action in this environment. But my fear of Claudine's potential viciousness should I entangle myself in her and Jacques's games was certainly a reason to refuse Jacques definitively. Remembering Claudine's flight into the dark night and given her propensity for creating scenes, I could imagine her turning against me with the venomous sting of a viper.

At that moment I realized that Jacques was getting to the stage where further reasoning, or even answering him rationally, was dangerous. I told him that I'd like to drop the subject and continue after dinner. We sat down at the table and Roland served the first course, baby North Sea shrimps with cocktail sauce.

"No! I will discuss it now!" Jacques said, stabbing the tiny shrimps. "I want to know why you won't sleep with my son. After all, it would change nothing in you! It is only one more added to a long list. You know you'd really enjoy it. It would be different for you. Have you ever slept with a very young boy?"

"No," I said quietly, answering only to avoid enraging him.

"Then you must *try*! You are old enough now to find it interesting, indeed. I remember when I was Philippe's age I slept with several older women and I remember how exciting it was. And they seemed to enjoy it. Well?"

"It is not something I care to try. Anyway, he's under age. It is actually a crime." I wondered whether to speak rationally or try to appeal to Jacques through some other ridiculous scheme.

Jacques got up from the table and set a fire in the fireplace. He looked back at me as I finished my dinner to gain strength for the potentially rough night ahead, and said, his voice hollow, "You are going to regret denying me this request. I want you to think about what you are doing."

"I will never have sex with Philippe, and that's final!" Despite the eventual outcome, I knew I had to take a strong position to quash his insane plan.

Jacques didn't say another word to me all evening. He refilled his cognac glass many times and smoked one thin Cuban cigar after another while he read. He went up to bed earlier than usual on this Friday night. I followed soon after.

As I looked around the bedroom I noticed that the shotgun had been moved from its usual place on the left side atop the tall dresser to the right, and also that several of my white St. Tropez dresses were lying on my chaise. I stood in the middle of the bedroom, frozen, unable to decide whether I could sleep in the same bed with Jacques. Cautiously I got into the bed, trying not to wake him, but he felt my presence and got up instantly and left for one of the guest bedrooms. Against all odds, I fell asleep immediately.

I awakened several times during the night and could hear him walking around downstairs. I called him on the intercom and asked him what he was doing. He said he was going to sleep in the pool house. I knew the house bar had probably run out of liquor and he was going to the pool house's supply.

The next morning I cautiously walked to the pool house. It was in complete chaos, with empty liquor bottles all over. The nude sketch I had drawn of Jacques one playful afternoon, which he had framed, was smashed and torn. Jacques was stretched out on the alcove bed, disheveled. He awoke when I came in and grunted something unintelligible in French. He gulped down the coffee and pushed the croissants aside. Then he got up and walked unsteadily toward the house without saying a word. I stayed at the pool, trying to think.

An hour later Jacques came out, shaved and in fresh clothes. He sat down on a garden chair next to me and started his angry speech, demanding how I could dare refuse to teach his son about sex. And then he started his usual tirade on all my past sins, speaking about each one as if he had never mentioned it before.

This went on for three hours nonstop. He was torturing me. He never raised his voice, only lectured in a low and even tone, which was more terrifying than if he had shouted. He stated his arguments with increasing intensity, giving the impression that it would never stop. I couldn't take it anymore and tried throughout his tirade to leave but he demanded that I stay and listen. The several times I got up to go he grabbed my arm and pulled me down.

I started to cry, sobbing bitterly, but he continued without softening his criticism. Throughout the hours he commanded me to answer his questions. And, like a recording, I gave him the same answers that I had given him on other sessions. Only this time it was different because I had finally realized that I was not dealing with a sane person.

Just as I became desperate, not knowing how long this cruel, abusive, increasingly vicious session would last, the phone rang and he answered it and left the house without a word. I overheard from the conversation that he was being called to help with some problem in Claudine's new house.

Had it been wise to refuse him so directly? Sleeping with Philippe was unthinkable to me. Yet, knowing Jacques's potential reaction, should I have given him an ambiguous answer and later backed out? Of course then I risked having another "deception" added to my list. Finally I came to the conclusion that either way, I was at an impasse.

On the previous evening his madness and persistent demands had almost made me lose touch with reality. There was no one to call; no place to seek help in this foreign country; I felt that my choices were limited. Pierre could only stop physical violence, not mental violence. Although Jacques had never raised a hand to me, it seemed possible now that he could harm me. He was further into his second personality than I had ever seen him. His eyes were without compassion even when I cried bitterly; the sight of my tears only excited him to increased cruelty.

"You are going to regret refusing my request," Jacques said upon entering the salon when he returned in the early afternoon.

Soon I overheard him speaking with Marie-Louise and

Roland, telling them to take a week's paid vacation. He told them they could leave immediately. Then I heard him call Pierre and dismiss him.

"We will not be needing you anymore. You may leave today," he said.

"But *Monsieur le Baron*, I take my orders from *Madame la Baronne*. Does she wish that I leave?"

"Yes, Pierre. Immediately," he said.

I panicked when I heard this and rushed to the pool house telephone to call Isabelle. She didn't answer. I rushed back to speak to Pierre.

"Pierre, you must stay! I need you!"

"*Madame la Baronne*, I cannot stay if *Monsieur le Baron* will not allow me to stay on his property. He just told me so. I'm sorry. I must wait until Baroness de Borchgrave returns from Switzerland. She'll decide if I should return and tell *Monsieur le Baron* so."

"No, you must stay *until* Baroness de Borchgrave returns. You must! You were hired to protect me!"

"I'm sorry to tell you, Sheri, I will not allow Pierre to stay." Jacques burst into the kitchen. "Now come outside with me."

It was actually a hot day; real Indian summer weather had returned. Jacques demanded that we lie in the sun as we had at the height of the summer. He asked that I give him a massage with ice cubes.

As I massaged him the ice melted quickly, cooling his long body. Then he said he wanted to massage me. He was very sensuous as he slid the ice cubes all over my body. He then asked me softly to reconsider my firm refusal of his plan. I explained to him once again that sleeping with his son could only have the most calamitous effect on all of us.

My answer made him furious and his ice massage became rougher. He rubbed the ice cubes into the sensitive interior of my vagina; it was cold and very painful. I cried for him to stop but he continued and then forced me to have sex. After satisfying himself, he got up and said, "You are going to regret refusing my request." He spoke only in French, as he always did during the worst attacks.

Soon the phone rang. Jacques handed the receiver to me. It was Isabelle. Unable to speak freely, I told her I had called to discuss what I should wear to Baron de Delvigne's party. I hoped that I could convey some alarm in my voice. I asked her whether she'd like to visit to try on gowns for each other, but she replied that she had other plans.

"You called Isabelle today!" he exclaimed when I hung up the phone. "You must have called her! I warn you, never tell Isabelle anything that goes on between us! Remember that! Do you plan to tell her about Philippe?"

I tried to be convincing as I told him I had not intended to do so. "Jacques, no. Never! That is something only between us!"

He poured himself a scotch. The drinking is starting too early in the afternoon, I thought. And then to my horror he began repeating my sins.

"If you continue this, Jacques, I will leave you. I am finally ready to leave. Is that what you've wanted?"

"You won't leave, Sheri. You like this life too much. The life I gave you. The life I can take away! I watched you at Count Alec von Kraft's soiree, dangling your jewels as you flirted seductively with him. You play the role too well. You won't leave! And as long as you stay, I'll punish you for your deception! Because you are not honorable. You don't know about honor. You will never understand our code. And as long as you stay I will make you suffer for your dishonesty. It's for your benefit. You need to be punished."

This was madness! Jacques's reasoning was insanity, and as he continued with his tirade I watched the sun go down, signaling another night ahead. I broke into a cold sweat.

My fear was so intense that I felt I was breaking. I couldn't bear any more. Years of this? Impossible! This would be the last night. I must leave for America. It was over! I couldn't control the images flashing through my mind. But what would he do to me tonight? What wicked games did he have planned? Would I be beaten, or tortured in some way? He'd never gone that far. But today he looked capable of anything.

"Tonight, my sweet, you have no will of your own. If you follow my instructions you won't be hurt."

"Hurt? What are you saying, Jacques? You'd never hurt me?"

"No. A gentleman never does that. But it is time you learned more about pleasing me. You never convinced me that you were so inexperienced. You've had plenty of lovers—or should I say men who violated you? Now, drink the cognac!"

He put on some loud jazz, and, strangely, put logs in the fireplace and lit it. A fire—on such a warm night?

"Now we start. You will listen. See that crown with the eight balls over the fireplace? As I've told you, it represents the baronial title. It represents a code of honor that goes along with it. You will never learn that code. Not having the operation was a big mistake."

"Stop this. Please, not again," I said imploringly.

"You will not talk. Here, drink some more cognac." He filled the large bowl to the halfway mark. "Your deception made me lose my trust in you. You can never regain that trust. You've committed so many sins! You lie!

"Take off your dress. Keep on the string bikini and go outside. Wait for me at the pool."

"No, Jacques. I'm going to bed. You can't force me."

He picked me up and carried me outside, down the four levels of stairs to the pool. He took me into the pool house and locked the door.

Cold chills ran through me. He won't be violent with me, I tried to convince myself. It's just a game. Yes, a game. To frighten me! He wants to control me. It's instigated again by Claudine. I'll let him have his sex and tire him out. It'll be over tomorrow.

He filled his glass yet again. His behavior was becoming very strange. He repeated the same speech. I knew I'd have to stop his irrational talk before he got more worked up, but how? How could I distract him?

"I can't believe I'll miss Count Michel de Vimont's hunt," he continued the litany. "That weekend is very important. All the top noble French families are there. He keeps the finest dogs and best-trained horses. His château is one of the most magnificent in France. I've gone for the last seven years. But what could you understand about that? Americans don't understand the refined pleasures in life. That is life as it has been lived for centuries. We follow the exact customs of the hunt as the nobles have done for hundreds of years. And then we feast at night. The oldest wines. Why am I telling you this?"

"It interests me, Jacques. Go on."

"No. I want to take you now. But in a different way. Let me see . . ."

I started toward the door, trying to force it open.

"Running away again! No, this won't do. I'll have to tie you up, so I know you'll be stationary when you give me pleasure."

He took an armful of heavy rope which was lying coiled on the ground and pulled me by the arms out into the yard. Then he dragged me up the hill into the dark orchard. I was terrified and could only moan, "Stop, Jacques, please stop."

"This is a sexy place," he said in a cheerful voice. He took the heavy rope and wound it around me, placing it meticulously as he circled the tree over and over. Then he knotted it at several places.

I closed my eyes and tried to remove myself mentally from the scene, forcing myself to remember happier times. I imagined myself back in Rio, Brazil during Carnival, for college spring break. It was a crush of people, excitement all around. I let the tight ropes around me represent people joyously crowding around me and dancing with me to the intoxicating rhythm of the samba.

"Open your eyes! I want you to look at me." He took off his smoking jacket, laid it on the ground, and removed his shirt. He removed his pants and folded them neatly and placed them atop the pile. Slowly he pulled down his small G-string pants. He had an enormous erection.

Then he walked away toward the pool house.

I didn't want to imagine what he planned next or why he'd left. Had he forgotten something?

I was back in Brazil. Rio! I was on Ipanema Beach in the glaring sun, looking out at the magnificent ocean, land and mountains behind, and the statue of Christ on top of Corcovado peak protecting the city, Jacques bending over me, caressing my lips with his . . .

He returned with the bottle of cognac and our glasses and poured another half glass and lifted it to my lips, forcing me to drink. I let it drip out and down onto my body.

"Now, that's sexy," he said. And he licked the cognac from my breasts and stomach between the ropes. He ended with a sharp bite on my left nipple.

"Jacques! Stop!"

"Are you ready to tell me how many lovers you've had?"

"Ten," I said.

"Oh, ten! Well, isn't that a round number. But should I add zero and perhaps multiply that by—what?"

"Why are you so cruel? Why?"

"All right. You'll tell me one day before you leave." He poured himself more cognac. Then, looking into my eyes as they searched his face for answers, he forced himself into me.

I closed my eyes and stayed on the beach watching the group of dancers and percussion players who had spontaneously assembled to dance in the setting sun.

"You're enjoying this! We'll have to come out here more often. Unless, of course, you leave for America soon. We can watch all the fruit ripen. It is good meditation. Now, let's count out some more lovers. Where are we? We're up to what? . . . About a hundred?"

"I have forgotten all of them. There is only you. I loved you, Jacques."

"Love! Love! We don't talk about love anymore. Your love and life with me is over. It's over forever! Try to grasp that. And leave me!"

I remained silent. He was now too drunk for me to even try to bring him out of his irrational state.

I was in agony. The ropes had so little give and the bark of the tree was rough against my back.

Please let this end, I was thinking, as he fell to the ground, exhausted. He lay there, eyes open, not speaking, not moving. My husband. The man I had once loved.

Finally he got up, obviously in a daze, and untied me. Then he collapsed again.

I walked cautiously away toward the house and went up to our bedroom. The shotgun and pistols were on the vanity table, moved again from their usual spot on top of the desk. I couldn't decide whether to sleep in our bed or go into one of the guest rooms. I finally decided I'd sleep in the bed so as not to antagonize him by hiding in one of the guest rooms.

I didn't fall asleep until early morning. And he never came back to our room.

When I awakened later that morning and went out onto the balcony I looked toward the orchard. He wasn't there. The rope and our clothes were still on the ground near the tree, but I couldn't look longer than a second. Then I spotted Jacques, at pool side, looking as if he were again putting together the huge *Playboy* Bunny puzzle; I could see colorful pieces spread out around one side of the pool.

Chapter 17

$\mathcal{A}$s I made breakfast, I rehearsed how I'd tell Jacques I was leaving. He had hidden all the keys to the cars and still held my passport. What would I do? I felt completely helpless, and a depressing fog was settling over me once again, as I kept asking myself why I hadn't left after the last incident, why I had deluded myself that life could ever be normal with Jacques.

"Good morning," he said warmly as he walked into the kitchen. "So . . . What would you like to do today? Maybe go to Loiroi and do some horseback riding?"

Jacques was in high spirits, his behavior completely normal. It was just like all the other times when he had played out his fantasies to their extreme. It broke his mood and then he returned to his first self.

"Horseback riding . . . No, I don't think I'm up to that," I said. "Why don't we take a ride and visit Gérard and Hélène?"

"No! I thought you'd learned by now that plans with any of our friends and family have to be arranged well in advance. We could never just call and say we'd like to come today."

"Well, then, could we go out for lunch to one of the farmhouse restaurants?"

"Let's go out to dinner instead and relax during the day. It's still warm enough to lie out at the pool and even swim. I'll heat up the pool. You know, I was thinking, next summer we won't spend the whole summer here. We'll go to St. Tropez for a month—maybe I'll take another yacht from the business and we'll also cruise the Mediterranean for a few weeks. Would you like that?"

"Sounds fine," I said quietly, knowing that I would no longer be with him come summer. I was sickened by the way he spoke after his bizarre mood of the past days. The insidious bribery of good times to come was starting—his way of assuaging my confusion and sadness.

"You don't seem too enthusiastic, *chérie* Sheri. Would you prefer to go someplace else? Someplace new, another adventure?"

"Whatever you want," I said, trying not to sound too negative.

"I know! I'll take you to India. Off the coast of India are the most exquisite islands—the Maldives. There is a Club Med there. A nudist Club Med. It is supposed to be the most exclusive of the clubs. Do you want that?"

"Yes," I lied.

"All right, I'll make arrangements to go for Christmas. Then we can travel a bit around India. It will be a perfect time to tour. Not too hot then. I'll think of other islands we can visit in the area near the Maldives."

While preparing lunch I searched through the pantry to find where Roland and Marie-Louise kept food and cooking utensils, and I spotted my car keys hanging on the pot rack in Roland's pantry. I quickly took them and hid them near the garage.

After lunch he suggested another swim in the pool and said he would start the heater. "You'd like a long swim, wouldn't you?"

"Fine. I'd like that," I said. He seemed to know he had gone too far this time, and was alarmingly tender and solicitous toward me.

In the late afternoon we brought towels and pareos to the pool and dived into the clear water. The swim shook me out of my malaise and gave me a spurt of confidence to broach the subject of the trip.

"Jacques, I'd like to take a short trip to New York to visit my mother."

"She's coming here in several weeks. Why go now?"

"I'd like to go there. I want to see my friends and family. I need to get some perspective on my life."

"How long would you plan to stay exactly?"

"Two weeks."

"Two weeks! That's too long."

"I must stay two weeks to get some rest. Things haven't been exactly smooth with us lately."

"You don't fool me!" He looked at me with a skeptical smile.

"What do you mean?"

"You're going home for longer than that. You are leaving me, aren't you?"

"No! I'm just going for two weeks to regain a sense of myself. I've been lonely here at times—without friends of my own. People need not only a husband or wife but friends around them to confide in, to advise them." I wanted to bite my tongue, to take back those words—confide, advise. But it was too late.

"Ah! So you are seeking advice if you should stay with me. Is that it?"

"No. I—"

"I know you are leaving me. And I won't let you go! That's final."

"Jacques, you can't control me. I am going for a visit."

"Go into the house. Here's your pareo. Make us veal cordon bleu. Start dinner now. It isn't easy doing all the cooking yourself, is it? Maybe that's why you need a rest. Don't worry. Marie-Louise and Roland will be back soon. And Sheri, you will not go to New York!"

"I'm sorry, Jacques. You can't stop me."

"I have your passport."

"I'll speak with your mother."

"I will not allow you to go. I love you. I need you with me. I love you more than you'll ever know." We walked back into the house and he poured us a scotch. "I won't let you go to New York and be with your lover. You must be going to visit a lover!"

His expression changed and I could see that he was about to become that strange person who knew no limits or reason.

I was frantic.

"There is no lover! What are you talking about? I want to be with my mother!"

"I love you. If you leave me I'll be unhappy the rest of my life without you. You can't go!"

He started pacing back and forth from the window to the bar, his strides so long that he covered the distance in a few steps.

"Cook dinner now! I need you. Don't leave me!" His words became desperate. "You *are* leaving me, aren't you?"

"No, I just want to take a short trip home. I need it."

"You *are* leaving. I can tell you're lying."

"Jacques, stop this!"

"Prepare dinner. I would like fresh french fries with the veal cordon bleu. Take out the potato cutter."

I walked into the kitchen, dizzy and weak with fear. In a daze, I started to beat eggs and prepare the veal when I heard him running up the stairs with a thunderous noise. He had rarely run at any time since I'd known him; his movements were always slow, and slower when he was angry.

Terrified that he had run upstairs to get his shotgun, I grabbed a raincoat, snatched the keys from my hiding place, and ran to my car.

As I drove away, my thoughts became stronger, surer. I deserved no punishment. I had acted in good faith. I had come to make a happy life for us. I hadn't deceived him. Now I knew I must leave, before I broke down completely. I must leave! I must run—run . . .

But where would I go? Where could I stay the night?

I drove aimlessly around the village for what seemed more than an hour, undecided what to do or where to go. The American Embassy was closed on Sunday. The banks too, of course. I had no money to check in to a hotel. No passport. No license or identity card if the police stopped me.

I saw a bar still open on this Sunday night. Dressed only in a transparent silk pareo, pool thongs, and the raincoat, I entered the bar in a frantic state and asked the bartender if I could use the telephone.

In my state of confusion I had difficulty speaking French and it took time to explain to the bartender that I wanted to use his phone, not a coin box telephone—which he had pointed out to me—because I didn't have a coin. I told him I'd pay him the next day. He finally agreed.

I telephoned Jacques. "Why did you run up the stairs?" I asked.

He answered in a sad, resigned voice. "I decided to let you leave for America. I ran up to get you your passport and papers. I will make reservations for you tonight—a suite at the Amigo Hotel in Brussels. You can pack a few things and stay there tonight. Then we'll discuss your leaving tomorrow. Come home and I'll give you your passport."

I suspected it might be a trick, but I had to risk it. I needed to get my passport, or at least some money.

My head spinning, I drove back to the house. I left my motor running, turned the car facing out of the driveway, and left the car door open. I found the front door key in its usual hiding place and opened the door quietly, crossed the hall, and opened the door leading into the living room. I stood frozen to the spot. A terrifying sight! There was six-foot-six Jacques sitting in front of the fireplace on a child's chair. He sat before a roaring fire, in front of which was a huge pile of clothes and papers.

"Jacques, what are you doing!" I was trembling with fright.

He turned around slowly on the tiny chair and with piercing demonic eyes stared at me without speaking. His image was stamped indelibly on my mind.

Then he said in a hollow voice, "I am burning your clothes—all the beautiful dresses I ever bought you. I am burning our wedding pictures and every photograph I have of you and of us together. And all the negatives! You will *never* wear my dresses to seduce another man! I am burning every trace of you! Go home! Get out of my life! I am burning you out of my life!"

He stared at me for long seconds with inhuman, glazed eyes. And then, very slowly, he turned back to the fireplace, picked up my treasured geisha kimono, and threw it into the fire. I watched it burst into flames.

Horrified, I ran back out to my car and drove away.

I was sure that in Jacques's twisted mind those dresses had become me. There was no doubt in my mind after seeing his destructive performance in front of the blazing fire that he was capable of killing me. I could never return to Ginal. I would never feel safe with him again.

My mind was exploding with confused, shocking thoughts and the strangest images. My whole life in Belgium flashed through my mind like a fantastic newsreel. The people at the wedding—so icy—their faces now distorted. The medieval castles. The crowns with the eight balls. The funeral painting. I saw myself crouching in the bell tower at Loiroi. Jacques and his friends—the horsemen—came after me and forced me off the edge of the tower. I felt as if I were falling through the air in slow motion, into the murky weed-filled moat.

I couldn't stop the haunting images: the burning, Jacques's demonic eyes, the smoke and crackling flames.

I pulled the car over to the shoulder of the Autoroute. I screamed hysterically and wept bitterly as the cars zoomed by. I was in shock. I hardly remember how I made it to Isabelle's apartment in Brussels that night.

Chapter 18

Isabelle was waiting for me, looking anxious, her face another shade of white below its powdered white surface. She immediately handed me a clear fruit liqueur to calm me and asked me to tell her exactly what had happened. I talked nonstop for what felt like an hour, my French now coming easily, the phrases rolling off my tongue, the days and nights of pent-up words, never let out in response to Jacques's mad questioning, finally pouring out of me.

Isabelle listened intently, not saying a word, until I was finished. "Sheri, my darling sister-in-law, I am going to tell you what Mamie and Marc did not have the courage or decency to tell you," she said with a fiery intensity, downing her glass of *framboise* in one determined gulp. "And forbade me to tell you! But I will no longer keep silent! You deserve to know the truth. It was unfair for you to have gone through such a ghastly time! Disgracefully dreadful!

"Throughout the years, Jacques had many attacks, crises

we called them, just as you described. We were all sure he was cured about four years ago when he left Claudine and started seeing you. Because after he met you he never had a crisis. We all marveled and cautiously hoped that you had the power to influence him. Change him. But as soon as I heard about the trouble you had immediately after your marriage, I just knew that Mamie should alert you to the possible dangers ahead." I listened in a mixture of shock, anger, and relief at finally hearing that I hadn't imagined that something sinister was lurking, something deliberately being hidden from me.

"Of course your not having the breast implants really set him off. Oh, Mother was furious at you! All her hopes that you had changed Jacques were shattered! Dashed. From that time on she turned against you. Completely."

"When did he start acting like this? The crises . . ."

"Even as a child, he'd been moody and difficult, but his severe problems started when he got married. Claudine was the wrong woman for him. She fueled his insecurities constantly. He became violent with her. Very violent. Many times over the years, she'd arrive at this house in the middle of the night. Black and blue marks all over her body. One time Jacques slammed the car hood down on her while she was checking the motor, injuring her back and her face."

I was horrified as Isabelle spoke. Mamie had lied to me. Marc had lied. I could hear their words, "Rest assured he will not be violent, only self-destructive."

"Claudine had to be hospitalized for a while after that and Mamie took him to a doctor for treatment. He was supposedly cured of his violent tendencies.

"But Claudine was still afraid of his moods and she begged Mamie to get the guns out of the house. He had quite a gun collection and she was right to be afraid with all the drinking and fighting still going on. Well, one time when

Jacques was very drunk and having a bitter fight with Claudine, he shot at her point-blank but missed because he was so unsteady and inebriated. It was in their bedroom and Alain, only six years old then, witnessed the whole thing."

Hearing this, I was horror-struck. He had tried to kill his first wife and they had let a second wife come onto the scene and just take her place as another target! They had put my life in jeopardy, a criminal act. I listened with escalating rage as Isabelle went on.

"After that Mamie finally managed to get the guns out of the house, convincing Jacques that Catherine needed them to protect the castle after a series of thefts. The guns he has now he only got recently. He needs them for hunting. Mamie couldn't stop him.

"Maurice, Gérard, and Hélène are aware of his condition, and Maurice is the only person other than Mamie and Marc who knows the doctor. I'm shocked that Mamie didn't tell you to get in touch with Maurice if you needed help."

"A doctor?" I blurted out. "And no one told me." Isabelle shook her head in compassion. Everyone knew and watched me struggle, desperate for answers. Even Hélène and Gérard. I didn't blame Isabelle, because I could see she was controlled by her mother. All the statements they had made since the wedding echoed in my thoughts like voices in a horror movie: "Jacques's moods, just don't let them get out of control." "Nonsense! he needs no doctor." "Just wait a few days until the mood passes. Don't antagonize him." Even Marc had shown his lack of ethics, not telling me why he had suggested I leave for America after the first bad incident, and then watching me stay.

Isabelle poured us another *framboise* and said how happy she was that we were finally having a heart-to-heart talk. "I really love my brother so much and am so sad he is once again displaying his bad side. This will all calm down and you must go back to him." Then she continued to tell me more shocking things about Jacques's double life. Little by little, mysteries that had plagued me over the months were solved. I had been in extreme danger.

As she spoke on animatedly about the most depraved behavior, I realized Isabelle took it all in stride, finding many of the sensational incidents of sexual play quite expected, including a woman being taken sexually by two men at a time. Isabelle too was unbalanced. I remembered Mémé and Mamie telling me repeatedly that Isabelle was childlike and could never keep a secret—"all of Belgium" would know— and from the way she poured out her stories, it was as if a child were blurting out a big secret, unabridged and with minute detail. I marveled that she had not come forth with this "big secret" of her brother's violent past before in so many months, and realized that the mystery of Jacques's insistence that I not see her alone was finally solved.

Suddenly she dropped her dramatic tone, as if to show that the discussion of the crisis was over. "You know, Jacques tried for many years to convince me to have the breast operation," she said now coquettishly. "But I always refused. Can I see your breasts?" I untied my pareo and showed them to her. "What's he talking about? You have small breasts, but they're quite charming. Oh, my brother is daft. Look, your body is sexy and cute."

This was all so insane. She now chatted on about gossip and about herself and I tuned her out, my mind spinning, fitting together the puzzle. I tried to make myself grasp and believe what I had just heard. Jacques was, without a doubt, a dangerous double personality with a long history of extreme incidents, a past that probably could fill a book of horrors. It wasn't my imagination; this was not something I'd wake up from. The horrors that he had created for me —the near gang-rape at the castle, the cracked mirrors at the dance studio, the scene at the tree, the final fire—filled my book of nightmares completely. How will I ever recover from this? I wondered.

When Isabelle finally reached Jacques on the phone after many tries, he was in an incoherent state, mumbling on about taking out the new BMW to come to her house, having an accident and demolishing the car, leaving it there and walking home, from about two miles away. She told him I was there with her and he became furious. He insisted she make me leave at once. "She is the devil who has come from overseas to destroy our family," he said. "You are in danger by keeping her there."

Isabelle repeated everything he was saying to me, and for a while I could see that he had managed to scare her. He spewed fantastically absurd accusations, which became more and more wicked. She looked over at me with doubt; he could be so treacherous in his fabrications, I now saw. Finally, when she hung up, I broke down completely, crying uncontrollably.

"Poor Jacques. He's suffering so much," she said softly in resignation. "Don't worry, I don't believe him. I won't turn you out. He's in torment that he's driven you away. I know him so well. He just said to me, 'I will never love another woman like I love Sheri. I will never feel that intense passion with anyone else.' "

When Isabelle said this, it became clear to me why I had suffered such indignities and hadn't left after the first incident. Jacques's power to love, to make one feel the intensity of his love, overwhelmed one's senses, drowning out all conflicting emotions. Isabelle and Jacques loved each other deeply and Isabelle could accept all his deeds. But unlike his sister, now knowing the full extent of his sadism and sexual violence, I couldn't love him unconditionally as she did, and I certainly could never return to him.

"Promise me that you will never tell Mamie or Marc what I told you tonight about Jacques's past," Isabelle said. "Especially not about his trying to kill Claudine! Mamie would cut off all my finances. She's done it before. Promise me!"

I promised her and she led me to the bedroom. I lay in bed crying. Isabelle soon came back into the room, sat on the bed, and tenderly put her arms around me. She whispered to me to stop crying, that everything would be all right, kissed me good night, and hugged me tightly. She kissed me on the cheek and then kissed me again, but this time on the ear. Suddenly I felt her put her tongue inside my ear, revolving it slowly and breathing deeply in a sexual way.

Her seductive kissing brought on the creepiest feeling imaginable and drove me deeper into a dark, dense chaos. I felt vulnerable, spent, and nakedly exposed. Although I should have been immune to sexual depravity after all I'd been through in the noble circle, in my emotional turmoil, this lesbian advance made by my own sister-in-law when I was already a victim of her brother's sexual assaults was just too much, a stinging overload to the senses.

I shook my head, nudging her away, and said I wanted to sleep. She hugged me tightly one last time, stroked my face, gently kissed me on both eyelids, and, unembarrassed, left the room. To Isabelle, giving comfort apparently meant giving sex, whether to her brother or her brother's wife. Sex was Isabelle's cure, which she undertook with the sweetest of intentions.

The next morning, Isabelle was in a strangely happy mood, seeming exhilarated by the high drama of my escape into the night and relishing her role as my protector. She strutted animatedly around the house, pacing as though thinking out the situation, taking charge. She fussed, searched for just the right outfit for me to fit the crisis mood, found a demure black dress and a simple pair of black pumps. A perfect look, she declared. "Poor, poor *chérie* Sheri. We'll work it all out. Let us not try to think this out ourselves until we speak to Gérard. He'll think for us. He'll surely know what to do."

She called Gérard and arranged that we go there that afternoon. I was relieved that he would see us immediately, because by now I knew that the nobles scheduled appointments for days later, never the same day.

My morning-after shock was more profound than that of the night before; the light of day made the nightmare real in all its glaring and revolting intricacies. I needed to discuss what I'd been through to somehow make sense of the madness, and Gérard was the voice of reason in this circle, probably the one who came closest to my estimation of someone normal.

Upon our arrival at Gérard and Hélène's, the four of us immediately sat down to a long discussion, and they expressed their horror at my harrowing story. Of course they knew of Jacques's past, but they had been convinced that he had changed under my influence. They had had no idea of my struggles. We continued to discuss my dilemma at dinner, and Gérard blamed Mamie and Marc for not warning me and not giving me the name of the doctor. From the way he spoke I had to assume there were yet even more severe acts of violence than Isabelle had revealed. Again the suicide of the young governess came into my mind, and I took courage and asked them to tell me the story.

They all froze at the question, looked at each other, and remained mute. Finally, after a long charged silence, Gérard spoke. "I cannot discuss this with you." He paused and added, "You were very lucky your marriage ended this way. You obviously should never think of going back."

It was clear from their reaction that Jacques had either killed the governess or driven her to kill herself.

After dinner Gérard called me into his library to speak privately. He reminded me that he had been a member of the Belgian Bar Association before his retirement and advised me to get a lawyer at once, warning that in Belgium if the spouse leaves the conjugal home and stays away more than three days, the other spouse can get a divorce on the grounds of abandonment. I cringed, remembering that a lawyer at the American Embassy had told me just that when I called him right after the wedding. Gérard said that a lawyer should immediately write a letter to Jacques saying that I had not abandoned the house, had only left out of fear; otherwise I could expect to have no rights under the law. "Go to the American Embassy, file a report, and have them recommend an attorney," said Gérard.

The next day I went to the American Embassy, where I was given a list of lawyers. I chose one at random.

Fortunately the lawyer I chose spoke English and agreed to write a letter immediately saying I was represented by his law firm and that I had been forced to leave the conjugal home because I had been in danger. In a long session I described my terrifying experiences to him and told him that I wished to leave the country as soon as possible. He said that I shouldn't leave until the separation agreement had been drawn up; that could take at least two weeks.

I asked whether it was possible for him to send me the papers in the United States. "For certain procedures," he said seriously, "you must be here. Unless you want your husband to get an instant divorce on the grounds of your abandoning him and returning to the U.S. I think you would be very foolish to have had such injustice done to you and not seek justice." He scrutinized me closely, real compassion in his eyes; he looked distinguished and seemed trustworthy. "If you win a divorce you have the right to live in the conjugal home with support for many years, until the time you choose to remarry, if you so choose. Don't you think you are owed that after the violence done to you?"

"How could I ever live here? I'd always feel in danger of more violence."

He explained that in my case he could try to have the court order Jacques to provide a residence in the United States. Also he would seek financial support for me until I could start working and fully support myself. He said he was well aware of what the noble circle was like, then said bluntly that it would take a great deal of money and influence to fight them in court and asked whether I was prepared for such a fight. He wanted me to think it over and come back to see him the next day. He then urged me at once to leave Isabelle's apartment, where he felt I might be in danger, and suggested that I go to Gérard or to a hotel, which he could arrange for me.

The time had finally come to break the news to Mother of the end of my marriage and admit to the horrifying chain of events that had led up to my escape from the house as my clothes were destroyed in a fire. Until this time, had I called her, I would only have cried, probably not been able to utter a coherent word. It was one of those dreaded calls that one hates to make to a parent—the ones that start with "Something has happened. I am not hurt physically. Where do I start . . ."

Naturally Mother began crying along with me when she heard the hell I had been through. But soon her reaction turned to outrage over the family's putting my life in danger. She didn't dwell on her emotional shock, but instead coolly managed to advise me how to proceed. She'd wire money immediately for all the expenses, told me to ask the lawyer what his retainer would be and she'd send a check, and said we'd speak twice every day to handle each eventuality as it arose. Thankfully Mother was very level-headed in emergencies and gave me courage. Had she fallen apart, I surely would have too; I think she knew that.

I wrote Isabelle a note telling her I'd left and would call her later to let her know where I was, then drove to Gérard and Hélène's home, an hour by car from Brussels, without even calling them for permission to come.

No one was home. Even the maid and butler were out. I sat in the car waiting for them for two hours. Sitting in the car in their driveway, hoping not to be seen by neighbors, I felt shame and fear; shame that I found myself hiding like a fugitive, fear that Jacques might appear.

When Hélène got home, she was rather alarmed to see me at first. When I explained my fear, she graciously agreed to let me stay with them for a few days, until I could make other arrangements. Gérard arrived home shortly afterward. He asked me to hide my car in the garage, just in case Jacques thought to come there. He said that if they had to leave me alone at any time during my stay and Jacques arrived, I should go straight to the butler's quarters and remain there; the butler would have instructions to protect me.

Gérard advised me to tell no one that I was staying with them, except, of course, Isabelle; he called her immediately to tell her I was there. Hélène took me upstairs to my quarters—a magnificent room with a four-poster bed, antique French furniture, artworks, and a huge adjoining bathroom. I was struck with the biting irony—a palatial hideout for a fugitive from the nobility.

Hélène, in her sweetest and noblest manner, asked me whether I had absolutely everything I needed to make me comfortable. She offered profuse excuses that she had no new soap to replace the slightly used bar. This little exchange confirmed yet again that the nobility's priorities were always first fixed on etiquette, even in crisis. Before Hélène left my room she asked me exactly what I wanted for breakfast and at what time her butler should serve me.

Waking up in this tranquil and pastoral setting with cows, sheep, and horses grazing on the vast property of rolling hills and meadows, I felt as if I had stumbled onto the wrong movie set. The pace was slow, Hélène and Gérard calm and gracious, their household run with Swiss-clock precision. In fact, the many clocks in their collection rang out the passing hours. In the morning, Gérard worked in his library while Hélène did her gardening. At 1:00 P.M. sharp, aperitifs were served by the butler on the terrace, and afterward we sat down to a full-course lunch with wine. That evening at exactly 7:00 aperitifs reappeared, and Gérard and Hélène were dressed for dinner. I of course was still in my one demure outfit with black pumps. A many-course meal again was served, and the impersonal and favorite topic, the analysis of foods and wines, was reopened. My crisis was not discussed. The maid and butler rang out at every opportunity: "*Madame la Baronne*, does *Madame la Baronne* wish this, does *Madame la Baronne* want that?" And again I felt it overwhelmingly ironic that my noble life in this circle had just ended and here I was in the most serene setting as an honored guest—my last hurrah in Belgium.

I slept peacefully in my palatial room, allowing myself the full day and night to calm down and try to stop the haunting thoughts and images, but the next morning I awoke to cruel reality. When I came downstairs, Isabelle was already there waiting to take me back to Ginal to pick up some clothing, identification, and other essentials. She had already found out that Jacques had gone to the office that day and that the servants were not at the house, as at all the other times when he had been out of control and had asked them to leave.

We arrived at Ginal. I stayed in the car while Isabelle cautiously went inside and looked around the house and garage to be sure Jacques was not there and then beckoned me in. I ran upstairs, frantically threw anything I could find, shoes and other essentials, into a suitcase, and ran back down. I glanced around the kitchen and living room. The house was in shambles. The eggs and the veal that I had started to prepare on Saturday night were still on the kitchen counter. In the living room empty liquor bottles were everywhere, the ashtrays overflowing, and there were no pictures of me in the frames; he had probably burned them all. I could not force myself to look toward the fireplace. Then I jumped into the car and Isabelle and I sped off.

I had another appointment with the lawyer in the afternoon. He urged me to try to talk to the family to see whether I could work out some amicable settlement with them. To my shock and dismay he warned me that I had no evidence of anything that had happened—not that my husband was violent, had tied me to a tree in the garden, not that he had burned my clothes, not that he was anything but a fine nobleman—and unless certain family members would testify to his nature, I was completely without proof. He predicted that the family would close ranks against me and not testify to a word of my story. He lamented that had he known I was going back to the house, he would have advised me to fill a sack with ashes from the fireplace as proof that clothes had been burned. He then urged me to go back to Ginal again and do so, but accompanied by a member of the village police.

Following his advice, I returned to Ginal with an officer. The garage door did not open with my radar button. I went to the front door and the other door; my keys did not fit. All the locks had been changed and the radar combination altered. The police officer made a report.

When I presented the police report to the lawyer, he said I had gotten an essential piece of evidence that would ensure that Jacques could not get an immediate divorce from me on grounds that I had abandoned him.

Gérard applauded my action in getting the report. He was completely and enthusiastically on my side. He abhorred what the Borchgraves had done, especially Mamie, and fired my anger against them.

Buoyed by the two lawyers who sought justice for me, I snapped out of my pitiful state and gathered my fighting spirit. The terrible experience I had endured could have been avoided if Mamie or Marc had warned me of the dangers. I was angry. Gérard and my lawyer were right; I couldn't just leave without seeking an explanation, an apology, or even an acknowledgment. My life had been played with cruelly. Gérard insisted there should be some compensation. Hélène also agreed and said she would arrange a meeting with Mamie.

I could hear Hélène and Mamie's muffled conversation going on in the salon while I waited on the terrace for over an hour. Finally Hélène came out and asked me to wait in my room, where Mamie would see me. Mamie knocked on the door. When she walked in, she coldly and abruptly announced that she had only a few minutes to give me.

"It is so sad what happened. So unfortunate. A pity. A pity," she said arrogantly, shaking her head. She lamented the sad facts for a while and then said indignantly, "I can do nothing about it. Nothing. I can't take sides. You are two adults involved in a marriage and it is your responsibility to resolve it, not mine."

"Two adults!" I exploded. "No. One adult and one out-of-control, violent man. The violent uncontrollable person's parent must assume responsibility. You should have warned me. Now you must help me."

"I am very sorry," she responded icily. "But since you went to a lawyer, I cannot talk to you. You brought this matter outside the family to a public forum and now I cannot help you in any way. It was you who got Jacques into this mood, and now you must face the consequences. And you would be surprised how much violence goes on in these circles. The highest circles."

"Does that make it right?"

"Women live with it! I warned you to live with him first. But you were so sure of yourself. I told you that you could know nothing of his character from only pleasurable vacations with him."

"But why didn't you tell me that he had a double personality and could be so insanely irrational? You called it only swings of moods! Why didn't you see to it that he got medical help? And why did you not give me the name of his doctor?"

"He's an adult," Mamie snapped and actually raised her voice. "If he wants professional help, it is his decision. I have nothing to do with it. I'm rushed, and I really must go." And she walked toward the door. "I won't be back in Brussels for another month. I will be traveling. And of course, now that you have gone to a lawyer, it would be best if we didn't see each other again."

And then, in a display of grotesque kindness, the most outrageous demonstration of noblesse oblige imaginable, she kissed me three times on each cheek and walked out abruptly, saying, "Pity it ended this way. *Bonne chance.*"

Fortunately Gérard and my lawyer had prepared me to expect nothing but hostility from the family. There was no remorse, no apology, not even a kind wish for the future. I was infuriated to be treated like a discarded object.

I knew that the only one who would show compassion was Mémé. I drove to Brussels to say goodbye. To my anguish, she wouldn't let me in. After some persuasion, she opened the door and said coldly, "We have nothing to speak about. You have been very dishonest with Jacques. He told me the whole story. In our circles we do not tolerate dishonesty. I have nothing further to say to you." Not wanting to challenge or upset an old woman further, I left brokenhearted. My lawyer had been right. All the doors were closing.

As I drove to Hélène and Gérard's to be back in time for their all-important 7:00 P.M. aperitif, I was once again enveloped in a dark stupor, a twilight state in which my mind played all sorts of tricks. I couldn't believe this was happening to me. I suddenly realized I'd better just get away from here, take the next flight out and not expose myself to more cruelty. But then it struck me. I had to make Mamie pay for her crime. I couldn't let her get away with casting me out, almost as if into the sea, to float back to my side of the great ocean.

That night I told Gérard and Hélène I was making the move to a Brussels hotel, arranged by my lawyer. They appreciated this decision, as they were already embroiled in a family dispute; calls were coming in from the family condemning them for having given me shelter. Again both urged me to fight for justice and not let the family dispose of me without some form of compensation.

When I called my mother and told her of Mamie and Mémé's reactions, she said, "If you must have answers to make sense of this, go to Marc. He's a monk and he will surely take responsibility." I called the abbey and Marc agreed to meet with me at Adriane's apartment.

Marc and I arrived at the same moment early the next morning and entered the apartment together. Everything had been draped with sheets, since Adriane had left for another long trip; it was an eerie feeling to see all the paintings, artworks, and furniture covered. This visit was probably my last to the apartment, and already it was concealed from me. I glanced around for the final time at the living room and dining room, the scene of many memorable occasions and critical talks—the first luncheon encounter with the baroness, the wedding reception, the dowry discussion, and the weekly luncheon. Now it looked like a morgue.

Marc, wearing his habit, was somber and distant; he opened our discussion like a formal meeting. He uncovered only a small spot on the couch for me and one directly facing it on a chair for himself. Then he took out his notes. Without preamble, he began his opening statement. "The question that both my mother and I have been wondering about is why you wanted personal stationery."

Knowing precisely what he was driving at, that I was being directly accused by him and his mother of marrying Jacques for the title, I was furious, but I decided to answer him, mimicking his arrogant lecturing style. "In America, personalized stationery is essential for proper communication. All thank-you notes and other communications are written on personalized letterhead."

"This is not a good answer. Isn't it possible that you liked the sound of the title and wanted to start using it? Is it possible that you wanted to marry Jacques to secure the title baroness for yourself?"

"I am not a title hunter, if that is what you and your mother are implying. Titles have no value in America!"

"I have another question," Marc said, unfazed. "Why did you visit Mémé so often?"

"I enjoyed talking with her and listening to her marvelous life stories. My visits to her really cheered me up after some harrowing weeks with Jacques."

"It seems to me that you were trying to get information on the family for some reason. Were you trying to find out about the family holdings?"

"These interrogations were inspired by your mother!" I burst out in anger. "And that question is an insult! An outrage! I am disappointed in your judgment for asking it!" I took out my notes as he had done. "And now I have a few questions for you.

"Why wouldn't your mother help me? Why has she treated me like an unwelcome stranger? And most importantly, why wasn't I told that Jacques had a doctor who treated him when he was violent in the past? It was morally wrong of you and of her not to tell me. You're a monk! How could you have kept it from me?"

"My mother is old," he answered, in calm control. "She's had problems with Jacques for years and years. She needs some peace. Expect no help from her. Nothing will help." He sighed in an exaggerated way. "Our discussions are futile. Go back to America. Turn the page! Jacques will never change. Turn the page! After all, the whole situation only involves barely a year of your life. In America you will find the right man who will suit you."

"How can you say it has been barely a year of my life? Marc, my life was in danger. Therefore, it was your mother's responsibility and yours to warn me! And now it is her responsibility to acknowledge this."

"I will not answer for my mother," he said. "She has had a hard life and has had enough of this whole thing. You're young. Just turn the page!

"Poor Sheri. For a while you really made progress with Jacques. He seemed like a changed man. We had hopes that it would all work. But you must accept life. And let us not make it difficult for all concerned. You are a great girl. I've admired you. Really admired your energy and perseverance. You are lucky it is ending this way. I have to get back to the monastery. I am happy I talked with you. I wish you good luck in America."

He directed me to the door and kissed me goodbye, three times, alternating cheeks. He showed no emotion.

The gates of the castle had closed.

The meeting left me trembling with outrage. The family had not warned me, had not helped me during my terrifying episodes with Jacques, had knowingly let the situation deteriorate to the point where I was in extreme danger, and now took no responsibility for me. I was an unwelcome stranger who was no longer useful in their plans. It was astounding that they expected me to turn the page, silently leave for America, and vanish from their lives forever. In my mind, a crime had been committed against me. I was an innocent victim of their conspiracy of silence.

The next day, Isabelle called and frantically insisted we meet. She gave me the address of a restaurant in the old city, a secret place she said she went to when she didn't want to be seen.

"I must tell you what has been going on," she began in a hushed tone, although we had total privacy. "Jacques is totally out of control! He is determined to find out where you are staying! He told me that I must cooperate with a trick he is planning. Of course I will not do it, and that's why I'm here. He told me to get a message to you through Gérard. He wants to return all your clothes and possessions. Then he wanted me to trick you into giving me your address on the pretext that I would deliver your clothes. Then he would have your address, and who knows what he would do to you! He's been worse than ever, because Mamie is away. He has severed all ties with Gérard and Hélène, accusing them of being traitors to him and the family. He has threatened me by saying that I would regret it seriously if I ever helped you in any way. Sheri, because he forbids me to see you or talk to you, except to carry out his trick, I am putting myself in danger. But I felt I had to warn you, since you've been harmed enough. In fact, he has threatened to do physical harm to me. He has been drinking heavily and hardly going to work. Even Claudine is afraid to see him in this condition. He continues to repeat that you are a devil and you are out to destroy the family. Why are you staying here in Brussels? You really should leave for America.

"Since you left Hélène and Gérard, he has been trying to find out where you are. He sometimes drives around Brussels at night looking for your car. He's put a lot of pressure on me because he believes Gérard has your telephone number and feels that I could get it from him."

Isabelle repeated how sad she was that things had happened this way. She left me with another strong warning to be careful and to leave Belgium as soon as possible.

Although I had one more week to wait until the court session when separation papers would be drawn up, I decided to heed Isabelle's warning and book a flight out that week. My attorney had me sign a statement in court and said he would proceed in my absence.

As I waited for the day of the flight I went out infrequently, almost hiding in the hotel, spending the time writing in my journal the final updates on the last days with Jacques and my two weeks of wandering after leaving Ginal. Writing was the only way to harness the exploding emotions that seemed to continually erupt in me; the mixture of shame,

outrage, sexual debasement, anger at the family's indiffer-
ence, fear of Jacques's still threatening presence, was potentially lethal, and directing my thoughts onto paper kept me
from breaking. Mother called every few hours. We were both
in such a state that we needed to be calmed and soothed by
each other's voice. We both feared that Jacques in his devious
way would find me. I had visions of him waiting for me at
the airport with his hunting rifle.

I left the hotel only to visit the American Embassy and
apprise the consular officer of the latest developments. My
lawyer had told me that he might be the only witness later
on who would testify that anything unusual had happened
to me. He would keep a record of my statements. When I
expressed my fear to him that my husband might be at the
airport waiting for me, he didn't find the fear exaggerated.
He said he'd arrange for an American Embassy escort to take
me to the airport, through customs, and onto the plane. He
said to put my car into a long-term parking lot and he'd
advise the family where it was. He asked that I not leave the
hotel until the guard arrived.

On the morning of my departure, the Embassy guard
picked me up and drove me to the airport. The consular
officer was waiting for us there and said goodbye. The guard
then escorted me through customs and onto the plane.

$\mathscr{E}pilogue$

$\mathscr{B}$ecause of the antiquated legal system in Belgium—bureaucratic procedure upon procedure, with an endless series of witness hearings held at intervals of a year or more—my divorce case dragged on for years. The system didn't allow the parties to argue the case back and forth at the same session; one party would be heard the first year, the other party the next. It was a nightmare. Never once was I allowed to testify in my own behalf. Just when I became resigned to the fact that the case would go on for years more and perhaps would never end, my Belgian lawyer called on October 23, 1989, announcing that I was a widow.

My lawyer advised me to come to Belgium to start the inheritance case. "And it will be a process, Sheri. You must fight the sons. They are claiming that since you were almost divorced, you don't deserve to inherit anything. The rest of the family, of course, is horrified at the thought that you, an American, now hold their family title . . . for your lifetime

. . . now the only person in the family who will ever be able to use the title baroness! You realize that they will fight you with all their might to keep the property in the family. But you have a good chance. You are clearly the widow. There was no divorce. In Belgium that means part of the estate."

The next phone call I received was from Jacques's last girlfriend, Simone, who had been living with him since I had left. She urged me to meet with her when I arrived in Brussels, promising she'd fill me in on the years since I'd left and tell me the circumstances surrounding his suicide. I couldn't help wondering whether her contacting me might have been instigated by the family, but promised to meet her.

I arrived in Brussels the following month and contacted Simone. She turned out to be intelligent and sympathetic, and it was soon evident that it was her own idea to see me. Simone had an urgent need to share the real story of Jacques's end. She told me how sorry she was for all I'd been through, and admitted to similar frightening times with Jacques. Almost unbelievably, she had chosen to stay with him for years, controlling him with one weapon, her threat of leaving him. Whenever things got too bad, she left for her apartment in Brussels. But listening to her claims of strength, choice, and control, I still detected a definite emotional damage. She wore it like a battered woman. She had fallen into the same trap I had, believing that occasional aberrational behavior was the exception rather than the rule. Mine was the mistake of a young person that had unalterably affected the course of my life; hers was a mistake made at an age when she could have better judged the situation, and I knew that soon she would reproach herself for having wasted so many years. It was as if we were Jacques's two widows, sharing the tragedy of having been deceived by a man with a cleverly disguised evil side.

Simone described the suicide scene to me in full detail. She said she had come to trust and respect me after she had read the transcript of the court case, which she had found in a chest after Jacques's death. He had given no warning, but had behaved quite strangely the month before the deed, and for several weeks his demeanor had been markedly different. That summer they had not taken the traditional trip to St. Tropez. His decision not to go had struck her as very odd. He had been in a mood for most of the summer, and she had been uneasy about questioning him. He had not seemed depressed, but preoccupied and joyless, drinking more heavily than usual—that is, beyond the lavish style of drinking that they had maintained for years.

She went on to tell the dramatic events of August 6, a day that strangely resembled my fateful last day of years before.

In the morning, after a night of sleepless roaming, drinking, and moaning, Jacques looked like a zombie. He took all the computer tapes with records of his business dealings and submerged them in boiling water. One by one he burned away years of records. She couldn't stop him.

Suddenly he rushed up the stairs to the bedroom. Simone remarked, as I had, that she had never heard him run up the stairs, only walk up quietly. Thinking that he was going to get a gun to shoot her, she escaped from the house in a panic and went to a neighbor's house. She drove by the property a number of times during the day and later as the sun was setting, and noticed that Jacques had turned on every light in the house and on the surrounding property. Terrified at the eerie sight, she tried to reach her daughter, who was to arrive home from her university that evening.

She waited at the entrance to the property and was able to intercept her daughter, and they both went to the neighbor's for the night, too afraid to return home. She had called throughout the day, but Jacques did not answer the telephone.

The next morning, she returned to the house with the neighbor at her side. They called out for Jacques from outside the house, again upon entering, and as they proceeded up the staircase. In the bedroom, at the balconied window that overlooked the expansive forested property, the same spot from which Jacques had often shot pheasants from the window, he lay dead in a pool of his own blood.

During my years of separation from the Baron de Borchgrave, while the divorce case was going on, I still was in contact with members of the baron's family. Uncle Gérard and Aunt Hélène corresponded with me regularly throughout the years. They remained unwaveringly on my side and in letters often expressed their outrage at the Borchgraves' (especially Adriane's) treatment of me and the family's unwillingness to settle the matter out of court. Uncle Gérard testified to Jacques's violent behavior, and his testimony was one of my few proofs that anything unusual had gone on in my marriage. The rest of the family, notably Adriane, Marc, Catherine, and Claudine, tried to claim that I had abandoned my husband and basically was uninterested in the role of a good Belgian housewife—these two points being legal grounds for divorce in Belgium. A long session in court was spent with the family members each claiming that I didn't keep up the flowers in the garden of the conjugal property, that I let them all wither and die, and hence I was uninterested in maintaining a home and being a good Belgian wife. They also concocted a tale that I caused my husband shame (another ground for divorce) by frequently visiting his grandmother and telling her "sex stories." When questioned under oath, Mémé, then in her late nineties, try as she might couldn't recall a single "sex story," which the family had undoubtedly drilled into her for weeks, and spontaneously made the unsolicited comment that she so enjoyed it when I picked her up to spend the summer day at Ginal because she loved sitting in the garden, where the flowers were so breathtakingly beautiful! These skirmishes were characteristic of the entire charade of a case I endured under the Belgian legal system, and they continued into the inheritance case.

Uncle Gérard died recently. Mémé died several years ago, having achieved the century mark. Isabelle and I remained friends through the years; I often saw her on my yearly trips to Belgium for court rounds. On my last visit, Isabelle was in terrible physical and mental shape. Her spirited, coquettish nature could not withstand the three consecutive deaths of loved ones: her only son, Bernard, in a car crash, her lover Gérard, and her brother Jacques. Claudine's botched-up breast enlargement operations have resulted in years of complications. The baron's last girlfriend, Simone, also underwent a breast operation; she testified to this fact in court, to the visible alarm of the woman judge hearing the inheritance case.

And finally, after her son's death, I met with Adriane (no longer do I call her Mamie) at her insistence for dinner in the winter of 1990 to discuss the inheritance case. She remained convinced, though I was her son's widow, that I deserved nothing. But she wanted to settle with me for a sum that would barely have covered my legal expenses for a year. She still rarely goes to any social event that is "mixed," travels to her friends' villas in Cannes and Marbella, goes on her British garden tours to smell the English nobles' flowers, and continues to make the rounds to all her old lady friends' castles, where they have a grand time drinking up the best vintages from their deceased husbands' wine cellars. But even through all of Adriane's merry times, I'm sure she can't block out the highly unpleasant thought—or she might say the "dreadful" thought—that a savage American holds her family's noble title for life.

As for me, the recuperation was very slow. I came home distraught, unfocused, a person out of her element. A broken spirit.

I lived under the strange stigma of being a deposed baroness back in America, an enigmatic figure whose life was dramatically suspended. I was ashamed, even though I knew I hadn't failed, but others thought I hadn't cut it in the noble circle.

Periodically, before the suicide, detectives watched me, and calls came from members of Jacques's family trying to create a climate for reconciliation—they claimed Jacques was under treatment and had changed. My life was in such limbo and confusion that for fleeting moments I actually considered going back—mainly, I think, because plummeting from such a lofty place and then trying to live a normal life seemed impossible. With such a crashing fall inevitably came loss of self-worth and self-respect.

I got a job working in an art gallery in SoHo once again. But coming back at the same level I had been at when I had left felt demoralizing. The men my age whom I dated didn't know how to handle me after hearing even the barest sketch of my story. The older men enjoyed being with a titled person and found me unique. Yet if any relationship developed, I became afraid at their slightest display of authority. A request to change my dress to something more casual could set off a panic attack. I held the irrational fear that all men could metamorphose into violent demons. I was lucky on one front, however: I got back just in time not to lose the lease on my Manhattan apartment. After I had sufficiently recovered to take their teasing, my friends never failed to remind me of this uncannily lucky timing.

The pain wouldn't go away, so I tried escape. I worked for Club Med for three summers in Tahiti, Greece, and Mexico. I taught waterskiing, gave English lessons to the French-speaking directors, even greeted guests in the restaurant as a hostess. I had a few summer flings in a protected environment and felt my fear of men—of their violence and their capacity to change—go away, and I felt my trust coming back.

But when I restarted the season at the art gallery in the fall, the pain returned. After the third year, I left my job and started my own art dealership. Seeing my spirits still so low, Mother suggested we take a trip, and we booked a tour to West Africa. And on the trip, while in Dakar, my romantic life took an interesting twist. History almost repeated itself.

I met a young man exactly my age from one of France's wealthiest families. He lived with his father on a 400-acre estate and game reserve. Handsome, very sportive, very French (meaning romantic and sensuous), Jean-Luc actually asked me to marry him the week I met him in Senegal. He urged me to rush my Belgian divorce. He was there on business, just as Jacques had been in Bucharest.

I hadn't been excited about someone for years and didn't think it was possible again. Another overseas relationship started up, with constant love letters and travel.

I was determined to know Jean-Luc thoroughly in his home environment before making any decisions and spent time with him in Normandy on his hunting reserve and also at his home on the coast.

My decision not to move to Europe and marry him came about quite suddenly through a telling incident. His father had divorced his mother to marry his mistress. One day while Jean-Luc, his father, and I were finishing dinner, a small poodle ran across the property and then back again. Jean-Luc's father excused himself from a lively conversation about his elephant hunting in Chad and rushed out.

When I asked Jean-Luc why his father had left, he told me that the poodle was a signal from his new mistress that she was awaiting him at her home on the next estate. I then asked Jean-Luc whether he approved of his father's exploits and whether he would have a mistress.

He answered, *"Ma chérie,* I am French . . . Life is pleasures. When we are married and you are older and involved with your horses and children, I will also pursue my pleasures. As you will yours, I'm sure."

I didn't debate the point further, but soon phased out the relationship, knowing I didn't belong in this life and deciding that I wanted more than pleasure-seeking with a husband who would surely divorce me after a time to marry his mistress.

Jean-Luc's society, though not noble or depraved in style, had many similarities to Jacques's circle. The value system was simply off, to the American way of thinking. I declared my European experience over and, like so many women, have resumed the odyssey to find the right partner—but this time, right here in the United States. I hope my search will end in time for me to have a child.

Sometimes, especially when working on this book—turning my frightening experience into a creative work was the single most important factor in my recuperation—I've dreamed what life would have been like had Jacques been the man I thought he was during our three-year romance. It could have been an idyll. Sometimes I picture myself with two good-looking children, well-behaved like all the little nobles; I would live in the family castle, planning dinner parties, tending the gardens, replenishing the wine cellars, shopping for the cheeses, and creating the superb erotic history that Jacques had promised that night on the terrace of the Amigo Hotel, "that few women will ever know . . ." But now I well realize that I had it wrong from the beginning; Jacques's noble world was no fairy tale; it was the world of dangerous liaisons.

The most dreaded Chinese curse is "I wish you an interesting life." For an interesting life you must pay the price. I've certainly paid it. In all this, however, I achieved personal growth, and I rediscovered my upbeat nature and spirit, my sense of humor and of fun. My breasts are probably the only part of me that survived this experience as they were before—no growth.

After the baron's suicide, the experience took on a finality, and it was then that I reconciled myself to my mistake in marrying him. I came to terms with the fact that I had been very young and that almost any young woman would have fallen prey. I gained a greater sensitivity toward people whose lives have been thrown off course by events that suddenly descend upon them.

I've learned instinctively to recognize warning signals and shun "dangerous men." And men are no longer the overwhelming priority of my life. My career, now as a travel writer and an author, takes precedence.

And finally, an inevitable by-product of this experience, one which I didn't think that I would master in my life, is that I thoroughly understand the erotic dimension of life and also the darker side of existence. I've learned the limits that I wish to set for myself, and I can also recognize and choose to avoid those who seek the outer limits in sex.

It was a fairy tale gone haywire. I thought I'd find happiness in the land of castles, nobles, and ancient traditions, but instead I found the dark side. And the dark side is a place where I never again want to travel.